Praise for Treating Adult Children of **Relational Trauma**

"Psychodrama is one of the most effective treatments of PTSD and developmental trauma that I am familiar with, and Tian Dayton has written a terrific manual to serve as our guide. Psychodrama helps to make our inner world visible and manifest what we struggle with, not so much by words, but by actions, making the invisible observable and measurable. Operating in a space where important people from our past are recreated in the living present, and where we can experience and manifest our confused inner world, we can finally say the words that were never spoken, and allow feelings to emerge that could not be expressed back then. Working with others in three-dimensional space, as psychodrama does, can not only uniquely create a timeless experience where past and present can merge to help us reconfigure our mental alignment, but also provide profound reparative experiences."

—**Bessel van der Kolk, MD,** professor of psychiatry at Boston University School of Medicine, president of the Trauma Research Foundation, and author of the #1 *New York Times* bestseller *The Body Keeps the Score*

"We store the imprint of trauma in our bodies as 'snapshots' frozen in the nervous system that tell the story of how the body-mind experienced trauma. Therapists need to understand what the living, sensing body is telling us in order to help clients heal. Tian Dayton's approach to embodied therapy using psychodrama informed by Somatic Experiencing® allows the body's unspoken voice to come forward and be heard. In this treatment guide, Tian has provided us with an unparalleled approach for treating relational trauma that confirms what we know to be true: Bringing the body into healing is a crucial component of recovery. I highly recommend this book to anyone who is treating the pain of unhealed attachment wounds."

—**Peter Levine, PhD,** developer of Somatic Experiencing® and best-selling author of *Waking the Tiger*

"Tian Dayton has done the field a tremendous service in making the active, experiential components of psychodrama and sociometry available to the layperson in the form of sociometrics. In my role as chief clinical officer at Phoenix House, she worked with me and several trainers in getting sociometrics to the staff in over 100 treatment programs. The clinical staff consisted primarily of entry-level staff and still they were able to implement the skills of sociometrics in the form of feelings floor checks, timeline work, letter writing, social atoms (on paper), and other activities with fidelity and competence. Importantly, the staff embraced these activities with enthusiasm and excitement. These skills profoundly increased the engagement of the staff and transformed the level of clinical services provided at the treatment programs. I can't thank Tian enough for having the amazing intellect that was able to transform components of psychodrama and sociometry—skills that take years to learn—into the easy-to-implement sociometrics that get clients out of their seats and into the here and now!"

—**Deni Carise, PhD,** adjunct clinical professor at the University of Pennsylvania

"Tian Dayton is brilliant, and her work on sociometrics is groundbreaking for addiction and other mental health disciplines due to the nature of incorporating psychodrama and sociometry into treatment. We at NAADAC are so thrilled with this work that we are partnering with Dr. Dayton to create a certificate program in order to advance training and skills for therapists and counselors to help heal their clients. Not only does this work heal the clients, but it is cyclical—it also heals the counselor as they use it! The value and need for adult relational trauma treatment is huge due to the environmental issues we have all been faced with these past years, and as we heal the adult clients, they can heal their children and grandchildren. I am excited to learn and use this model for skill development and, more so, for the generational healing I have been doing in my own family to grow generations of health, recovery, and happy lives!"

—**Cynthia Moreno Tuohy, BSW, NCAC II,** executive director of NAADAC, the Association for Addiction Professionals

Treating Adult Children of Relational Trauma

85 Experiential Interventions to Heal the Inner Child and Create Authentic Connection in the Present

Tian Dayton, MA, PhD, TEP

Treating Adult Children of Relational Trauma

Published by
PESI Publishing, Inc.
3839 White Ave
Eau Claire, WI 54703

Cover and Interior Design: Emily Dyer
Editing: Marisa Solis

ISBN: 9781683735700 (print)
ISBN: 9781683735717 (ePUB)
ISBN: 9781683735724 (ePDF)

Printed in the United States of America.

Dedication

I would like to dedicate this book to those I have trained over the past three decades in psychodrama, sociometry, and relational trauma repair sociometrics, and to my training groups in New York City and online. Many of you have been part of bringing this work forward, and I know it will continue on in your capable hands. You are in my heart.

About the Author

Tian Dayton, MA, PhD, TEP, is a senior fellow at The Meadows, the author of fifteen books, and the creator of Relational Trauma Repair-Sociometrics (RTR-S). Dr. Dayton was a professor of psychodrama at New York University. She is a fellow of the American Society of Group Psychotherapy and Psychodrama (ASGPP) and the former editor-in-chief of *The Journal of Psychodrama, Sociometry, and Group Psychotherapy*. She has received numerous awards, including the Marty Mann Award, the Mona Mansell Award, the Ackerman/Black Award, and the ASGPP's lifetime achievement award, scholar's award, and president's award.

Table of Contents

List of Interventions

Acknowledgments

In my professional lifetime, embodied forms of therapy have moved from the fringes to the cutting edge of the mental health field.

Thus it has been an exciting time to be someone who works with experiential, embodied forms of therapy. In the 1980s, Bessel van der Kolk opened the conversation as to why talk therapy was insufficient in healing trauma. Peter Levine brought the body into therapy, giving it a sentient presence and a voice through his method of somatic experiencing. And Stephen Porges provided the polyvagal theoretical lens through which to understand not only what is happening in the body and mind of the client but the interaction and coregulation of the group. Further, Dan Siegel's work in interpersonal neurobiology provides another underpinning for the importance of keeping methods welcoming and safe so that participants don't need to defend themselves but can be open for healing. Their contributions to the mental health field have forever changed it for the better. I have spent the last three decades interweaving these groundbreaking theories of neuropsychology with psychodrama and sociometry.

My introduction to experiential work came through Sharon Wegscheider-Cruse in 1980. Sharon's work with families of addicts, and my family specifically, changed my life and career direction. Sharon was trained by Virginia Satir, who was in turn trained in her family reconstructions by psychodramatists in applying a social atom process to family therapy. I did this experiential work for several years before I came upon psychodrama in the mid-1980s in New York City.

Psychodrama, created by Jacob Levy Moreno, known as the father of group psychotherapy, was the first mind-body therapy. Encountering psychodrama from the hands of its creators, and recognizing the brilliance of its techniques and the efficacy of its methodology, was another career event that changed my life. Integrating the understanding, warmth, and mission-driven passion of the addictions field with the incisive skill of psychodrama and sociometry has been a rich, satisfying, and at times electrifying journey.

Zerka Moreno, J. L. Moreno's wife and a continued co-creator of the methods of psychodrama and sociometry, wanted what he wanted: for psychodrama and sociometry to "heal all of mankind," to reach all who needed it. They felt that they had something that could change the world and regretted that psychodrama had become confined only to the mental health field. In that spirit, Zerka was ever supportive of my own adaptation of the method in treating those in the addictions and broader mental health fields. Zerka's no-nonsense way of doing this work, always keeping the discipline of the method consistent and lines of execution clean with her open-mindedness and creativity, gave me a solid theoretical and methodological base from which to work. I am also indebted to Robert Siroka, whose training as a psychologist informed his seamless integration of psychodrama with group therapy and, in his case, with humor and healing.

Another important thank-you goes to Cynthia Moreno Tuohy, NAADAC's executive director, and Jessica O'Brien, NAADAC's director of training and professional development, for partnering with me to produce a certificate in relational trauma repair (RTR) sociometrics. Their clear-sightedness in seeing that this is the work that is needed, both for therapists to do their own healing and for those struggling with addictions of all kinds to find their path to recovery, is the inspiration for the NAADAC RTR Sociometrics certificate.

I also want to acknowledge, thank, and express gratitude for the addictions field and all of my colleagues and friends in it. I love working in this field. There is a shared passion for helping others because "we've been there"—we know the pain and wreckage that living in the wake of addiction causes. And we have known the miracle of recovery, whether from addiction, codependency, or adult child issues of relational trauma. Because this is frontline work, this field allows for a latitude of experimentation: We do what we see works. We embrace what helps our clients get better. It has been in this spirit that I have developed RTR sociometrics. Although I have drawn all of the basic theory from the best in our field, I have adapted to meet the pressing needs of therapists who need to learn an experiential approach that is manageable for them to learn and engaging, healing, and educational for their clients. Sociometrics takes the mystery out of using experiential, embodied forms of therapy in working with relational trauma for both the therapist and the client.

Finally, I want to say a big thank-you to Kate Sample at PESI Publishing for bringing this book forward with such grace and clarity. Her understanding of the importance of creating user-friendly materials for therapists is the impetus behind this book. And thank you to Marisa Solis, whose gift for bringing forward the core concepts of complex material has been so helpful. She has used her acumen in helping to shape the material in order to create an accessible and user-friendly guide for therapists. Thank you to Gretchen Panzer for providing an editorial attention to detail, flow, and accuracy that contributed so greatly to making the book work for therapists. The team at PESI has been a real example of professionalism and a great pleasure to work with.

Introduction

With the advent of trauma and neurobiology research, there has been a steadily growing awareness that trauma, including relational trauma, can have a lasting effect on the body and the nervous system, as well as on the mind and the heart. For this reason, the body needs to be a part of the therapies we use in treating posttraumatic stress disorder (PTSD) and complex posttraumatic stress disorder (C-PTSD).

Put plainly, talk therapy is insufficient in healing trauma.

Bessel van der Kolk and Peter Levine noted this 30 years ago, and today more than ever clinicians are accepting that words alone are not enough to help clients revisit and repair the psychic frozenness and dysregulated inner states that can result from relational disruptions. Because of the way the body processes—or sometimes doesn't process—trauma, we need to observe and deconstruct how the nervous system may be holding on to emotional pain before we try to describe that pain in words.

We, as therapists, need to let the client's body show us how their past hurts evidence themselves when body states or memories from long ago become triggered today. The body holds the secrets of the unconscious mind, so what the client's body reveals offers a royal road to their unconscious. Unpacking what it is showing us, alongside the meaning the client has made out of painful interactions in their life, provides a path to shifting less-than-functional patterns from the past that they may be living out in the present. This is what bottom-up, experiential, and embodied therapy is all about—and why it has become recognized as a cutting-edge approach when it comes to healing trauma.

Trauma-Informed Therapies in This Book

This book offers experiential and embodied processes that are structured, disciplined, educational, and accessible. These processes are rooted in Jacob Levy Moreno's triadic system of psychodrama, sociometry, and group therapy. His were the first forms of mind-body therapy, in turn-of-the-century Vienna, happening alongside the work of such luminaries as Freud and Montessori. Moreno famously said, "The body remembers what the mind forgets," a prescient statement in light of the current popularity of neurobiology and the groundbreaking books, Peter Levine's *Waking the Tiger* and Bessel van der Kolk's *The Body Keeps the Score*. Sociometrics grew out of the principles of Moreno's methods and is based in solid theory and generations of refinement.

Initially, the mental health field looked at events to explain the at times devastating impact of relational trauma. Therapists used narrative to describe the impact of trauma, but narrative didn't address or heal what happened on the inside of people that changed the way they experienced themselves and their relationships.

Yet until those inner truths have surfaced and been processed, descriptive words are simply words, lacking the power to heal. That is why we need to incorporate into our sessions therapies that facilitate entering the inner states that hold the truth of our clients' experiences and that drive subsequent thinking, meaning-making, and behaviors. We need to let disowned and forgotten parts of the self come forward organically through a process that allows the body as well as the mind to participate.

When van der Kolk first said that words don't heal (2014), it changed the way I worked as a psychodramatist and sociometrist. Around the same time, I was working with Stanley Greenspan's (2009) research, which offered insight into how an emotional language is built in childhood through the myriad of meaning-laden gestures and movements before words ever enter the picture. Stephen Porges's (2004) introduction of neuroception and the social engagement system provided the scientific underpinnings to describe why sociometrics and psychodrama actually work. Dan Siegel (1999) introduced interpersonal neurobiology, shedding further light on the interactive nature of coregulation, and Peter Levine (1997) opened the conversation on how to let the body have a voice and how to observe and work with frozenness in the nervous system.

In addition to these influences, I used Maria Montessori's model of the prepared learning environment (1995), which allows the learner to choose the work they feel drawn to and positions the teacher as a catalyst between the learner and the prepared environment rather than the exclusive purveyor of knowledge.

With this rich wellspring of immense contributions to the field of mind-body understanding and childhood education, I developed my own sociometrics. I did this slowly over time to meet the needs of groups in therapy for relational trauma from the disequilibrating, toxic effects of living with addiction, being addicted, or both, as well as from the debilitating impact of living with mental illness, dysfunction, or both.

My objective was simple: to make experiential healing accessible, user-friendly, and responsible.

But first, there were a few issues that needed solving. While psychodrama had been incorporated into most treatment centers that recognized its profound role in treating trauma, therapists weren't always trained well enough to implement this very open-ended method safely. Because of this lack of understanding of the full method of psychodrama, there tended to be an overemphasis on each individual's "piece of work" and on a catharsis of abreaction as an end goal of role plays, which ignored a catharsis of integration.

I decided to use sociometry as a base from which to develop my approach, because it is easier to learn and safer to implement than psychodrama. In response to budget cuts and an increasing need for one professional to deliver therapy to potentially large groups, I adapted sociometric processes to make them significantly longer, offered many more possibilities for choice and member-to-member connection, and added psychoeducation.

Siegel (personal communication, 2019) advises that the vehicles we use to heal trauma feel welcoming and safe, so that people don't orient to them as unsafe and thus become anxious or shut down. Porges (personal communication, 2021) adds that if the methods we use feel threatening or overly evaluative, clients may feel a need to self-protect rather than enter into the healing process.

That's why I have developed my sociometric approach to feel welcoming, engaging, and nonevaluative by putting choice-making and connection, wherever possible, in the hands of the group members themselves. The role of the therapist is reduced and opportunities for meaningful connection among participants are enhanced, creating a living, real-time experiential process in which the group members become, as Moreno (1946/2019) advised, healing agents for each other. This simple, self-directed process builds autonomy, initiative, resourcefulness, and resilience.

It also counteracts the immobilization that can accompany trauma. Participants "warm up" both their bodies and their limbic systems through the movement-based processes of floor checks, timelines, and targeted role plays. This allows them to better access their feelings and share them in authentic, meaningful connection.

The processes themselves are structured and predictable because that's what the human brain and body likes in order to feel safe, and they're engaging because that's what human beings need in order to feel alive (Porges, personal communication, 2022). They empower clients to move through their issues at their own pace while still being motivated and stimulated. Clients can enter the inner states where pain, hope, fear, and dreams live, then vivify and share these parts of themselves with others. They gain insight through action, rather than interpretation. They create new meaning as they welcome back the parts of themselves that they have shut down and allow them to move and speak. They come alive on the inside, and that changes their interactions on the outside.

CHAPTER 1

When It Hurts to Love: What Is Relational Trauma?

Relational trauma, simply put, can occur in the context of our early attachment relationships when there are repeated ruptures in loving connection that regularly go unrepaired. Because children are dependent on their parents or caregivers for their very survival, they are especially vulnerable to experiencing deep fear, anxiety, and pain at rejection. Often characterized by coldness, indifference, dismissal, or invalidation of the child's emotions on the part of the caregiver, unrecognized and unhealed relational trauma, also called complex trauma, can wreak havoc on the child's ability to trust, connect, and thrive in relationships with others.

When clients have felt traumatized in their attachment relationships, they may live with a residue of unconscious physical, emotional, and psychological pain. If that childhood pain is not made conscious, it tends to remain compartmentalized and hidden. Then it leaks out sideways in a myriad of ways: as disgruntled facial expressions, undermining comments, and distancing or clingy behaviors. Years or decades later, when these clients become adults and create families of their own, the pressures of partnering and parenting can trigger these "forgotten" inner states. The very intense emotions of closeness, neediness, and vulnerability that are a part of our adult intimate relationships act as a trigger for all the unfelt, unhealed attachment pain of childhood.

In the same way that a soldier might hit the pavement when he hears a car backfiring because his unconscious interprets the sound as gunfire, our clients of relational trauma hit the ground emotionally and psychologically when yelling in the present reminds them of yelling in the past, or when stonewalling now hurts like stonewalling from long before. Once these lacunae get triggered, the client may experience conflicts not as their rational adult self but as the wounded child who lives inside of them.

All too often our clients interpret—or misinterpret—today's conflicts through the lens of the traumatized child of yesterday. But this interpreting is largely unconscious, and this is key in understanding adult relational trauma. Clients don't know *what* they don't know, and they don't know *that* they don't know. They may remember that they got hurt as kids, but they haven't been able to feel it and process the visceral contents of that hurt enough to move through and beyond it. So while the recollections can be conscious, the feelings and sensations woven into them are not. Adult relational trauma is pain from childhood that has remained unconscious and unprocessed that is replaying its unconscious visceral contents over and over again in adult relationships.

Event versus Relational Trauma

Adult relational trauma isn't necessarily the result of a list of overt events, because events are not the only way in which children get hurt. Because significant aspects of childhood pain are unconscious, in trying to describe their inner discomfort or reactivity, clients can feel at a loss for words. They can't necessarily find themselves in questions like "Were you sexually abused?" "Who hit you?" "Can you remember anything specific?" or "Did you witness abuse?" We, as therapists, need to understand that relational trauma can also occur at very subtle levels.

When a child is unable to get the face they love to turn toward them, when they feel they don't matter to the people they want most to matter to, it can leave a mark on them that lasts a lifetime. And if it is the parents who are traumatizing them by their coldness, indifference, or outward abuse, then that child is losing their first line of defense. The very people they are supposed to go to for comfort and reassurance are the ones hurting them.

Thus, for a small child being hurt by those they desperately want to be loved by, subtle as well as overt abuse can wreak a kind of damage to their inner world and their nervous system that undermines their ability to comfortably create intimate connection as an adult. It shapes the way they see themselves, how they live in their own skin, and how they experience the intimate, shared space of relationships. It can teach them that relationships, which can hurt under the best of circumstances, can become overwhelmingly painful and difficult to live in.

The family is the first classroom on relationships—where the child is learning how to love, reason, and develop character, discipline, self-confidence, and a moral compass to live by. It's where they learn how love feels, what love means, and how it is actualized. It's where they learn how to hurt, how to restore inner calm, and how to manage and repair conflicts as they encounter the inevitable "slings and arrows . . . that flesh is heir to" (Shakespeare, 1601/2019, 3.1.59–64).

Children make sense of circumstances with limited psychological equipment; they think and reason through the tender, immature, and magical eyes of childhood. Children are dependent and little, and need someone big to make them feel safe, loved, and seen. If their parents are there for them in the myriad ways that create security and happiness, they can relax and trust. But if no one is there at the other end of the child's innocent attempts to connect, then they do not learn how to be in comfortable and authentic connection with others.

As Ed Tronick points out in discussing his still face experiment, children need loving contact like they need oxygen (Johnson, 2016). When this loving attention is denied to them, or when it is given intermittently or is based not on the child's but the parent's need, children can collapse inside. If no one shows any interest in where they have gone, they can just stay in that place.

Making the unconscious conscious is what this book is all about. We need to help our clients access these compartments and inner states so that they can feel and heal them. Sociometrics and role play bring these forgotten selves forward so that our clients can listen to what the selves have to tell them, observe them, and give them a voice.

My processes take out the guesswork for therapists. I've designed them to be easy to implement and to feel "safe and welcoming," as Siegel says (personal communication, 2021), so that clients do not feel a need to unconsciously reengage their defenses and self-protect—so that they can actually engage in the therapeutic process and heal.

Neuroception: Picking Up on Subtle Relational Signals

Neuroception, a term coined by Stephen Porges (2004), describes our innate ability to use intricate, meaning-laden, barely perceptible mind-body signals to establish bonds and communicate our needs and intentions. It's part of what Porges (2003) calls our social engagement system.

Neuroception is the process through which we learn to read the subtle signals coming toward us so that we can discern if we're safe to interact or if our nervous system needs to brace itself for zingers, rejections, competition, or criticism. Can we relax and be ourselves in this situation, or do we need to self-protect? If the signals we're picking up from those we depend upon are indifferent, cold, dismissive, or threatening, this neuroception system sets off an inner alarm, which is followed by a reflexive cascade of mind-body responses honed by eons of evolution to keep us from being harmed.

As children, we learn to safely experience and contain our emotions in many ways, but there is wide agreement that one of the primary ways this happens is in the arms of those who raise us. In the caring arms of our parents and caregivers, we learn to contain and tolerate our affective range of responses that we continue to build on throughout our development. We absorb the ability to self-soothe and self-regulate from our nourishing connection or co-state with our caregivers (Moreno, 1946/2019), and those skills then become ours—they become portable.

Successful self-regulation grows out of successful coregulation (Porges, personal communication, 2022). But in pain-engendering exchanges, "people are not able to use their interactions to regulate their physiological states in relationship. . . . They are not getting enough back from the other person that can help them to remain calm and regulated. Quite the opposite. The other person's behavior is making them go into a scared, braced-for-danger state. Their physiology is being upregulated" (Porges, personal communication, n.d.).

These mind-body responses are occurring beneath the level of our conscious awareness. As Porges (2011) writes, "The detection of a person as safe or dangerous triggers neurobiologically determined pro-social or defensive behaviors. Even though we may not always be aware of danger on a cognitive level, on a neurophysiological level, our body has already started a sequence of neural processes that would facilitate adaptive defense behaviors such as fight, flight, or freeze" (p. 11). Thus, when similar dynamics in adult relationships make us feel we need to self-protect, our intense response—based on our childhood experience—may still be unconscious.

How Trauma Gets Stuck in the Body

According to the work of Porges and Levine (1997), when the nervous system recalibrates into a braced-for-danger state, not only does the body remember this trauma response, but it can actually store and stay stuck in this mode. So even when the threat is gone, the body still perceives danger and its defenses stay engaged.

"The job of the autonomic nervous system," writes Deb Dana (2018, p. 17), "is to ensure we survive in moments of danger and thrive in times of safety. Survival requires threat detection and the activation of a survival response. Thriving demands the opposite—the inhibition of a survival response so that social engagement can happen. Without the capacity for activation, inhibition, and flexibility of response, we suffer." Sociometrics seeks to activate the social engagement system and train flexibility. One of Moreno's central goals of psychodrama and sociometry is what he called "spontaneity training."

Questions don't help our clients heal, nor do intellectualizations of what hurt them. They need forms of therapy that can access the state of frozenness that is held in the nervous system. They need therapeutic vehicles that allow them to talk not as the adult to the parent they have today but as the child to the parent they had when they were young. They need to give the child within them a body and a voice so they can enter into the inner relational states that shaped who they became.

When a child goes into a shut-down or freeze state over a long period of time, they can lose access to important parts of themselves that would allow them to feel whole and alive in intimate connection. The result is that they can feel disconnected from parts of themselves and those they love, and this becomes a way of functioning. They don't learn how to work through conflict—how to translate hurt or angry feelings into words, talk about them, and listen to others do the same. Rather, they have learned to hide their feelings from those close to them—and even from themselves—and to avoid deep connection.

Later in life, when these clients try to have intimate relationships of their own (with partners, children, or others), those parts of themselves that they threw out of conscious awareness or shut down as kids inevitably get triggered. Their inner world still braces for danger, only they're not aware on a cognitive level that this is what's happening. Feeling vulnerable or hurt can be a challenge for anyone, but for the client who has been deeply wounded in their attachment relationships, it can feel like a deal breaker.

The sheer intensity of intimacy with their children and partners presses on these unprocessed childhood wounds. Our clients can't explain why they feel the way they do. They simply don't have the tools to resolve and repair discord or conflict because they never learned how. They may not have developed a language to talk about what they were feeling, or even learned how to feel safe feeling deep emotion. What they learned was to run from or avoid their real feelings. And that is what they repeat.

During conflicts, adult children of relational trauma may regress back to feeling like a wounded, lost, or unseen child on the inside. They may see-saw between an urge to fight hard and an urge to collapse into the shame they felt at their own unmet needs for love, closeness, and contact—emotions they felt were forbidden.

When they get triggered and feel overwhelmed by such feelings, they fear not only what is happening *outside* of them but also what is happening *inside* of them. Then they want a culprit, a reason to explain why they're feeling so distressed and overwhelmed. So they project old hurt and anger from yesterday onto and into new relationships of today. They make their unfelt pain from childhood about what triggered it rather than what caused it to be there in the first place, never making the connection as to why their reactions are often so much bigger than the current situation merits—and why they feel so small inside even though they are now big.

This is how pain from one generation gets re-created and played out in the next generation unconsciously.

How Childhood Itself Makes Kids Vulnerable

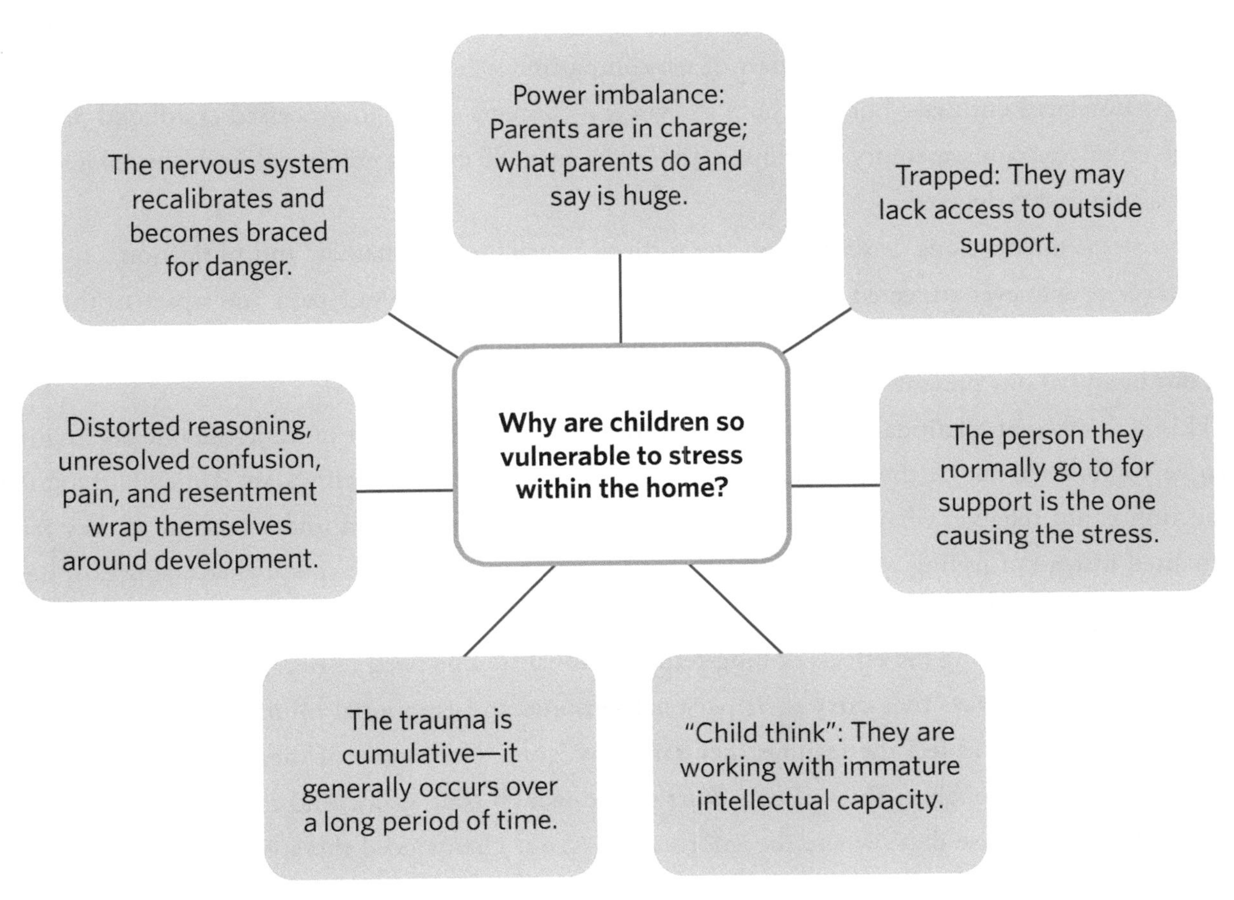

Fight/Flight: The Shutting Down of the Thinking/Reasoning Mind

In order to more fully understand why clients re-create dysfunctional relational dynamics, we need to continue to explore what other changes occurred on the inside as a result of what happened on the outside.

Along with the nervous system bracing for danger, there is another way that fight/flight/freeze manifests in the mind and body. Regardless of the situation—a baby trying desperately to get their parents' love and attention, a fifth grader who's been called on and can't come up with an answer they know they know, an adventurous hiker staring down a hungry bear—once fear or terror kicks in, the thinking mind shuts down, going temporarily offline (van der Kolk, 1987).

Nature does not want us thinking about whether we should escape from the danger; she wants us to just escape! So in moments of terror, our limbic system revs up to enable us to flee for safety or fight, and it forecloses on thought. However, and this is a big however, it continues to do its basic job of recording the emotions and sense memories that are part of the circumstance.

Because the thinking mind is temporarily shut down, we're not making sense of what we're experiencing. So we carry the imprint of the experience in the form of sense memories and emotions, often referred to as body memories. But there's no meaning or understanding woven into them. There's no storyline. We don't have a clear picture of what happened, especially if we're kids and no one is helping us make sense of it. So these unconscious mind-body feelings and sense impressions live unnamed, unexplained, and unthought-about. They are a part of us but not a part of us, compartmentalized, shrink-wrapped, and siloed as little, seemingly unrelated entities—but they hold the visceral contents of our unprocessed childhood pain. This mélange of unconscious memory develops a life of its own. It creates emotional and physiological land mines waiting to be triggered.

Because it's unconscious, it surfaces in the form of reenactment dynamics and projections. It attaches to whatever or whoever triggered it, and then we mistakenly attribute our pain and upset to the person who triggered it and may never make the connection that the pain from our past is being re-created and lived out in and as our present.

This is the face of relational trauma, the kind that the client often can't quite figure out because it can be so very subtle. It can be the product of living in a home where real feelings are denied and authentic connection is not reliable, where they cannot talk about what they feel and understand it, so they remain fragmented instead of feeling whole. Or it can result from a more obvious type of chaos, abuse, or neglect that goes unacknowledged and unrepaired.

Adults who are healing the effects of long-term relational trauma need to find plenty of ways to reenter the inner states and spaces that carry their personal sensorial and emotional information so that they can let down their guard and feel the feelings they ran away from. The modes of therapy we use need to feel welcoming and safe enough so these clients don't shut down all over again. And the interventions need to involve the body, because that's where the information is; our clients need therapies that restimulate these inner states and that reintroduce safe connection with the self and others. To do this, the body as well as the mind needs to find its voice.

PTSD and C-PTSD

Posttraumatic stress disorder (PTSD) in the DSM is seen as a chronic set of long-term symptoms that manifest after experiencing or witnessing one or more traumatic events. It can also be pain from one part of life that is shut down and resurfaces later—days, months, or years after the event or circumstance has passed. Much research has been done on Vietnam War veterans, for example, to understand why they still suffered from symptoms such as nightmares, somatic disturbances, and mood disorders long after the war was over (van der Kolk has contributed greatly in this area—see Tippett, 2013; Williams, 2021).

The diagnosis of complex PTSD (C-PTSD), which was introduced in 1988 by Dr. Judith Herman (1997), refers to a more cumulative or chronic type of relational trauma. It can occur when primary attachment relationships do not support a healthy, sustaining, and nourishing connection—in other words, when someone feels unseen, unheard, or not loved for who they are. C-PTSD can also occur when one's relationships feel disruptive, neglectful, or abusive or when one's home or world feels disordered and unsafe. The anxiety of living without what feels like genuine and sustaining connection can cause, for example, a small child to withdraw or shut down parts of themselves so that they can continue to function and remain connected to the people they need in order to survive. Years or even decades later, that unprocessed pain emerges, making the natural vicissitudes of intimacy or conflict that are a part of close relationships feel overwhelming or even dangerous.

As Siegel explains:

> Trauma can occur any time that we've encountered an experience that overwhelmed our capacity to cope with what's going on. So if we're an adult and we have trauma, it's going to have one kind of impact. But if we're a young child and we experience trauma, especially in relationship to those we depend on, our caregivers, then the trauma takes on a different kind of impact. That kind of betrayal by our caregivers leads to all kinds of ways where the developing brain, for example, doesn't develop the kind of integrative circuits that it otherwise would. So developmental trauma, which means abuse, neglect, or both early in life, has been shown to result in impairments in the growth of the fibers of the brain that take differentiated areas, like the left and the right or widely separated memory systems. The brain, in other words, compartmentalizes pain, and doesn't create a kind of relational coherence. (personal communication, 2021)

But out of sight is not out of mind. Compartmentalized, unprocessed pain leaks out and cries for help in the form of free-floating anxiety or depression or symptoms such as nightmares, backaches, emotional or muscle constriction, rage, violence, or urges to self-medicate. It also reappears as we repeat dysfunctional behaviors from the past in our adult relationships in the present.

Symptoms of PTSD and C-PTSD

PTSD and C-PTSD have many overlapping symptoms and manifestations because all trauma is processed by the same human system. Trauma leaves its trail of pain in the body, emotions, mind, and spirit. Understanding some of the manifestations helps to make clients aware of how trauma may be living inside of them. The following handout, which is designed for you to share with your clients, describes many of the common symptoms of PTSD and C-PTSD.

Client Handout

Symptoms of PTSD and C-PTSD*

Posttraumatic stress disorder (PTSD) and complex PTSD (C-PTSD) are diagnoses that describe the symptoms people often have after experiencing traumatic events or situations. The following list explains some of these common symptoms.

- **Problems with self-regulation:** When you have experienced trauma, you may have broad swings back and forth between feeling overwhelmed with intense emotion and shutting down or going numb. When you feel angry, afraid, or anxious, for example, you go from zero to ten, and ten to zero, with no speed bumps in between. You have trouble regulating your emotions, and that can lead to difficulty regulating your thinking or behavior. This cycling is sometimes called black and white or yo-yoing.
- **Hypervigilance/anxiety:** When you're hypervigilant, you scan your environment and relationships for signs of potential danger or repeated relationship insults and ruptures. You may constantly try to read the faces of those around you so that you can protect yourself against perceived danger. You're always bracing for danger, waiting for the other shoe to drop, or walking on eggshells. This can create problems because you may perceive danger even where little exists or become overly reactive to perceived slights, making it difficult for others to connect with you or even driving a situation toward problems (van der Kolk, 1987).
- **Hyperreactivity/being easily triggered:** Living with relationship trauma can oversensitize you to stress and make you feel compromised in processing deep emotion. Consequently, you may overrespond to stressful situations, blowing conflicts that could be managed calmly out of proportion. You become easily triggered, overreacting even to simple, day-to-day frustrations such as slow-moving traffic. Stimuli that reminds you of your relationship trauma, such as feeling helpless or humiliated, can trigger old vulnerability. Yelling, criticism, and even certain facial expressions may trigger a stronger reaction than is appropriate to the situation. This hyperreactivity can affect your relationships, your work, and other areas of your life.
- **Emotional constriction:** Growing up in a home where the expression of genuine feeling was not encouraged, along with the emotional numbing that is a part of the trauma response, can cause you to have a restricted range of feelings that you are comfortable feeling and expressing (van der Kolk, 1987).
- **Loss of trust and faith:** When your personal world and the relationships within it become very unpredictable or unreliable, you may experience a loss of trust and faith, both in relationships and in

* Adapted from Dayton (2011)

life's ability to repair and renew itself. Restoring hope is incredibly important in healing relationship trauma. Having a spiritual belief system can be helpful in this regard (van der Kolk, 1987).

- **Unresolved grief:** Experiencing relational trauma involves suffering profound losses. These might include the loss of parents to rely on, the loss of family members, the loss of a feeling of safety and normalcy, the loss of the secure family unit, the loss of trust, the loss of a stable and smooth early development, and the losses of comfortable family events, rituals, and holidays. You may need to mourn not only what happened but also what never got a chance to happen.
- **Traumatic bonding:** Traumatic bonds are unhealthy bonding styles that tend to be created in families where there is significant fear, primarily when there is an abuse of power or authority (Carnes, 1991). These bonds have a tendency to repeat themselves—once you have experienced a traumatic bond, you will likely create traumatic bonds in other relationships throughout your life, even without being aware of it.
- **Learned helplessness/avoidance:** When you feel you can do nothing to affect or change the situation you're in, you may give up and collapse on the inside. You may develop learned helplessness, losing some of your ability to take actions to affect change or move a situation forward. You may also avoid people, places, and things that threaten to trigger your unresolved past anxiety (Seligman & Maier, 1967; van der Kolk, 1987).
- **Confusion:** The cognitive dissonance that results from relational trauma can cause you to doubt your own perceptions. You may be repeatedly told that what you see and sense is not really happening, and this denial and deception can bend your reality. As a result, you may become confused. You learn to doubt your own feelings and your best thinking. Eventually, you may avoid coming to conclusions and decisions, and this avoidance can grow into a defense that you slip into, a sort of zone that becomes a familiar hiding place.
- **Somatic disturbances:** The body processes and holds emotion. If you can't feel and heal your pain and inner stress consciously, your emotions may get stored in a sensitive body part and cause pain or other somatic disturbances. Examples include back pain, chronic headaches, muscle tightness or stiffness, stomach problems, heart pounding, headaches, shivering or shaking, and sleep problems, such as nightmares or flashbacks that intrude on our relaxation (van der Kolk, 1987).
- **Tendency to isolate:** When you have experienced trauma, you may have a tendency to isolate and withdraw into yourself when you are feeling vulnerable. You have learned to recoil into a personless world and take refuge in avoiding connection. Unfortunately, the more you isolate, the more out-of-practice you become at making connections with people, which can further isolate you.
- **Cycles of reenactment:** The reenactment dynamic is one of the most common ways that trauma from one generation gets passed down through subsequent generations. You tend to re-create those circumstances in your life that feel unresolved, perhaps in an attempt to see the self more clearly and master or resolve your pain, or perhaps because you are locked in circuits of

brain-body patterning that are largely unconscious. You repeat the relational patterns that are familiar to you, even if they do not work to get you what you really want.

- **High-risk behaviors:** Adrenaline is highly addictive to the brain and may be a powerful mood enhancer. After experiencing trauma, you may be more likely to seek this adrenaline rush by engaging in behaviors that put you at risk in some way, such as speeding, unsafe sex, impulsive spending, fighting, drug use, or working too hard (van der Kolk, 1987).
- **Survival guilt:** If you got out of an unhealthy family system while others remain mired within it, you may experience survivor's guilt, a term originally used to describe the experience of soldiers who left comrades on the battlefield. You may become overly preoccupied with fixing your family because the thought of being happy while your family members remain locked in dysfunctional ways of living can be very disturbing.
- **Shame:** Shame can become not so much a feeling that is experienced in relation to an incident or situation, but rather a basic attitude toward and about yourself. It can be difficult to identify because it may be so pervasive. You might experience this all-encompassing shame as a lack of energy for life, an inability to accept love and caring on a consistent basis, or a hesitancy to move into self-affirming roles. It may also play out as impulsive decision-making or, conversely, an inability to make decisions at all (Porges, personal communication, 2022).
- **Aggression against yourself or others:** Being abused as a child increases the risk for later delinquency and violent criminal behavior (Herrenkohl et al., 2016). It is also a highly significant predictor of self-harm behaviors (van der Kolk et al., 1991). Over the course of your life, you may have found yourself caught in a cycle of violence or having thoughts about harming yourself or others.
- **Development of rigid psychological defenses:** As a result of consistently being wounded emotionally, and not being able to address it openly and honestly, you may have developed rigid psychological defenses to manage your fear and pain. These defenses operate without your conscious awareness. Some examples are dissociation (experiencing altered states or gaps in your consciousness), denial (refusing to acknowledge certain facts, feelings, or thoughts), splitting (seeing yourself or others as either all "good" or all "bad," with no in-between), repression (forgetting painful memories, feelings, or thoughts), minimization (presenting events to yourself or others as unimportant or insignificant), intellectualization (dealing with problems in a purely abstract or logical way to avoid painful emotions), and projection (refusing to acknowledge certain traits in yourself while attributing those traits to other people instead).
- **Relationship issues:** After experiencing trauma within the context of your primary relationships, you may tend to re-create dysfunctional patterns of relating in the present that mirror unresolved issues from the past. This can occur through psychological dynamics such as projection (projecting your pain onto someone else or onto a situation), transference (transferring old pain into new

relationships), and reenactment patterns (re-creating dysfunctional patterns of relating over and over again; Hermann, 1997).

- **Depression with feelings of despair:** The limbic system regulates mood. When you are dysregulated in your emotional system from living through trauma, you may have trouble regulating feelings such as anger, sadness, and fear, all of which may contribute to depression. You might have dark ruminations or view life through a negative lens. Research both in animals and in people shows that stress or trauma early in life can sensitize neurons and receptors throughout the central nervous system so that they perpetually overrespond to stress (van der Kolk, 1987).
- **Distorted reasoning/disorganized thinking:** We make sense of situations with the developmental equipment we have at any given age. When we're young, we make childlike meaning, which may be laced with magical thinking or interpretations that are based on the natural egocentricity of the child, who feels that the world circulates around and because of them. This kind of reasoning can be immature and distorted. When your family unit is spinning out of control, you may tell yourself whatever is necessary to allow yourself to stay connected—that your drunk mother has the flu or that your sexually invasive father loves you best. You may deny the truth that is right in front of you in an attempt to make more palatable meaning out of confusing, frightening, or painful experiences that feel senseless. You may then carry this distorted reasoning into your adult relationships. If those who raised you used denial as a way to avoid looking at their own or the family dysfunction, that denial is another way that your thinking can become distorted.
- **False self-functioning:** When you feel that your genuine reactions aren't acceptable to those you wish to be accepted by, you may create a false self that is more palatable or popular with them, a presentation that you imagine will work better or that does work better in your family system, but that does not allow you to be your true self. Your true self is based on your spontaneous, authentic experience, and it makes you feel alive. Your false self, on the other hand, is a defensive facade—it may seem real to others, but it lacks spontaneity and leaves you feeling dead and empty (Winnicott, 1965).
- **Learning difficulties:** Your ability to focus in the present can be negatively impacted by trauma. Physiological hyperarousal interferes with your capacity to concentrate and to make sense of, draw meaning from, and learn from experience or teaching (van der Kolk et al., 1995).
- **Loss of ability to take in caring and support from others:** After experiencing trauma, you may feel emotionally numb or constricted. You might also be preoccupied with real or perceived threats because your brain and body are still on high alert. All of this may lead to a loss of your ability to take in caring and support from other people. Additionally, as mistrust takes hold, your willingness to accept love and support may lessen. You might be afraid that if you let your guard down, if you let connection feel too good, you'll only set yourself up for more pain when

the inevitable happens and you're disappointed again and again. So you protect yourself as best as you know how, imagining that by avoiding meaningful connection you will also avoid getting hurt (van der Kolk, 1987).

- **Self-medication:** Many trauma survivors experience a desire to self-medicate with drugs, alcohol, or other means. You may use substances as a mood regulator because your own skills of self-regulation feel compromised (for example, you might drink to help yourself feel more relaxed or numb intense emotions). You may develop an addiction that mirrors your parent's or that reenacts your childhood trauma (such as engaging in risky sexual behaviors as an adult after you were sexually abused as a child). As you recover, you will need to deal with both the earlier trauma and the substance use or compulsive behavior (van der Kolk, 1987).

How Do the Symptoms Play Out in Relationships?

I find that the most reliable way to understand the degree of unconsciousness that accompanies unprocessed PTSD or C-PTSD is by looking at the ways in which pain gets played out in the client's relationships without their awareness. Unresolved pain can reoccur throughout the client's life—and be passed down through generations—through the following relational dynamics:

- **Reenactment dynamics:** Childhood pain resurfaces and is re-created in adult relationships through unconscious dynamics such as projection, transference, or overreacting to or misreading others' intentions and actions. Often the client has no idea they are doing this; they cling tightly to their perception that the complications in their current relationships are their only problem, and they can be blind to the pain they are importing that is fueling conflict. They may well be with a partner who is doing the same.
- **Projection:** Because the client doesn't want to feel the pain that is getting triggered inside of them, they make it about the person who is triggering it. They want to get it out of their insides and onto someone or something else so they feel less confused and lost. They want a quick reason for why they feel bad inside, a culprit on whom to pin their pain.
- **Transference:** The client layers characteristics from their childhood relationships onto their present adult relationships (intimate, social, professional, etc.), which elicits certain behaviors from others.
- **Misreading:** The client interprets an interaction in the present through the skewed or scared eyes of their wounded inner child. As a result, they either overreact according to yesterday's expectations or elicit expected or anticipated behaviors from others.
- **Lack of emotional regulation:** This reflects the dysregulation of the traumatized nervous system, which remains set on a sort of orange alert. Dysregulation can manifest as emotional over- or underreactions ranging from rage, hysterics, or panic to shutdown, withdrawal, or flat affect. In rigid reactions wherein the client has trouble regulating their level of involvement, they are either all in or all out—they can only say no or they can only say yes (e.g., they overexercise, overeat, or overdrink, or they do the opposite).
- **Dysfunctional patterns of thinking, feeling, and relating:** The client has patterns of thought, mood issues, or ways of relating that don't lead to positive solutions or conflict resolution but rather continue the dysfunction throughout their lifetime and potentially across generations.

Understanding Trauma

Keep in mind that clients with PTSD will avoid thinking, feeling, or talking about what has hurt them in the past. It stirs them up inside, it intrudes on their peace of mind, and they're haunted by images from the past that they try to ignore. Much of it was never made conscious—they truly don't know it's there. Add to this that adult relational trauma can make them mistrust the very people they need to turn to in order to decode their complex inner world, and the dilemma is clear: Adult children of relational trauma may resist the very vehicles that would help them to heal, such as feeling, naming, and sharing the contents of their inner world with another human being.

In moments of high stress and terror, the prefrontal cortex shuts down, cutting off access to conscious thought and depriving us of one of our best ways of right-sizing feelings: understanding! Unless someone helps a child, for example, to understand what just hurt them and made them want to run, fight, or withdraw, their nervous system will not become calm and balanced again but will retain a feeling of being braced for danger.

As Peter Payne, Peter Levine, and Mardi Crane-Godreau (2015) explain:

> In response to threat and injury, animals, including humans, execute biologically based, non-conscious action patterns that prepare them to meet the threat and defend themselves. The very structure of trauma, including activation, freezing, dissociation, and collapse, is based on the evolution of survival behaviors. When threatened or injured, all animals draw from a "library" of possible responses. We orient, dodge, duck, stiffen, brace, retract, fight, flee, freeze, collapse, etc. *All* of these coordinated responses are somatically based—they are things that the body does to protect and defend itself. (p. 14)

It is when these orienting and defending responses are overwhelmed that we see trauma:

> The bodies of traumatized people portray "snapshots" of their unsuccessful attempts to defend themselves in the face of threat and injury. Trauma is a highly activated incomplete biological response to threat, *frozen in time*. For example, when we prepare to fight or to flee, muscles throughout our entire body are tensed together in specific patterns of high-energy readiness. When we are unable to complete these appropriate actions, we fail to discharge the tremendous energy generated by our survival preparations. This energy becomes fixed (as a snapshot) in specific patterns of neuromuscular readiness or collapse (i.e., mobilization or immobilization). The person then remains in a state of acute and then chronic arousal and dysfunction in the central nervous system. Traumatized people are not suffering from a disease in the normal sense of the word—they have become stuck in a hyper-aroused or "shutdown" (dissociated) state. It is difficult if not impossible to function normally under these circumstances. (Payne et al., 2015, p. 14)

Why Words Don't Heal

To illuminate why words aren't useful in resolving trauma, here is a story from a client, in her own words, that encapsulates how relational trauma feels inside a person and how it heals.

> It was a pretty typical summer's day. We were hanging around with our four-year-old grandson, Jake, and his sister, Marisa. Our daughter was waiting for friends to arrive. As is often the case, everything happened at once: Marisa and Jake were fighting, the guests arrived, the pasta was al dente, the broccoli was done. In an attempt to get our grandson out of a chaotic kitchen and tell him to behave, my husband and I did something we almost never do: We each grabbed a hand and began to drag him out of there.
>
> He immediately started crying. Based on our intense reaction, he thought he'd done something horrible. He kept trying to justify himself. When I realized this, I said, "Jake, we're not mad at you, and besides, there is nothing you could do that would make us stop loving you." He began to relax, but not as much as I'd have hoped. He'd had what was for him a traumatizing experience—he felt that he had been bad, that we were angry, and that he'd disappointed two of his most beloved people in his young world. Clearly, more repair was needed.
>
> I put my arm around him and said, "What are you feeling, sweetheart?"
>
> "I don't know, Gram."
>
> "Can you give me a word, maybe?"
>
> "Not really."
>
> "Maybe just one?"
>
> And then he said something I will never forget.
>
> "I'm trying, but I can't think of one. It's like pieces of me are scattered all over the room and I can't pull them together enough to give you a word."
>
> This whole process took about 25 minutes. Once he was able to describe what felt indescribable, to put words not on a *feeling* but on an *experience,* he was himself again in the blink of an eye. He slid off the couch and returned to playing.

Here is what I want you to take away from this story: Jake couldn't tell his grandma what *had* happened. He could only tell her what *was* happening *in the moment*—what was happening in his mind and body *now* as a direct result of feeling there had been a serious break in their empathetic connection.

This is exactly what trauma resolution looks like. When a client revisits their trauma and the body state they experienced at that time, they need to tell you what is happening to them *right now* in their mind and body as they relive the painful moments or dynamics. They don't need to relive the trauma itself, but they do need to experience or reexperience the disequilibrating feelings, thoughts, and memories that are a part of them. And then the client can find the words to describe these experiences, directly as they feel inside of them. Interpretation at these delicate moments can interfere with the deep healing that the client is doing themselves.

Clients' behavior grows out of body states and emotions that they slip into when they get triggered, so learning to translate their inner experience into words and talk about it brings conscious awareness around how their trauma lives inside of them and reproduces its contents over time.

This is where words are helpful in healing—when they are used not as a narrative about what happened but to describe inner states so those states can be reflected on and communicated to others in a way that moves understanding forward. The therapy is bottom-up; it starts with directly connecting with and experiencing inner mind-body states and it ends with verbal description.

The purely intellectual narrative is useless and distracting. It puts someone in their head but doesn't do anything to heal them. Questioning only makes a traumatized person feel even more inadequate because they don't know why they can't describe their trauma. To keep from feeling inadequate all over again, they might placate or say something that might please their frustrated therapist or, worse still, adopt their therapist's version of what may have occurred.

This is why embodied forms of therapy are so important. Without a vehicle through which to feel what goes on inside of their body, the client can't get the full picture of how their nervous system recalibrated both to stay safe and to, in some manner, stay in the situation, and they can't connect with the visceral memories that are actually the body states that are driving their behavior. These parts from the past need to be refelt and reunderstood in the present so the client can understand what happened to them and move beyond it.

The Importance of Resilience in Experiential Healing

When working through the pain of a traumatic past, it is important for the client to identify not only what hurt them but also what sustained them. Terrible things happen, but interwoven with those terrible things are often meaningful sources of love and support that help the client overcome their circumstances and go on to have a purposeful and meaningful life.

Understanding what makes up resilience helps to counter what researchers refer to as the "damage" model—the idea that if someone had a troubled childhood, they are condemned to a troubled adulthood or are operating without strengths (Wolin & Wolin, 1993). In fact, adversity can help us develop strength if we learn to mobilize and make use of the supports that are at our disposal.

One way to understand resilience is to know what it *isn't*. As Karen Reivich and Andrew Shatté explain in *The Resilience Factor* (2002), the following inner states are associated with a lack of resilience:

- Anger
- Sadness or depression
- Guilt
- Anxiety or fear
- Embarrassment

Being stuck in a chronic version of any of these feelings will make it harder for the client to live their best life. It's a good idea to spend some time reflecting on where these feelings come from and how to work through them so the client can develop the skills to tolerate and process these emotions, rather than allowing them to cycle around inside of them.

On the other hand, we can look at what resilience *is*. The Connor-Davidson resilience scale (CD-RISC) is a highly validated and widely recognized measurement tool. In developing this scale, Connor and Davidson (2003) identified the following as the basic qualities of resilience:

- Being able to adapt to change
- Having close and secure relationships
- Believing that sometimes fate or God can help
- Feeling that you can deal with whatever comes
- Drawing confidence from past success when facing a new challenge
- Seeing the humorous side of things
- Being strengthened by coping with stress
- Tending to bounce back after illness or hardship
- Believing that things happen for a reason
- Putting forth your best effort, no matter what
- Believing that you can achieve your goals
- Not giving up when things seem hopeless
- Knowing where to turn for help
- Being able to focus and think clearly under pressure
- Preferring to take the lead in problem-solving
- Not being easily discouraged by failure
- Thinking of yourself as a strong person
- Making unpopular or difficult decisions
- Being able to handle unpleasant feelings
- Having to act on a hunch
- Having a strong sense of purpose
- Feeling in control of your life
- Enjoying challenges
- Working to attain your goals
- Taking pride in your achievements

In chapter 12, you'll find several sociometrics specifically targeted to building and consolidating resilience.

Healing can hurt at times; after all, the client is reexperiencing the vulnerability and pain of early abuse or neglect. However, as they are able to translate these deep feeling states into words and share them—and reflect on and reorder them as they become more conscious—they gain a sense of mastery or "survivor's pride" (Wolin & Wolin, 1993).

To be able to guide your clients on this journey from trauma and shame to healing and pride, you will need a therapeutic "map." The next chapter provides just that: a walk-through of my sociometric approach to treating adult children of relational trauma.

CHAPTER 2

My Sociometric Approach: Embodied, Experiential Processes for Relational Trauma Repair

Adults with complex trauma histories can be fearful of feeling the hurt they carry inside, so they may have a pattern of avoiding doing exactly what therapy is asking them to do. On top of that, they may have learned to mistrust relationships, which are their very vehicles of healing. Therefore, structured group processes feel safer to them than a less structured approach. This is why a combination of sociometrics and targeted role plays is an effective, relational, and titrated way of healing relational trauma.

What Is Sociometrics?

Sociometry—which is part of Jacob Levy Moreno's (1946/2019) triadic system of psychodrama, sociometry, and group psychotherapy—is the measurement of social choice, meaning the decisions, both conscious and unconscious, that are made regarding interpersonal affiliation. At its most basic level, sociometry addresses the various aspects of human connection. I have designed my sociometrics for group therapy settings, to create psychoeducational, titrated healing processes that can easily be adapted to the needs of any population. The word *trauma*, which can feel loaded to clients, as they think they have to come up with their most painful event, need never be mentioned. The relational healing and building of the skills of self-regulation, coregulation, emotional literacy, and resilience are baked into the processes themselves.

Sociometric exercises allow for movement throughout the entire process so that the limbic system can warm up, and this makes clients more able to access their emotions. It's rather like how walking together with a friend helps us to talk more freely—when the body is in motion, the limbic system warms up and feelings flow more easily. When the participants are on their feet, engaged, and connecting with themselves and each other, a good part of their healing and relational repair is already happening.

Sociometric processes also serve as a warm-up to role plays. Warm-up is everything in using role play. If you do role plays without sufficient warm up, your clients may have a harder time getting in touch with their inner world and the work can become forced. You are then at risk of using interpretation or pushing to get the client's work moving. When psychodrama is too controlled or in any way pre-planned, the unconscious doesn't pull forward that mélange of feeling, imagery, and role relationship that allows clients to embody and reveal the emotions the body is holding that let them "show us rather than tell us" how it felt during moments of conflict, closeness, distance, and so on.

Warm-up also lessens the risk of retraumatization because the client is dealing with what is organically coming forward for them in that particular moment, without being told or pushed toward any particular work. We are not putting them on the spot, but guiding them through an experiential process in which they feel a sense of control.

For all these reasons, I use sociometrics before engaging my clients in a role play. Two interventions in particular form the core of my approach: floor checks and timelines.

Floor Checks

Floor checks provide experiential learning on the symptoms of PTSD/C-PTSD, resilience, and posttraumatic growth, as well as a deep dive into the many manifestations of emotions such as anger, fear, grief, anxiety, depression, and forgiveness. Clients interact with research-based information written on cards placed on the floor. The therapist asks questions about how that information applies to each individual, and the clients themselves decide which feelings or symptoms they identify with at any given moment in response to the questions. In this way, feelings and symptoms can be felt and then translated into words and elevated to a conscious level wherein they can be reflected on and communicated to others. Floor checks encourage proficiency in emotional literacy, which is so important in consolidating the gains of embodied therapy and developing the kind of emotional intelligence that will allow them to make health-enhancing life choices.

The role of the therapist and any iatrogenic effects that could result from a client feeling misunderstood or overdiagnosed are lessened. Clients can better relax as they are given personal agency and autonomy—experiences that trauma-engendering exchanges often take away.

The structured, interactive, and repeated process of floor checks allows clients to feel secure in their participation. They gain insights into their own disease process, becoming stakeholders in their healing. And as they share all of this with others and listen to others do the same, they repair relational deficits and practice new ways of genuine and attuned relating.

Because floor checks are embodied and experiential, the client can actually experience what regulation of intense emotions feels like. This is why sociometrics does not need to be intense or have specific interventions in order to heal—because the interventions themselves are healing and reparative, and the potential for insights and skill building is baked into the processes themselves. The processes are also manageable for therapists to learn so that they can be incorporated where experiential work is needed to invigorate existing programming.

How I Developed Floor Checks

Robert Siroka, the founder of the Sociometric Institute and a trainee of Moreno, recalls that Moreno used to say, "I use psychodrama to get people in the door so that I can teach them sociometry" (Giacomucci, 2021). This statement always interested me, and it took me many years to fully comprehend the meaning.

I had been trying to integrate research with sociometry to make it more practical and educational for treatment centers, to better serve those who were delivering therapy to large groups of clients and with insufficient training in psychodrama. I was using Bowlby's (1982) four stages of loss as a locogram, and while it worked, it was limited. There were only a few options to choose from, so the warm-up process wasn't long enough to provide a process that offered enough choices so that it could be used for sustained psychoeducational processes in large groups. Nor did it offer enough moments of incremental, titrated healing and skill development. It was, however, educational, so that part was working.

In an attempt to create processes that I could use in my frequent program development for treatment centers and clinical groups, I arrived at one group having scrawled many feelings on pieces of paper to provide more options for choice-making, and I scattered these around the floor. I asked criterion questions to move the process forward—and the rest was a moment in my life that I will never forget. In front of my eyes, people healed each other. Over and over again they made choices in response to questions I asked and eventually invited them to ask as well. They laughed and they got teary. They were creative and spontaneous with their own questions and responses. They cracked jokes and supported each other through tender and revealing moments.

The process regulated itself because it was structured, and I could see that the group liked this—they understood that they needed to get to the point, make use of their sharing time, and listen as others made use of theirs. They wanted to hear from each other. They saw that if they chimed in, they didn't have to be on stage; they could be part of a group and still get their "work" done. And they knew that they didn't have to open up on every question if they didn't feel like it. They relaxed, and it was almost gamelike: fun but predictable.

The process got a bit intense but never seemed to get *too* intense, because the group, through natural empathy and limbic regulation, regulated itself. If someone seemed to need a little holding, the group saw to it. They regulated each other; they became an organic container. Because the clients felt in charge of their own process, able to choose what and how much they were willing to do, they didn't have to plow through resistance. They titrated their own level of participation. They self-regulated and co-regulated. People seemed more willing to open up when others were doing the same and when the opening up had a clear beginning, middle, and end. There was safety in numbers and safety in structure.

And I removed myself as the font of knowledge—this is very important. Adult children of relational trauma have learned to mistrust people who are telling them who to be. I created a process wherein the choice of what clients identify with is in their hands. It is they who say, "This symptom feels right for me but that one doesn't," and "This is how much of this symptom or feeling I am experiencing, and now I will tell *you* how I am experiencing it rather than having you tell me."

At every possible and ethical juncture, I put their healing in their hands. I provide endless opportunities for structured encounters throughout each process so group members can access each other around the feelings, symptoms, or age that they have in common at that moment. They can choose whom to share with and how much to share. They can practice feeling and connecting as they share who they are on the inside. Then they can take in sharing, caring, and support from others. In this way they become healing agents of each other.

After seeing how well my floor checks were working, I sunk into the research on feelings. I began to see not only *that* the *Feelings Floor Check* (page 52) was healing but *why*. I made the connection between trauma and addiction, or why resolving feelings through something this simple could work with resolving unconscious trauma and reduce relapse. People often relapse because their emotions are unmanageable for them; they avoid their feelings and then, when triggered, they are at risk for self-medicating to manage feelings that feel overwhelming. The *Feelings Floor Check* was helping them learn to tolerate deeper feeling states and translate them into words, share them, and listen as others shared. They were developing emotional and relational literacy through a contained, titrated, communal process.

As the *Feelings Floor Check* continued to grow in use, I wondered if the same approach might work for, say, grief or PTSD. I had found lecturing on trauma symptoms to be a somewhat overwhelming process for therapists and clients alike. People often became flooded with their own identification of the material being explored, especially in the early days of trauma research before the field had had a chance to absorb it. Unlike many forms of therapy, treatment for addiction includes education, giving the client up-to-date information so that they can wrap their minds around their own disease process and take responsibility for not only getting sober and emotionally sober, but staying that way.

I decided to pull the list of trauma symptoms off the chalkboard and put it onto the floor. I wondered if this change in format, along with including more options, would make it better. It changed everything. Suddenly learning and healing became integrated and experiential. There were revolving groupings of people who could share with the whole group or with each other, clustered around a particular symptom they had in common. The process could hold many people for a long time—for as long as the group was engaged in it. And because the process itself was self-sustaining, I became much less relevant; the participants didn't need to keep looking to me for direction or reassurance because they had each other. As long as I kept the questions flowing in an attuned manner and kept the room safe, the process almost ran itself.

Again, I was amazed at the brilliance of the participants. Given the right information, they intuitively knew how to use it. In front of my eyes, resistance and boredom evaporated. There was excitement and energy in the room as people moved around on their own and chose symptoms they identified with, then shared why they did. Lucid, moving, impromptu case examples started popping up all over the room, providing windows into the participants' inner worlds. In fact, the spontaneous things that people shared were a better illustration than any case example could possibly be in illuminating the trail of unresolved, repetitive trauma. And the more people shared, the more people shared—they were, as Dan Siegel says, "inspired to rewire."

As the participants shared, they healed. They gained empathy for each other and compassion for themselves. They learned to take in support from others and to give it. Their sense of isolation fell away, and they began connecting in vulnerable ways that created a deepening and widening circle of connection.

A prompt such as "Walk over to a symptom that your family of origin used to struggle with" became a way of looking at intergenerational issues that did not necessarily seek to overpathologize the family, but illuminate what struggles from yesterday might be being imported into today's relationships.

And so floor checks became a staple of relational trauma repair.

I have since developed a variety of floor checks, adapted to different symptoms and treatment goals; you will find these throughout the rest of the book. The floor check process itself is flexible, allowing for your own customization. Even mid-session, you or the group members can choose which prompts to give based on the cards available. You can also ask participants to "Walk over to someone who said something that moved you or that you identified with, and share with them what it was that caught your attention" as a way of extending the process and deepening connections.

Prompts inevitably create some moments that feel triggering, but it becomes a safe way to unpack these moments. For example, "Which feeling do you avoid feeling?" might be a triggering question that leads a client to realize that they avoid certain emotions. They could then reflect on why this is the case as a soft entry into trauma work. To help clients build resilience, you might include prompts such as "Walk over to a symptom that you feel you have made progress in managing," while questions like "Which feeling do you have trouble with when you encounter it in someone else?" help people begin to see how relational dynamics that may date from childhood have affected the way they relate and react in adulthood.

Clients often find these exercises enjoyable and almost gamelike, as well as deeply healing. The process feels safe enough that they tend not to overengage their defenses, thus allowing them to make gradual moves from states of dysregulation to coregulation in relational connection with others (Porges, personal communication, 2022). Their insights happen through an active process of sensing, feeling, sharing, and listening. Your job as the therapist, then, is to keep the workspace safe and the process moving. Trust the reparative experiences inherent in mobilizing and embodying the human social engagement system. Allow the floor check to work its magic.

Timelines

The timeline intervention helps clients focus and reflect on experiences from their past, present, or future. The *Attachment Timeline* (page 74) can be used as a developmental intervention. Throughout their walk on the timeline, as the client revisits moments or dynamics along their developmental continuum, they are able to cast role players to represent themselves or others at a particular age. They can bring a role relationship, whether with themselves or with someone else, from the past into the present—for example, they might do a role play with a part of self, talking from their adult self today to a child or teenage self.

Through the *Resilience Timeline* (page 224), clients can recall times when a great decision was made that set a pattern of positive change, or embody and thank someone who supported them, or revisit a part of themselves they wish to acknowledge or celebrate.

Timelines also serve as a warm-up to role play by allowing clients to encounter and talk to themselves or others in real (rather than imagined) form. By the time the client is warmed up through the floor check or timeline process, they know who they want to talk to and what they want to say. The psychodrama is therefore shorter and more focused. The therapist doesn't need to do as much directing, so there is less room for error through overinterpretation and overmanagement.

Like floor checks, timelines create many incremental moments of engagement that allow people to make use of the miraculous healing power of coregulation that pulses through any group. And from this experience of coregulation, participants are able to have an embodied felt sense of self-regulation that they can make portable and take into their own lives. In Stephen Porges's words, "Self-regulation grows out of successful coregulation" (personal communication, 2022).

How I Developed Timelines

When I first began working with trauma, I often ran into what people were calling "memory loss" around trauma. The more I dug into the research, the more I became convinced that all the components of "memories" were there, trapped in the body, so to speak. Yet these "memories" hadn't been thought about because the thinking mind had shut down from fear and never processed the "memory" through feeling it, naming it, and talking about it. If it had, the "memory" would have been elevated to a conscious level and could be accessed to reflect on it.

I wanted to find a way that clients could contact these hidden parts of themselves, bringing them out and onto, in this case, a piece of paper. I wondered if writing things down in order might help people create enough context that more recollections would come forward.

I invited clients to draw a line on the long end of the paper, divide it into five-year segments, and then jot down relational dynamics, circumstances, or events that hurt them, that felt derailing, that shut them down, that they still felt stuck in, or that they felt traumatized by. As the clients shared their timelines, their issues became more real and they saw what they had not seen previously. They could identify how pain had been carried and repeated. They saw how unresolved trauma dogged their trail because it was hidden. They could identify periods in their lives when not much trauma had occurred; some felt surprised that even though nothing "bad" had happened, their hypervigilance and unresolved pain from previous times in life made them feel as if the pain was still continuing. This was how, over the course of a couple of years in the mid-1980s, I developed the *Attachment Timeline.*

The original paper-and-pencil timeline was a more than sufficient process, but I wanted to make it more experiential for the whole group. So I tried putting numbers along the floor and inviting group members to "Stand up and walk over to an age in your life where you still feel trapped in time, where you are being drawn, where you have something to say. Now talk to the people near to you about it."

People just got out of their chairs and knew where to go, sociometrically aligning themselves by age. The hurting babies could talk to each other, the rebellious teens, the lost young adults. They had something to give each other that felt special and dialed in, the way people in recovery do. Again, the therapy wasn't coming from me, but from and *with* each other. I was providing a framework and educational information that could focus and ground their work and then questions to move the process along, but the process itself belonged to them.

Last, I tried inviting clients to "walk the timeline" one at a time. Initially, I just said, "Do a soliloquy as you walk along," but the process grew as people did it. They began to create a sort of bottom-up narrative as they met themselves at various ages along their timeline. I would invite them to talk with themselves at any particular age if they appeared warmed up to do so, so organically attachment dramas became focused by age or a period in life. Participants could do a drama reconnecting with a part of themselves or bring in an attachment figure and do a drama with them. They remembered what they had forgotten—they reconnected with hidden selves or revisited and repaired relational dynamics. This process is called *Walking the Attachment Timeline* (page 79).

The *Resilience Timeline* (page 224) was also a wonderfully consolidating experience for clients that worked to counter the idea that trauma is all damage. As clients identified moments along their development when they made good decisions that sent their lives in a positive direction that they built on, they smiled, felt full and good inside, and took ownership of their strengths and their ability to meet challenges. As they participated in *Walking the Resilience Timeline*, they clearly felt good about telling the group how strong they had been, how hard they had worked, or what great choices they had made. They were proud of themselves. And they expressed gratitude toward those who had given them help and support when they most needed it—both other people and parts of themselves.

Targeted Social Atoms

In addition to creating the interventions of floor checks and timelines, I began using the social atom, originally developed by Moreno, as a way to explore relational issues on paper in order to see the relationship network and gain some insight into the proxemics involved in any given constellation of relationships. The client can "show" their own experience through the way they position relationships on the page vis-à-vis themselves, rather than talk about these relationships in the abstract. For example, different people may be distant from or closer to, bigger or smaller than, and overlapped with or farther away from the client themselves. People who do not appear on the client's atom may be significant by omission, which also fills in the story.

Sociometry seeks to measure levels of attraction and rejection within a system as a way of gauging levels of relatedness. The social atom allows clinicians to create snapshots or maps of relatedness within any given system at any given moment in time, or a model scene that encapsulates dynamics over a period of time. It is a full and rich process in and of itself, or it can be a springboard to targeted role plays with whatever person or part of self clients feel warmed up to talk to.

A social atom can also be a map used to create a sculpture on stage (see *Sculpting the Social Atom*, page 93). This sculpturing offers a way to show the relationship network (for example, the family system) rather than talk about it. I always use a stand-in to represent the self so that clients can reverse in and out of the sculpture as they feel the need. As part of this sculpturing, Moreno (1946/2019) encourages the client to *do*, *undo*, and *redo* the relational experience so that they see the network as they experienced it, then work through the relational issues that seeing this in live form brings up, and finally redo the relational experience as they wish it had been by positioning the family as they'd have liked to experience it. In every stage role-playing can be done.

My Approach to Trauma-Informed Psychodrama

As I traveled all over the country training clinicians in psychodrama, a troublesome issue that I encountered again and again was that they didn't feel they had adequate training to do it well. This was, of course, a legitimate concern and why I created my own sociometrics. Another challenge was that psychodrama is completely open-ended—anything can be enrolled (the term we use to describe a participant in the scene acting and speaking as another person, part, feeling, etc.) and worked with. While as a psychodramatist I relish the freedom this offers, as a trainer working with attachment trauma it becomes a problem.

Initially I thought that more training in psychodrama would address these issues; however, over the years, even in those with significant training, I was seeing psychodrama that wasn't necessarily trauma-informed. When we work with trauma, it's as important to fully understand all of the research in neurobiology that informs how the mind-body processes trauma as it is to have psychodrama skills. Without this understanding and integration of interpersonal neurobiology, psychodrama is still profoundly healing but not necessarily suited to titrated work in healing relational trauma.

I was also concerned that there was too much focus on an intense catharsis of rage and pain, a catharsis of abreaction, without a catharsis of integration—without, in other words, attention to titration and integration or a calmer role interaction, still deep but more measured and nuanced.

Also, there was an emphasis on a client's "piece of work," which is a complete misunderstanding of the dynamics that underlie the group process. In a good psychodrama group, everyone is healing all of the time, whether through being a protagonist, role player, or witness. There is no emphasis on a piece of individual work, because that ignores the healing going on all of the time. Another problem is that therapists would structure an event that was frightening, which could shock someone all over again.

Over the past 30 years, I have combined the theory of Bessel van der Kolk, Stephen Porges, Peter Levine, Sharon Wegscheider-Cruse, Zerka Moreno, Stanley Greenspan, and Dan Siegel in creating a trauma-informed approach to psychodrama. With trauma-informed psychodrama, the work is relationally oriented, not event oriented. What we're treating when working in a trauma-sensitive manner is what happened on the inside of a person as a result of what occurred outside that shaped the way they live in their body and their relationships. We're revisiting not the event or dynamic, but the mind-body that recalibrated itself in order to protect the inner self that felt threatened and overwhelmed.

Role Plays

While it isn't necessary to do a role play in order for healing to happen, a targeted role play can allow a client to experience a connection with themselves or another, to explore a role dynamic that has felt frozen inside of them. If they choose to, they can embody and encounter significant people from their lives or inner parts (e.g., "my depression," "my wished-for self") through targeted plays. As Richard Schwartz, the creator of internal family systems (IFS) therapy, puts it, it allows for an "unblending" of internalized roles (2021).

Embodiment and role relationship are two key components of trauma-informed psychodrama. One of the main goals is to work to move from dysregulation to states of coregulation. Trauma-informed role plays access and work with Porges's social engagement system by stimulating feelings and sensations that are warmed up by the role relationship. If a client is bringing dysregulation or frozenness to the therapy space, their nervous system is likely activated, stimulated by the memory of the role relationships they are dealing with. As these role relationships are embodied, we see neuroception in action—how the client experienced themselves in connection or lack thereof. It is the embodiment of what Siegel refers to as interpersonal neurobiology.

As a client enters the moment when they may have experienced what Porges describes as a parasympathetic breakdown, their therapist and group members can help them move from a state of dysregulation to coregulation through embodiment and thoughtful use of psychodrama techniques such as doubling and role reversal.

Feelings can be felt and words come pouring forward, helping to restore a felt sense of intimate connection that may have been shut down. Clients find the parts of themselves that had to go underground for protection so that they can heal them and take them to other relationships they may want to have.

Doubling can help them put words on inner states that they sense but can't quite describe; it can also help them feel seen and witnessed. Role reversal lets them temporarily leave the confines of self and move into another role. This can restore flexibility and spontaneity as they move in and out of their own rigid point of view, seeing themselves and their interactions that had their origins in childhood through their more mature eyes of today.

The role play incorporates gestures that are intentional and imbued with meaning and purpose that we need to read as part of the role relationship. We can see what Greenspan and Wieder (1998) describe as "feedback loops" that incorporate body, sound, and eventually words, all of which allow one human being to understand another (p. 34). We can see where these loops may not have been adequately completed and work toward repair. Clients can say and do what they couldn't say and do then. They can experience what they didn't have and bring in what they would have liked to have through casting "reformed auxiliary egos" or role players that can portray more ideal forms of the relationship.

Once adults in recovery from childhood relational trauma understand what they did to self-protect—once they enter those inner states, experience them, and only then translate them into words—they understand that those protections are likely outdated now that they're empowered, fully functioning adults. They see how they get stuck in their early defenses and recognize that when they continue to sink back into these childlike defenses, they undermine their ability to have healthy, adult, two-way connection and empathy. They realize that when they brace for danger inside, their nervous system upregulates and they blurt out all the anger and hurt they never got to say as a kid from that child state of mind, projecting and transferring pain from yesterday's relationships onto today's. Now that they understand, they have a choice. They can do it differently.

In psychodrama we help the client embody or concretize a role relationship and move through it *before* we ask them to reflect on it through words alone. Rather than trying to describe inner states before they have embodied and experienced them, clients can embody role relationships in which they experienced pain and they can feel and express that pain through action. Then they can redo the relational dynamic as they would have liked it to be and gain a felt sense of what a more nourishing dynamic might be like. They can take in love that they may have blocked and practice behaviors that are more satisfying.

I have seen how remarkable the simple act of role-playing can be in allowing participants' true feelings to flow so that they can restore their felt sense of connection with another person or with the another who lives inside of them as an introject—the internalized role or carried presence of another person that remains within them. Even if the client can't repair a relational rupture with a specific person, they can repair it inside of themselves so that they can take that repair to their next relationship and stop re-creating pain. When they have those pieces of themselves back, when they have been reintegrated into them in a processed state rather than remaining frozen and hidden, there is a restoration of the capacity for pleasure and trust in connection.

The real-life test of healing is then to observe if the client's spontaneous reactions to situations that used to give them trouble change. When they are triggered, do they have more clarity around what's going on and avoid getting stuck in it? Can they move past triggered states and let them go more easily? Can they love, learn, and let go more freely? Have they changed on the inside, and do their outside interactions feel or look different? Have they healed on the inside so they can be different on the outside?

Experiential Letter Writing

For clinicians who don't feel in a position to use the more standard types of role play, I have worked out a structured approach to adding a role play by building out the practice of letter writing that the addictions field uses so successfully. In the *Experiential Letter Writing* process (page 44), clients write their letters, then read them to empty chairs or group members representing the people receiving them. Clients can also follow this process to write a letter they wish to receive and have it read to them. This can be a memorable and important role play that is easy to do, and you can incorporate other psychodrama techniques as they seem useful.

The skillful combination of psychodrama and sociometrics that I have just described offers an engaging, effective approach to healing relational trauma. Now that you understand the key concepts of my approach, you are ready to explore more specific themes, treatment goals, and interventions. The remaining chapters in this book focus on particular feeling states, behaviors, and methods, offering tailored exercises for each.

CHAPTER 3

Empathy Training: Self-Regulation and Coregulation

From the time we come into this world, we resonate in tune or out of tune with our primary caregivers (Schore, 1994). Babies and small children are wired by nature to bond with their parents for their very survival. This bonding phenomenon is at the basis of self-regulation and coregulation: Without it, parents wouldn't pair-bond long enough to stay close to and nurture their young, and a baby might wander off and get lost; babies also wouldn't have the capacity to develop the skills of self-regulation and coregulation.

This powerful human mind and body urge is at the base of our social engagement and survival system (Porges, 2004). When the system is disrupted, all involved can experience it as a shutdown of this connection apparatus. To heal these shutdowns, we need therapies that include the body and other people, and that reengage and repair this system.

A baby's nervous system is actually developed partially outside the womb, in the arms of those who care for them. Each tiny interaction between parent and child builds the neural capacity within the infant that will allow them to self-regulate and coregulate (Schore, 1994). So from the very beginning, a parent is co-creating the neural equipment that will allow their child to live comfortably both within themselves and in connection with another human being.

When this profound need, honed by eons of evolution to ensure our survival, is refused or is met unreliably or intermittently, the child can experience it as potentially dangerous. In order to survive this refusal of connection and maintain some semblance of feeling intact on the inside—to preserve their most tender sense of self—they may shut down parts of themselves that are hurting too much. They learn to connect with other parts of themselves but not all of themselves.

But while the yearning for connection can be dulled or numbed, it is never really gone. It too often gets replaced by something far less nourishing, like technology, frenetic activity, drugs, compulsive sex, food—anything to feel alive and connected, soothed and related to something, even if that something isn't alive.

This is where an embodied, relational form of therapy is so helpful in treating adult relational trauma. We are not treating the event or the painful relational dynamic itself, but the effect it has had on the client's inner being. We're helping the client to be better able to identify moments when they feel dysregulated and come out of these states toward a more comfortable and regulated way of connecting with themselves and others.

As the body is directly involved in role-playing, it can *feel*. For example, therapists can see and protagonists can describe the shiver that is going through their body or give a color, shape, or texture to the tightness in their chest (Levine, personal communication, 2022). It's as important in trauma work to read what the body is telling us as to hear the words coming from the protagonist.

My trauma-informed approach to floor checks and psychodrama works within a regulated range of affect. This doesn't mean that I don't allow for the release of powerful emotion, simply that it is by no means a goal. The important goals are to:

1. assist the client in learning to move from states of dysregulation to coregulation;
2. absorb a felt sense of coregulation and self-regulation through providing a direct experience with those states;
3. develop a language for the expression and management of inner states; and
4. develop greater flexibility and confidence in connecting with their own inner states and with others in authentic ways.

Role Play: Talking to the Right Person, at the Right Place, at the Right Time

When a client has had problematic relationships with their parents, when they grow up, if they try to work things out with their parents, they can find themselves feeling as if they're not heard all over again. Even though their parents may be calmer, less stressed people, or sober if they were once addicted, they may not be open to this kind of self- and relational reflection. Your client may feel like they're talking to the wrong person at the wrong place and the wrong time.

Psychodrama, through bringing these role relationships from the past into the here and now and structuring a role play, lets the client talk to the right person at the right place and the right time and as the child they were when the pain occurred.

For example, rather than talk to the mother they have now, 20 years after the fact, your client can talk to the mother they had then. They can return to the embodiment of the child self or adolescent self and talk to the parent they had at that age. They can blurt out feelings and say now what they couldn't say then. Or they can have the tactile experience of climbing back into the lap of the parent who became lost to them and being held by them.

While we cannot ethically do that holding as therapists, we can do it through surrogates on the psychodramatic stage. The yearning for touch that didn't happen can arise in embodied therapy, so to receive that hug or holding from the role player representing the person from whom the client longed for it can feel wonderful and restoring.

In using role play to work with developmental deficits, all we need to do is allow the child in the client to talk to a role player representing the parent they had then and the truth pours out. The role lets the client reach back into the psyche in which the self was shaped and bring it onto the stage for examination. As participants embody these roles through action, they loosen their grip on their insides; through role reversal, they can step into and out of roles with increasing ease. It opens a door into the unconscious that, once jimmied open, casts a light that grows incrementally or sometimes floods the room.

People often come to therapy because they want to learn to be better at intimate relationships. The relationships that our clients enter into as adults restimulate the unconscious parts of themselves, motivating them to heal their younger selves. Our clients have a choice: They can unconsciously give what they got—re-creating and passing down dissociated or shut-down relational dynamics—or they can face and process the blocks and disconnects that are getting stimulated.

Role play offers a way to talk *to,* rather than talk *about,* a person with whom the client has issues. Through the use of surrogate role players, clients can bring a relationship dynamic that may have felt disrupted or distressing (or, for that matter, wonderful) back into an alive, interactive state that feels real in the moment.

Participants can also use role play to embody and reconnect with parts of themselves. They can talk directly to their wounded inner child, the hurting adolescent, or the disappointed or despairing adult. Or they can talk to the hopeful, spiritual self or the innocent and playful self that they may have lost a satisfying connection with or that is hiding and waiting to be rediscovered.

The process should be protagonist led—do not impose parts or characters onto the protagonist. Your role is to keep the process feeling safe enough so that it can continue to move forward, and the best way of doing that is through insightful use of technique rather than intruding on the protagonist's process with too many suggestions or interpretations. Techniques such as doubling, role reversal, role reversal interview, and soliloquy can be used thoughtfully to keep the process moving. Remember, the stage belongs to the protagonists; we directors are there in service of their drama.

The Power of the Embodiment of a Role: The Core of Reenactment Dynamics

Therapists often underestimate the power of concretizing or embodying a role. Adding to that, we may underestimate the exponential power of embodying or concretizing that role in relationship to someone else. Through role play, and the simple power of embodiment, clients reenact the dyadic role relationship on the outside as they carry it on the inside. They revisit and reshape dynamic role relationships as they live within them. They look for someone to play their parent or sibling and say to them what they wish they'd said as a child. Or the client reverses roles and becomes their parent, then acts toward that person in the way they experienced them—they give what they got.

Moreno (1946/2019) defined *role* as "the actual and tangible forms which the self takes" (p. 242). When a client talks from their role of self to an attachment role, they are entering the unconscious relational development that has occurred over a lifetime. The visceral contents of the inner states—the feelings, sensory content, thoughts, and body states—are stimulated and pour forward in the words, gestures, body shapes, and sensations, which show how they experienced the role and what they have internalized from years of playing it. The client isn't talking *about* their relationship with their parent or sibling; they are entering the world, the inner space where it lives, and bringing it back to life.

When therapists don't understand the power of simply concretizing a role in current space and time—allowing the protagonist to choose someone to embody it, then place the relationship onto the stage in whatever distance, closeness, proxemic, or power dynamic as it feels inside of them—they miss the power of embodiment. Then the therapist may try to "amp up" emotion to "get things going." But there is another way that is easier on everyone, one that allows the innate power of embodiment to unfold.

When the protagonist takes this journey of embodiment, they are slowly entering into the inner spaces where the role relationship lives inside of them and showing us how it lives. They are revisiting the core of a reenactment dynamic so that they can understand how it lives within them and how it fuels reenactment dynamics. Clients internalize not only others as introjects but also the full role dynamic, whether it is a satisfying, nurturing one or a trauma-engendering one. Making these dynamics conscious lets our clients see more clearly how they may be passing down pain through the generations; they also get practice in doing things differently.

Role Play Techniques

Doubling and role reversal are the two directing techniques that I use most often in role plays. I also use role reversal interview and soliloquy. These techniques are valuable additions to your psychodrama toolbox; you can use them in the basic role plays in this chapter, as well as in the other exercises throughout this book.

Doubling

Doubling offers an embodied, experiential way to connect or reconnect with the inner self, or to give voice to parts of self that may live in silence. Another group member stands behind the protagonist and adopts the protagonist's behavior and movements, expressing what they feel is going on inside of the protagonist. Alternately, the protagonist can stand behind their own chair or take a step back and double for themselves to deepen a felt sense of their own inner workings. Doubling is true empathy training if it is real and attuned. It enhances empathy for the self and the other person.

Clients are sometimes concerned that they won't get it "right" when doubling; however, there is no "wrong" doubling. If the person who is doubling presumes something that isn't accurate, the person being doubled for is encouraged to say, "That's not it; *this* is actually what's going on inside of me." This simple sentence not only alerts the person doing the doubling that they are not accurately tuning in on the protagonist, but it lets the protagonist refine and tune in more accurately on what they feel—it trains them to be in good touch with themselves.

On the other hand, when someone doubles and hits the mark, the protagonist can really feel seen and witnessed on the inside. It's a great sensation and builds trust. If a client has felt unseen, which is part of the experience of relational trauma, it helps them gain the experience of feeling seen and understood.

Group members can double for the protagonist (or the protagonist in role reversal) only. In other words, they cannot double for role players, which can make the drama confusing and make the protagonist feel distracted or even ganged up on.

Role Reversal

Role reversal provides practice in connecting with the inner world of another human being or another part of self. The client changes places with another person and, for a moment in time, becomes them—embodying their role, thinking as they think, feeling as they feel, acting as they act. The client leaves their own self and embodies the self of the other to gain a felt sense of both ends of an interaction.

This is intimacy training, helping the client see through another's eyes. Paradoxically, although it may seem or feel risky to leave the self and momentarily become another, it actually strengthens the client's sense of self because they gain a new perspective on themselves and more understanding and empathy for another. Whether a client can successfully reverse roles and speak from another person's point of view can tell you a lot about their level of relational empathy and intelligence.

And if it's a part of themselves the client is reversing roles with—perhaps a depressed, anxious, frozen, or wished-for part—the technique helps the client illuminate this part, experiencing it with more clarity and separateness. They can experience themselves as less "blended" with that part, as Richard Schwartz might say.

Role reversal can be taught to clients by calling "Reverse roles!" as the need for it emerges spontaneously in a role play. Times when a role reversal is called for include:

- When there is a direct question that only the protagonist knows the answer to. Don't let role players make things up; the protagonist is the one who holds the answers from their own life.
- When you sense the role play wants to move forward and reversing roles will allow it to do so.
- As a way of "role training" the role player or auxiliary ego. The protagonist can show the other person and how they experience that other person.

Please always use the term "reverse roles"; do not say things like "switch places." This keeps the language crisp, consistent, and predictable.

Role Reversal Interview

While a client is in role reversal, the therapist can interview them to help guide and deepen the experience. The therapist asks questions, and the client in role reversal responds as that other person, showing the therapist and the group how that person acts, thinks, and talks. The experience for the client as they answer questions as that person is unique. They may be surprised at what comes out spontaneously in a way that gives them both an inside look into that person and the experience of standing in their shoes.

Soliloquy

The soliloquy is an opportunity for the client to take a break from the drama and talk about what is going on for them on the inside. It is often referred to as a "walk and talk" because the therapist and the client walk around the scene as the client soliloquizes their inner experience of the moment. They can take the stage for a while and reveal, both to themselves and to the group, the inner workings of their mind—how they are perceiving the drama from deeper layers within themselves.

Experiential Letter Writing

Letter writing is what we call a *near-psychodramatic technique*. In its most basic form, group members write letters and read them to an empty chair or a role player. Clients can write as their child self to a parent or adult self, or they can write from the self at any time, including the self they are today, to a future self, to someone who was there for them when they needed them, to someone they admire and want to be like, or even to a favorite pet or stuffed animal—in other words, to anything or anyone.

I created experiential letter writing to provide a very contained form of role play that incorporates all of the role-based theory of psychodrama but doesn't require the kind of training psychodrama needs. Writing and reading letters is a powerful intervention in and of itself. It allows clients to fully say what they need to say, as the letters are never meant to be sent.

Clinical Exercise

Basic Role Play

Role plays, also called vignettes, can be done about anything that emerges. A role play can be an intrapsychic scene where the protagonist meets parts of the self, an interpersonal scene where they talk to others, or a scene where they speak to metaphoric images, pets, or even objects that represent something of significance to the protagonist. The protagonist can talk to anyone or anything—for example, "I want to talk to Dad in one chair and Dad's rage in a separate chair" or "I'd like to talk to the person I want to become."

Role plays can be short and relatively straightforward or longer and more complex, depending on the material being explored. They can include two or more roles. (Even if the protagonist is talking to an empty chair, the chair is the second role.) A basic role play in true psychodrama always incorporates doubling and role reversal. Other techniques, like role reversal interview or soliloquy, are optional.

Goals

- Provide a simple, user-friendly dramatic form that doesn't require a full, classical psychodramatic setup.
- Allow a protagonist to create a small role play with themselves or others.
- Allow for more than one person to be the protagonist in a single group session.

Steps

1. After the protagonist has warmed up and knows to whom they wish to speak, invite them to choose one or more group members to hold or play those roles for them or use an empty chair to represent a role. Let the protagonist set the scene themselves, including any chairs or other objects, as part of their warm-up. The setting can be any place, real or imagined, that the protagonist chooses.
2. If the protagonist likes the idea and there is enough time, they can "role train" each auxiliary ego before officially starting the role play by reversing roles with that character, assuming the body posture and gestures of that person and saying a few things as or from the role of that character in their drama. The protagonist can show the auxiliary and the group who this person is to them. This is also a great way for the protagonist to continue warming up to their own drama. Then the protagonist reverses back into their own role.
3. Ask the protagonist, "What would you like to say to this person or to this part of yourself?"

4. Allow the scene to develop, following the lead of the protagonist. Use doubling and role reversal wherever appropriate.
5. When the scene seems to be drawing to a natural close, invite the protagonist to say the last things they need to say to each character.
6. Have the role players return to their seats for deroling and sharing. Deroling allows the role players to brush off those roles and become themselves again. Ask them to say, "I am [their own name]; I am no longer [the name of the character]." Then ask them to share how they felt while playing the role: "Playing [the name of the character], I felt . . ." Role players often have interesting insights from being in the role. Once they have deroled, the role players can also share anything that came up for them from their own lives if they choose to.
7. Invite the group members to share any identification from their own lives, if they wish to do so, using this format: "What came up for me from my own life while witnessing your drama was . . ." Group members should not use feedback or mirroring while sharing in psychodrama; if they do, gently remind them, "In psychodrama, we share what came up for us from our own lives." The protagonist has opened themselves up in a vulnerable way, so no advice or feedback should be given at this time.

Variations

- **Somatic Experiencing:** If you're familiar with Peter Levine's somatic experiencing work, it can be helpful to the protagonist if you slow down the role play process and allow more of the body feeling to come forward into awareness. Ask the protagonist, "What is going on in your body as you embody this role? Can you describe it? If that part of you had a voice, what would it say? Does it have a color or a shape, and if so, can you allow that color or shape to get bigger, then smaller—to pendulate along with your inward and outward breath so that it becomes more modulated?"
- **The Empty Chair:** This is a classic one-to-one technique, but it's also user-friendly in group and telehealth sessions. For example, if a client is talking about someone they feel pain around, I simply say, "If they were sitting there, what would you say to them?" As the client talks to the empty chair, their feelings surface and the drama flows. I use role reversal as needed, and if I double, I simply ask, "May I double for you?" and then double from my own seated position so as not to take over the space too much. When the role play is finished, I let the client continue to process in any way they wish to.

  To use this technique in a group, place two chairs facing each other in the center of the group. Invite the group members to begin a role play by saying, "Put someone you want to talk to in the empty chair. Or put a part of yourself—for instance, yourself at a particular age, or your innocence, or your depression, or anything you like—in the chair."

- **Telehealth:** The somatic experiencing variation (described earlier) works well online because it can be made interior—it doesn't require a lot of reversing roles, and the protagonist can use the role casting and embodiment as a warm-up to exploring what feelings come up while playing a particular role. This can also help the protagonist understand that certain feelings associate more with certain roles and not others.
- **In Group:** The empty chair technique (described earlier) works well in groups, including as a closure or follow-up technique for those who have been warmed up from watching another group member's drama. They can do their own role play talking to a person or part. This allows many pieces of work to be done in one session using the initial, longer role play as a warm-up.

  For an even simpler closure technique, I sometimes put what I call a "finishing" chair in the center of the circle and invite anyone who's warmed up to do a short role play. They can remain in their own seat while talking to the finishing chair. Role reversal and doubling can always be included. This can also be considered a form of action sharing.

Clinical Exercise

Learning How to Double

Good doubling helps clients connect with deep inner states—with what is not being spoken by the protagonist but will benefit from being put into words. It allows the protagonist to feel supported, witnessed, and seen from the inside. It can also be a way of putting words to the swirl of imagery, thoughts, feelings, and sense memories so that the protagonist's limbic world can be clarified and reflected on by the thinking mind.

Use doubling as a part of any role play. Remember that doubling should only be done for the protagonist or the protagonist in role reversal, not for other role players. Once a group gets the hang of doubling, it can be done at any point during a role play or the group process, whether the group is seated and sharing or doing a spectrogram, locogram, floor check, or timeline. When someone seems to be longing to say something but appears stuck, or otherwise seems like they could use some identification, another group member can ask, "Can I double for them?" or use the hand signal of waving two fingers. After doubling, you can ask the person who was doubled for, "Did that feel right?" They are free to accept the doubling, reject it, or put it into their own words.

Goals

- Tune in to what's going on at a deeper level within the protagonist or group member.
- Help clients build emotional literacy and intelligence.
- Create group cohesion and build trust.
- Give several people in the group a chance to feel involved in experiential work.

Steps

1. Let the group settle in and begin to share about their week or whatever is going on for them.
2. Invite the group members to each share a sentence about where they are at the moment, either in the group or in their lives. Invite the group member who is sharing to get out of their chair, stand behind it, and "double" for themselves, sharing what might be going on for them at a less conscious level. Explain that the double speaks what isn't being outwardly shared—what is unconscious, hidden, or harder to say.
3. Once the group members have had an opportunity to double for themselves, invite them to try doubling for each other. Explain that the idea here is to help someone come to the awareness of what might be going on inside of them that they aren't even necessarily aware of. It is not an interpretation but simply putting words to what a group member feels is not being spoken out

loud. The double should feel like an inner, witnessing presence; it should make the person being doubled for feel seen from the inside.

4. Continue giving the group members the chance to double for themselves and for others. This can become a very lively process.

Variations

- **Telehealth:** Doubling works over telehealth exactly as it does in person. It's a great way to liven up an online session. It's very important that all microphones are on and everyone is in their window for it to happen smoothly. If mics are muted, there are gaps in participation that keep the process from feeling spontaneous. Group members can wave two fingers to indicate when they want to double, or you can allow them to simply jump in at any point.
- **One-to-One:** Doubling can occur at any time during one-to-one sessions. The client can double for themselves or you can ask, "May I double for you?" After doubling, say, "Did I get that right? If not, just correct it." The protagonist is always right—never insist that they accept a doubling statement that doesn't feel right for them. I do not get out of my chair in one-to-one, as I think it creates an odd power imbalance when there is only one client present. The client can do as they wish.

Clinical Exercise

Embodied Role Reversal

Through reversing roles, clients can traverse the boundaries of self, leave it temporarily behind, inhabit the role of another, then return to the self, a little bit changed and expanded on the inside. Surprisingly, this process has the effect of consolidating a stronger sense of self, allowing the client to feel more flexible and less threatened by entertaining different points of view.

Goals

- Tune in to what's going on at a deeper level inside someone else.
- Help clients to feel less trapped in their own defenses (Yablonsky, 1976).
- Help role players understand how the specific roles that they are going to play will be perceived by the protagonist (Yablonsky, 1976).
- Help clients develop empathy by standing in another person's shoes momentarily.
- Allow clients to experience themselves from the role of another or see themselves as another person might.

Steps

1. Let the group settle in and begin to share about their week or whatever is going on for them, or do any kind of warm-up that works for the group. Or you can wait for real issues to emerge through sharing so that group members have someone in mind that they'd like to talk to.
2. Set up two chairs in the workspace facing each other. (Or participants can stand facing each other.)
3. Invite the group members to identify someone or something from their personal life that they wish to talk to in a role play. This could be anything—a person, a part of themselves, a pet, an object, or a concept.
4. Have the group member who will be going first choose another group member to play the role they have designated. (Or an empty chair can be used for the role—this can be a good way to do a bare-bones role reversal.) Begin the role play by inviting the protagonist to talk to this character.
5. When the moment is right—typically, when the protagonist asks a question, says something that requires a reply, or says something that only they have the necessary information about (other role players should not make things up; the information should always come from the protagonist)—invite the protagonist to reverse roles. Now the protagonist embodies the role

of the significant person, part, or thing while the other group member takes on the role of the protagonist.

6. A good way to deepen the protagonist's experience of reversing roles is to invite them to "double for the role you're now in"—that is, when they are in role reversal, they can stand behind that chair they are in (or take a step back) and double for the other person whose role they are now playing. Doubling in this way helps the protagonist gain a deeper sense of being the other person.
7. Continue these role plays; it's fine to do a few in a row. They can be surprisingly satisfying and they teach the skills of role reversal in an easy, organic way.
8. When the role plays come to a natural closure, the group members can return to their chairs and share with the various protagonists what came up inside of them from their own lives while witnessing the protagonist's drama. They can also derole if they played a role in a drama.

Variations

- **Role Reversal Interview:** This technique, which is featured in the next exercise, works well when incorporated into these role plays.
- **Telehealth:** Role reversal can be tricky to do on a telehealth platform. I ask clients to move their screen to one side or the other to indicate a reversal; this works pretty well but not perfectly. You could also have clients hold up cards with the names of the roles being represented. I don't change names on the screen, as it takes too long. If a client has a chair in their own space, I often direct a role play through the telehealth window. This works well and I can invite them to double or reverse roles as I would if they were in the same room with me.
- **One-to-One:** Role reversal in empty chair dramas with one client is user-friendly and very satisfying. You can incorporate it into any role play that you do. Inviting the protagonist to double while in role reversal works beautifully. I also like to incorporate the role reversal interview technique (as described in the next exercise).

Clinical Exercise

Role Reversal Interview

This is one of my favorite techniques. I first learned it from Zerka Moreno and have extended its use. This technique gives the protagonist a chance to show, rather than tell, what someone in their relational world was or is like. Asking questions of the protagonist while they are in role reversal allows them to respond spontaneously as the other person or as that part of self.

If it is an attachment figure from early in their life, you get a sense of who raised them and how that person acted when the protagonist was young. Parents are people, and people change—sometimes the parent that the client had as a child is different from the one they have as an adult. If the protagonist is doing a role play with a part of themselves (e.g., the depressed part, the addict, or the inner child), this technique allows you to gain information and history in a way that's much more inventive than a traditional client interview. And it gives the client a visceral experience of a part of themselves or another person.

The protagonist's memory should come forward in an easy and relaxed way. Keep your questions simple; don't be intrusive, just interested and companionable. Remember, the stage always belongs to the protagonist—it is their life we're investigating.

Goals

- Build relational intelligence and a felt sense of "being" another person.
- Give clients a longer experience of sitting in the shoes of another.
- Deepen the experience of sensing another person from the inside out.
- Get a first-hand view of how the client has internalized someone from their past or present.
- Create ways to explore introjects.

Steps

1. Ask the protagonist whom they would like to talk to in order to gain a deeper sense of that other person or part of self and their relationship. If they are having trouble thinking of someone, you can do a short guided imagery exercise by asking them to close their eyes, breathe, pay attention to their body and inner world, and then consider who lives "rent free" in their head, whom they carry inside themselves for better or worse, whom they have issues with and would like to understand better. Or they can talk to a version of themselves they would like to become in what psychodrama refers to as a "future projection" drama.
2. Proceed with a role play by asking, "What would you like to say to this person?"

3. Call "Reverse roles!" one or more times as the role play progresses. At some point when the protagonist is in role reversal, actually sitting in the chair or standing in the role of the other person, you can begin to interview them.
4. Start by saying, "May I ask you a few questions?" With their permission, continue with questions like "What's your name?" "Why do you think the protagonist brought you here today?" and "Would you tell me a little about yourself? Your family? Your own childhood? The protagonist? Your relationship?"
5. Continue to ask whatever else you feel will be useful but not aggressive. The questions should be easy and sensitive, and as always, let the protagonist be in charge of the material they choose to bring forward. Let the protagonist act like that other person—they are showing you how they perceived that person.
6. When the interview seems to have drawn to a natural closure, ask the protagonist to reverse roles back into themselves and say the last things they want to say for now to the other person or part of self, to end the scene.
7. After the interview, continue with the broader role play or move into sharing and identifying.

Variations

- **Telehealth:** Role reversal can be difficult to do over telehealth; however, of this category of techniques, I find that the role reversal interview is the easiest to do online. The client can use their own empty chair, first talking to it and then sitting in it for the role reversal.
- **In Group:** Doing this exercise in a group gives you more options throughout the process:
    - The protagonist can invite another group member to play the role. Allow a role play to move forward using role reversal and doubling.
    - When the protagonist is in role reversal, you can ask them if it's all right to ask them a few questions. You can invite the group to join in asking questions. They will need to be able to modulate their questions, take turns, and be sensitive to the protagonist's experience. Too much questioning may get in the way of the protagonist's process.
    - Group members can double for the protagonist in role reversal whenever they wish to.
    - After the protagonist has finished their role play, you can either move into sharing and identifying or invite another person to do this exercise and then share after more than one has been done. Invite the group members to share what came up for them from their own lives while witnessing or participating in the drama.

Clinical Exercise

Experiential Letter Writing

It is amazing to witness how much feeling can arise when a client is talking to an "empty" chair—which is, of course, not empty at all but filled with the felt presence of another person from the client's life or a part of the client's self. It is a testimony to the power of the introject. This exercise joins that power with the healing and/or closure technique of letter writing, which the addictions field uses so successfully. Experiential letter writing is a powerful and versatile technique in which clients write letters and then read them to empty chairs or role players. Importantly, the letters are never sent to the people to whom they are written; the exercise is simply a psychodramatic release for the clients.

Letters can be written to virtually anyone or anything. When resolving grief issues, the client can embody a person they feel loss around and talk to, rather than about, them; as they do, they revisit themselves in this dyadic connection. Or they might embody the loss through a surrogate representing a part of self, regaining access to the wounded inner child, the hurting adolescent, or the disappointed or despairing adult. They might also talk to the hopeful, spiritual self or the innocent, playful self that they had lost a satisfying connection with. Feelings that were never expressed, including goodbyes or thank-yous that were not said, can finally be released and processed.

If you're working with addiction, protagonists may benefit from talking to the substance or behavior and reversing roles to embody it, speaking as it so that they can pass through that feared boundary of slipping into the addiction, becoming it, and never getting out again. Protagonists may also want to talk to a part of themselves that they are letting go of along with the addiction (e.g., the fun drunk, the life of the party, the bad person) or to a part that they are building (e.g., a responsible self, a fun-loving, free-spirited self).

Here are some other examples of letters that can be written:

- A letter to an experience, a job, a house, or similar
- A letter of forgiveness to the self
- A letter forgiving another person
- A letter asking forgiveness from someone else
- A letter to some aspect of the self (e.g., the hurt self, the successful self, the angry self, the addicted self, the codependent self, the wished-for self)
- A letter to the self or an aspect of the self at a particular time in life (e.g., the child self, the adolescent self, the self after a breakup or traumatic moment)
- A letter expressing anger toward someone

- A letter telling someone about a hurt
- A letter to someone expressing a desire for reconciliation
- A letter to a substance or behavior that the client is letting go of
- A letter to some part of the body (e.g., a part that has been removed, a despised part, a cherished part, a part that is in transition or aging, a sore part)
- A letter to a time in life (e.g., a missed younger self, a feared older self, a younger working self if the client has retired, a self before their children grew up and left home)
- A letter expressing gratitude toward someone
- A letter the client wishes to receive
- A role reversal letter in which the client writes from the perspective of another person, a part of the self, or the self at a different time in life, expressing what the client wishes that person or part would say to them

Letter writing is a powerful intervention in its own right, and it can also be useful as a closure technique for any of the experiential processes in this book. If a lot of feelings come up for group members during a session, they can continue to process these by choosing someone to whom they feel they have something to say and taking a few minutes to write a letter.

Goals

- Provide a contained way to incorporate psychodrama into programming.
- Provide an experiential vehicle through which feelings can be processed, expressed, put into words, shared, personalized, and placed into context.
- Help clients clarify, articulate, and grieve loss openly.
- Allow clients to embody a lost person, part of a person, part of self, time of life, substance, or behavior.
- Help clients recapture their connection with frozen, discarded, or dissociated inner states.

Steps

1. Invite the participants to make themselves comfortable, either in their chairs or somewhere in the workspace. You might play soft, ambient sound or instrumental music during the letter writing.
2. Explain the letter writing process. You can share the examples of potential letters listed earlier in this exercise to help them generate ideas. Ask them to begin their letter with "Dear (name)" and end it with an appropriate closing and their signature. Encourage them to write anything that

comes to mind. Emphasize that this letter is not meant to be sent, but to release feelings. It works best to write quickly, not thinking about how it sounds.

3. After giving them time to write their letters, move into reading them. If the group is large, you might have them break out into pairs or clusters. If you are staying in one group, place two empty chairs—one for the person reading the letter and one to represent the person, part, or other entity to whom the letter is written—facing each other in the center of the group.
4. Invite the group member who is sharing their letter to imagine that the person, part of the self, or other entity to whom the letter is written is sitting in the empty chair. Or they can choose another group member to play the role.
5. Invite the protagonist to read their letter to the empty chair or role player. During or after the reading, you can invite the protagonist to double for themselves, to reverse roles, and to double while in role reversal. You can also double for them or let group members jump up and double.
6. When the protagonist has finished their letter or had a chance to say something else if they chose to, invite them to "Say the last thing you need to say for now" and end the role play.
7. Move into sharing and identification, allowing everyone to do personal unpacking and to share from their own experience. Keep the sharing on a personal basis; it is not a time for advice-giving, feedback, or questioning.

Variations

- **Telehealth:** Letter writing is easily adapted to telehealth. If the group is large, you can use breakout rooms for reading the letters and come back as a full group for continued sharing and closure. If a client wishes to use the empty chair technique, they can find an extra chair in their own physical space or call in on another device and talk to the black box that appears—an adaptation that I've used in my own training groups and have found to be surprisingly evocative. Clients can also choose a member of the telehealth group to read their letter to or have it read to them. Group members can also double for the letter writer/protagonist.

CHAPTER 4

Floor Checks and Experiential Check-Ins: Mobilizing the Social Engagement System

Floor Checks

There are a variety of techniques available to bring a group together, deepen their connection through identification, and help them build and practice skills experientially. My go-to—and what I consider my most valuable contribution to the field—is the floor check. This exercise facilitates profound healing and connection within the group. It contains all the necessary components for healing relational trauma and building resilience. Floor checks are easy for therapists to implement and highly engaging for clients.

In a floor check, information about the subject matter being addressed or taught in treatment—such as PTSD symptoms, manifestations of fear and anxiety, or resilience and posttraumatic growth—is written down on cards that are placed on the floor. Participants are asked questions that prompt them to move toward the card that reflects their own experience; in this way, they sort themselves into groups based on a symptom, feeling, or other quality they have in common.

While a presentation or lecture on trauma-related topics can feel passive or even overwhelming to clients, the floor check offers interactive education and healing. Clients are given the freedom to cut their own paths through the material being explored. Each time a client shares their experience—for example, how a symptom of anger manifests for them—they are offering a living case study that teaches and normalizes an otherwise embarrassing subject. The inherent message is: *It's okay to come forward and open up. We can all learn something from each other. We can grow together.*

It often happens in groups that, after a couple of prompts, a buzz develops in the room. At this point, I ask criterion questions to move the process along, but no one really hears me. Well-meaning onlookers or assistants sometimes whistle, make noises into the mic, or put their arms in the air to get the group's attention, but I quickly explain that this is exactly what I want, what I have learned to expect and even look for—a measure of engagement. The group members are more interested in each other than in me or in what's coming next. They are in the present and connecting through a relational process that is healing, playful, and profound.

I have done floor checks for many years, in many venues, and they never disappoint. They are consistently effective across groups of all sizes, ages, genders, cultures, and races. They take the burden of having to be always "on" off the therapist, and they motivate the group to become active co-healers and co-regulators such that 85 to 90 percent of the activity centers around the group itself. The curriculum is always new and always tailored to the group, because the content comes from the participants themselves.

Floor checks offer so many benefits, in fact, that even if your only takeaway from this book is to do floor checks, you will be adding an experiential, psychoeducational component to your programming that will help to heal relational trauma and build resilience.

Turning on the Social Engagement System

Floor checks heal by turning on the social engagement system. They enliven the human drive toward connection and then offer many ways for group members to connect in nonthreatening, meaningful ways. In so doing, they offer reparative interactions for attachment deficits through a process that's engaging and supportive; as Siegel says, they are "inspired to rewire."

Clients feel safe because they are standing on their own feet, grounded, oriented in the room, and cutting their own path at their own rate through the choices presented on the floor cards. The process is nonevaluative, so clients needn't worry about doing it "right." It's structured and predictable, so once they know it, they can get creative and spontaneous.

There is also an intellectual rigor that is very satisfying in the understanding of the symptomology of any given exploration, be it grief, PTSD symptoms, or the many ways in which fear, anxiety, or anger might manifest. All systems are engaged in the process of self-discovery, and the body, too, is invited in. The word "trauma" need never be mentioned. The relational healing is baked into the floor check process itself.

I recommend providing as many points of person-to-person connection as possible. Group members can share with the full group or, if the group is large, in dyads or clusters. Breaking out into subgroups ensures that each person has time to share and to give others attention and interest. Through repetition, clients experience many incremental moments of healing.

Being Playful

It is well known that children who are in traumatizing situations need to play, to interact spontaneously, in order to avoid becoming symptomatic. Without play, they are more likely to shut down or withdraw into themselves. Adults, I think, need something similar in order to heal relational trauma. They need to free the shut-down child inside of them. They need a process that has no specific goal other than to enter into the activity—one that has easy onboarding and offboarding, feels spontaneous and engaging, and puts them (at least somewhat) in charge. They need to relearn how to have lighthearted, nonevaluative interactions with others in which everyone has an equal status and all input is welcome and valued.

When clients can actually see what the rest of their community is doing, when they are resonating face-to-face in a group, they mirror, learn, and practice new behaviors. They try them on for size and get immediate feedback through action. Then these new connections give birth to more connections in the brain, which influence more experiences and more behaviors, and so on. The emergent process actually takes on a life of its own and influences itself: It becomes a feedback loop for change (Dayton, 2022).

Over time, clients develop the skill set to elevate the kinds of unconscious pain and anger that drive dysfunction to a conscious level, where they can be examined in the light of day rather than acted out upon unconsciously.

Developing Feelings Fluency

Reexperiencing numbed feelings in therapy can feel scary. The same fear the client felt as a child at the short end of a power dynamic can kick in and leave them feeling little and threatened all over again. Floor checks reverse the loss of agency and connection they may have experienced as children and create mobility and connection. Through a structured, relational process, clients can bring their frozen inner spaces out of hiding, feel the internal states that they get trapped in, and then find words to describe and share them. The process gives clients a bottom-up path toward words.

Floor checks allow feelings to be slightly triggered by the information on the floor cards that are part of the prepared learning environment (Montessori, 1995). Because the clients choose how they respond to the prompts, they are in charge of which feeling or symptom they are feeling and then translating that inner experience of identifying it into their own words and communicating it to others. They can also listen to others share without exploding or imploding.

As feelings get safely triggered, named, and translated into words, a language of emotion is developed and practiced; this builds emotional and relational intelligence. Floor checks, along with the *Attachment Timeline* (page 74), the *Resilience Timeline* (page 224), and *Experiential Letter Writing* (page 44), will give you all you need to introduce experiential paths toward achieving relational repair.

Benefits of Floor Checks

- Access the social engagement system in service of healing.
- Allow clients to move from states of dysregulation to self-regulation and coregulation.
- Teach the subject matter and research that are a part of understanding the dynamics of PTSD and C-PTSD.
- Restore personal volition by allowing clients to be choice makers and stakeholders in their own healing.
- Ground clients as they get on their feet, orient in the workspace, and move on their own.
- Allow clients to get safely triggered in a controlled environment, become aware of feelings, then translate their emotions and inner states into coherent sentences that can be shared spontaneously with others.

- Develop emotional literacy and provide practice in naming and sharing emotional material, as well as listening while others share without imploding or exploding.
- Engage and connect group members in a low-risk, supportive process.
- Build resilience by allowing group members to mobilize support and use their initiative, agency, and creativity in making choices.
- Support clients in becoming meaningful members of a group.
- Offer experiences in playfulness by creating room for humor, laughter, and joking that comes forward spontaneously.

Other Experiential Check-Ins

While floor checks are my program staple, they are not the only technique for bringing feelings out of hiding and into the room. I also recommend Moreno's locogram and spectrogram, as well as the step-in circle. Although these have limitations in terms of length and depth, as experiential check-ins, icebreakers, and warm-ups they are hard to beat. These processes can bring a group together and deepen their connection through identification in a matter of minutes.

Spectrogram

You can think of the spectrogram as a graph that is laid out on the floor. Participants are invited to stand in the location that best represents their self-assessment in response to each criterion question. For example, you could designate one end of the workspace as representing feeling extremely anxious (100 percent) and the opposite end as feeling no anxiety at all (0 percent); the participants would then move to stand at either end or at any point in between, according to the level of anxiety they are feeling.

This moving from one's seat and committing to a standing, choice-making position encourages a greater engagement in the process. Then, as people share, they express the thoughts and feelings behind their choice.

The spectrogram reveals significant information about the group very quickly; you can use it to understand anything from how the group members are doing in recovery to who is warmed up to do a role play. It's a great way to introduce the idea of feelings regulation because you can ask the clients to show how much or how little of a particular feeling or symptom they are experiencing.

Spectrograms are one of the most adaptable and user-friendly exercises in sociometry. They are flexible enough to accommodate a wide variety of group sizes, and the intensity is titrated by the client themselves as they respond to the criterion questions.

Locogram

The locogram is similar to the spectrogram in that participants are asked to stand in designated locations based on their answers to the criterion questions. However, in the locogram these locations aren't along a specific graph. For example, you might assign DBT categories to locogram boxes, then ask the group members to choose one to express what state of mind they are in at the moment: wise mind, emotional mind, or reasonable mind. This gives you a snapshot of where the group is at any given moment, and it gives the group a chance to consolidate their own feelings of the moment.

Locograms work well as an icebreaker in which the group members check in about how they feel about being in group. They can use the locogram to work through ambivalence or talk about how much they like being in group. Locograms give participants a way to voice resistance, which can help them let it go, laugh at themselves, or simply feel relief at having space created in group where they can be authentic.

Step-in-Circle

The step-in circle is a beautiful way to make it safe to be genuine. Participants stand in a circle and take turns stepping into the circle and making a statement about themselves; then any group members who also identify with that statement step into the circle as well. The statement is phrased as a question: "Who, like me, . . . ?" This opens the floor to participants taking the risk of announcing something about themselves for others to identify with, which can be anything from "Who, like me, likes spy novels?" to "Who, like me, was sexually abused?"

The group is entirely in charge of the content, and all they do is to step into the circle to show solidarity with that particular choice—there is no additional sharing or follow-up. Those who stepped in can pause for a few seconds and look around; then, once they step out, someone else puts a question forward. It is a quick, easy way to bond groups that feels safe and low-risk to the participants.

Clinical Exercise

Feelings Floor Check

This floor check helps clients build the skills of emotional literacy, regulation, and coregulation. It can be your staple activity when you want the group to explore feelings. It also works well as a warm-up to deeper role plays or experiential letter writing.

Goals

- Expand a restricted range of affect that can be the result of trauma.
- Allow the group to become comfortable identifying, articulating, and sharing emotions and listening as others do the same.
- Allow the group to connect with each other around vulnerable emotions, share, and take in sharing and support.
- Teach and develop emotional literacy and emotional intelligence.
- Help clients learn to tolerate and talk about positive and self-affirming emotions so that they are less likely to relapse over them.
- Introduce structured, welcoming, and safe processes that can even feel playful or gamelike.
- Mobilize each group member's self-engagement system in a relational context for a repeated experience of self-regulation and coregulation.

Steps

1. On separate pieces of paper, write feelings words such as angry, sad, mistrustful, anxious, despairing, self-conscious, content, hopeful, ashamed, guilty, frustrated, desperate, happy, serene, genuine, lonely, excited, empowered, or helpless. Have at least one paper marked "other" so clients can choose their own emotion.
2. Place the papers a couple of feet apart from each other, scattered around the floor.
3. Ask participants to stand on or near the feeling that best describes their mood in this moment.
4. Say, "Whenever you are warmed up, share a sentence or two about why you are standing where you're standing."
5. After all who wish to have shared, you can choose to repeat the process and ask participants to stand on another feeling that they are also experiencing. (Learning to hold more than one feeling

at a time helps clients tolerate living in gray rather than black and white.) Then have them share as before.

6. At this point you can vary the criterion questions. For example:
   - "Which feeling do you avoid feeling?"
   - "Which feeling did your family of origin avoid feeling?"
   - "Which feeling did your family of origin struggle with or get stuck in too much of the time?"
   - "Which feeling did you have trouble with in your family of origin?"
   - "Which feeling state triggers you when you encounter it in someone else?"
7. If you want to build resilience, you can include criterion questions such as:
   - "Which feeling do you like to be near in someone who is a friend or partner?"
   - "Which feeling would you like to experience more of in your life?"
   - "Which feeling used to drag you down, but you have learned how to manage it better?"
8. If you'd like to extend the process further, you can say, "Place your hand on the shoulder of someone who shared something with which you identified. Now tell them why you chose them." The entire group can do this at once, which can create a nice feeling of connectedness or even a bit of a buzz.
9. If the group seems warmed up to do more work, you can invite them to do a role play (see the *Basic Role Play*, page 35). Or you can have them simply sit down and share about the entire process and what came up throughout.

Variations

- **Telehealth:** Display the options to the group using a whiteboard tool, a shared document, or another method that works for you. As you ask the criterion questions, group members can call out their answer and say a sentence or two about why they chose it. Or, if the group is large enough, you can use the initial questions as a warm-up and then move into breakout rooms for continued sharing.

Clinical Exercise

Basic Spectrogram

This exercise allows you to quickly learn how much or how little of a feeling, symptom, or issue the group members are experiencing. It is useful for developing emotional regulation, getting people involved in the group process, developing group cohesion, and facilitating bonding as group members open up and connect with each other. You can modify the criterion questions to suit anything you wish to explore in the group.

Goals

- Provide a floor graph that group members can step into to represent the degree and intensity of a particular emotion, symptom, or issue.
- Help clients learn and practice the skills of emotional regulation.
- Help clients learn and practice the skills of emotional literacy and build emotional intelligence.
- Create group cohesion and build trust.
- Give everyone in the group a chance to feel involved in experiential work.

Steps

1. Designate an area in the workspace and explain to the participants that each end of this area represents an extreme—for example, one end of the workspace represents 0 percent and the opposite end represents 100 percent. Next, draw an imaginary line bisecting the area, representing the midpoint (50 percent).
2. Ask a criterion question and invite the participants to move to whatever point along the continuum best describes their response to the question. For example:
   - "How comfortable are you in group right now?"
   - "How satisfied are you with your progress in healing from relational trauma?"
   - "How comfortable are you when feeling your intense emotions, such as anger, need, or love?"
   - "How comfortable do you feel around others when they are feeling intense emotions, such as anger, need, or love?"
   - "How comfortable are you with adult intimacy, such as partnering, parenting, or close friendship?"
   - "How comfortable are you around the people you grew up with?"

- "How vulnerable do feel when opening up about your feelings?"
- "How good do you feel about your work life or other responsibilities (such as your education or caregiving responsibilities)?"
- "How good do you feel about your hobbies or other pursuits outside of your work or responsibilities?"
- "How comfortable do you feel about your body?"

3. Allow people to share, either with the full group or in dyads or clusters with the people nearest to them. (They are already sociometrically aligned from moving in response to the question, so sharing with those standing next to them is an excellent way to create moments of identification and connection.) Invite them to share a sentence or two about why they're standing where they're standing (e.g., "I'm at about a 50 percent comfort level in group; I'm glad I'm here, but I'm a bit anxious about what's to come."). This encourages the participants to reflect on, regulate, and share their feelings, then listen as others do the same.
4. After you have explored as many questions as you wished to or the group has reached its saturation point, you can invite them to return to their seats and continue to share or begin a role play, if someone has warmed up to do so.

Variations

- **Research-Based Spectrogram:** Basic spectrograms belong to psychodrama and are a part of sociometry; adding research to them is my own adaptation. Adding research allows spectrograms to become psychoeducational and focused more vividly and efficiently for treatment of particular issues, including adult relational trauma. The research-based spectrogram also allows clients to speak for themselves rather than being told what they "have." And it puts reflecting on the degree to which a client is experiencing any particular symptom in their own hands, which teaches tuning into the self, as well as symptom awareness and regulation. Any of the psychoeducational floor checks in this book can be made into a spectrogram.
- **Telehealth:** You can simply ask the criterion questions and invite the group members to rate their degree of intensity by holding up one to five fingers (with one being the least intense and five being top intensity) or by holding their arm sideways across the screen in a lower or higher position. You can also create the spectrogram using an interactive whiteboard tool: Draw a line and label the two endpoints and the midpoint, then invite the group members to add a dot or other mark along the line to represent their answer. Then invite them to share about why they have located themselves at that point.

Clinical Exercise

Basic Locogram

You can adapt this basic locogram to explore any issues that are relevant to the group you're working with—simply change the labels you assign to the different areas and the criterion questions you ask. The locogram works well as an icebreaker to give the group members a way to check in about how they feel about being in group. It also serves as a warm-up to other processes and encourages authenticity, sharing, and openness among the group members.

Goals

- Break the ice in the beginning of group.
- Allow group members to announce their preferences.
- Create group bonding and cohesion.

Steps

1. Identify the issue that the group wishes to explore (for example, checking in about how they feel about being in group).
2. Designate four areas on the floor to represent possible responses to the issue ("I am glad to be in group"; "I could take it or leave it"; "I wish I were somewhere else"; "Other").
3. Ask a criterion question ("How do you feel right now?") and invite the group members to move to the area that best describes their response to the question. If they feel ambivalent or between responses, they may want to stand between those areas.
4. Invite them to share a sentence or two about why they are standing where they are standing. Group members may spontaneously double for each other if this seems useful to the process.
5. If you feel that the group wants to make another choice, you might say something like, "Has anything changed for you since you shared just now? If so, change places and share from where you are right now."
6. You can invite further sharing by saying, "Walk over to someone who shared something with which you identify and place your hand on their shoulder. Now share with them why you chose them or how you identify." Or you may ask them to return to their seats for sharing or move into other processes like floor checks, timelines, social atoms, or role play.

Variations

- **Triggers Locogram:** Assign possible responses to feeling triggered—such as shame, anger, withdrawal, and placating—to the sections of the room. Ask criterion questions to explore the clients' feelings and behaviors when they are triggered: "Where do you tend to go when you get triggered?" "Where do you go when you feel rejected (or angry, sad, hurt, humiliated, etc.)?" You can also use this locogram spontaneously if clients get triggered during group. You can ask, "Where are you now?" or "Where did you go just then?"
- **Learning Locogram:** Divide the space according to key learnings or skills that you have been working on in group. Ask criterion questions like, "Which new learning do you feel you're making some progress in?" "Which learning makes you feel anxious to consider?" "Where do you feel stuck?" and "Where do you feel hopeful that you can change?"
- **DBT Locograms:** One option for a locogram based in dialectical behavior therapy is to have clients check in about their state of mind. Designate the areas on the floor as the wise mind, the emotional mind, the reasonable mind, and other, then pose criterion questions such as, "Which mind are you experiencing now?" "Which mind do you tend to spend the most time in?" and "Which mind would you like to spend more time in?"

  A locogram can also be used to explore how clients are using their DBT skills in their recovery, in their life, or even in group if they feel triggered. Use the areas on the floor to represent either the four categories of DBT skills (mindfulness, distress tolerance, interpersonal effectiveness, and emotional regulation) or specific skills that you have been working on. Ask questions like, "Which skill are you using now?" "Which skill would you like to use but are having a hard time with?" and "Which skill do you feel you're getting more proficient in using?"
- **Telehealth:** Display the options to the group using a whiteboard tool, a shared document, or another method that works for you. As you ask the criterion questions, group members can call out their answer and say a sentence or two about why they chose it. You can also create the locogram using an interactive whiteboard tool: Draw a large square, divide it into four sections, label the sections, then invite the group members to add a dot or other mark on the diagram to represent their answer and then share about why they are located at that point.

Clinical Exercise

Step-In Circle*

The step-in circle is a surprisingly powerful intervention that can be done for groups of any age or size who are open to exploring common threads that connect them. It's a great icebreaker in any setting. Because the group is out of their chairs and in a circle, there is an automatic feeling of engagement. The exercise starts to build group safety and cohesion through identification. It also builds resilience as the group members are invited to tune into themselves and make experiential "I" statements that allow them to feel in charge of their own experience. And the questions themselves help group members break through resistance to the process.

Goals

- Bond and engage a group.
- Normalize the subject matter being explored.
- Bring up difficult subject matter in a nonthreatening manner.
- Bring up playful subject matter in an easily accessible format.

Steps

1. Invite the group to stand in a large circle.
2. Explain the process: "I will ask a question starting with the words 'Who, like me.' If you also identify with what I say, take a step forward into the circle." Ask a few low-risk questions to warm up the group and to build trust and connection (e.g., "Who, like me, loves a good murder mystery?").
3. Invite the participants to ask their own "Who, like me" questions and continue warming up.
4. Once the group members feel at ease with each other, they may organically move on to greater openness (e.g., "Who, like me, has felt rejected in a primary relationship?"). This can be an awakening and surprisingly deep process for those participating. Allow the group to feel respectful and deep or playful and light as the energy moves. Allow the questions to go wherever the group goes as long as no one is being bullied or hurt. As group members step into the circle, they see each other and know that they share energy and alignment around that issue.
5. Once the group seems saturated, invite them to sit down and share about how it felt to do the exercise. If the group is very large, invite them to share in clusters with the people sitting nearest to them.

* This exercise has been contributed by Dale Richard Buchanan, PhD, TEP.

Variations

- **Tailored Circle:** The exercise can be tailored to any group by simply modeling the type of questions that you feel will be helpful and then letting the group come up with their own questions. In this way, you can both highlight commonalities and bring attention to differences in their experiences, including forms of privilege and oppression. For example: "Who, like me, is an addict in recovery?" "Who, like me, has children?" "Who, like me, has experienced racial prejudice?"
- **Telehealth:** This can be easily adapted to telehealth by asking the participants to raise or wave their hand when they identify with a question.

Clinical Exercise

Shame Locogram

This exercise can be done on its own or as a follow-up to the *Shame Floor Check* (page 62). Clients share what kinds of behaviors they are using to manage or cope when they feel shame, which helps them become more conscious of how these behaviors are impacting their relationships. Bringing the subject out of hiding and creating structured ways to talk about it can help to normalize shame so that it feels less overwhelming.

Goals

- Provide an easy way to concretize answers to a particular set of questions.
- Help clients gain clarity around how they behave when feeling shame.

Steps

1. Designate areas on the floor to represent the four categories of shame behaviors (Gilbert, 1998):
    - The hot response (sympathetic body response such as sweating or collapsing, or intense behaviors such as lashing out in rage)
    - Behaviors to cope with or conceal shame as it occurs (e.g., masking your facial expression, not sharing your thoughts or feelings)
    - Safety behaviors to try to avoid feeling shame or being discovered (e.g., perfectionism, self-medication, avoiding situations where you might experience shame, keeping secrets)
    - Behaviors to repair shame (e.g., self-soothing, apologizing to others)
    - Other
2. Invite the participants to stand in the section that they most identify with, or that best represents how they respond to feeling shame. If multiple sections apply, they may stand between those sections or choose one that they would most like to explore.
3. Ask the participants to share about the category of behaviors in which they are standing—for example, "Why did you choose this category?" "How do these behaviors play out in your life and in your relationships?" Group members may double for each other if this seems useful to the process.

4. You can repeat this process using other criterion questions, such as, "Where are you experiencing the most relief through getting help and processing you painful feelings?" or "Which response is the beginning of sending you into a shame spiral that you have trouble climbing out of?"
5. Move into another exercise or have the participants sit down and share about the experience.

Variations

- **Shame Letter:** Follow up the locogram with experiential letter writing. Participants can write a letter to the part of themselves that carries shame or to someone they have felt shamed by. They can share the letters with the group or in dyads or clusters, and they can read them to an empty chair or a role player.
- **Embodying Shame:** Invite the participants to share a sentence *as* the behavior they are representing. Group members can double for any behavior they are identifying with.
- **Telehealth:** Display the options to the group using a whiteboard tool, a shared document, or another method that works for you. As you ask the criterion questions, group members can call out their answer and say a sentence or two about why they chose it. You can also create the locogram using an interactive whiteboard tool: Draw a large square, divide it into four sections, label the sections, then invite the group members to add a dot or other mark on the diagram to represent their answer and then share about why they are located at that point.

Clinical Exercise

Shame Floor Check

The kinds of relational dynamics that engender trauma can engender shame too. When in the throes of feeling shame, the brain responds as if it were actually facing physical danger. The feeling generates a sympathetic flight/fight/freeze response in the nervous system, which is why it can make someone red in the face, sweaty, and anxious.

This floor check introduces and normalizes shame. It helps clients bring their shame responses to consciousness, understand what triggers them, and share them so that they feel less toxic and immobilizing to the self.

Steps

1. Write the following shame responses on separate pieces of paper:
    - Feeling frozen or in a fog, unable to act
    - Lack of spontaneity
    - Wanting to hide or disappear
    - Feeling like you have little impact
    - Being a perfectionist/hard on yourself/self-critical
    - Feeling like an outsider or that you are different or left out of normal groups
    - Feeling suspicious, anxious, or like you can't trust others
    - Wanting to shut people out or withdraw from connection
    - Sympathetic activation, like blushing cheeks, increased body temperature, sweating, or queasiness
    - Feeling that you can't be your authentic self/loss of identity
    - Feeling inadequate
    - Sunken body posture or not looking people in the eye
    - Other
2. Place the papers a couple of feet apart, scattered around the floor.
3. Ask any of the following criterion questions, or come up with your own. After each question, invite the participants to share with each other.
    - "Walk over to a manifestation of shame that is pulling you now."

- "Walk over to a manifestation of shame that you have long denied."
- "Walk over to a manifestation of shame that your family experienced."
- "Walk over to a manifestation of shame that you are here to work on."
- "Walk over to an effect of shame that you feel you have come a long way in mastering."

4. If you would like to give the participants practice in reaching out to others, say, "Walk over and place your hand on the shoulder of someone who shared something with which you identified. Share with them why you chose them."
5. Depending on what the group is ready for, you can sit down and share about the entire process or move into future projection psychodramas, inviting the clients to talk to themselves in the future after having moved forward in some of these areas (for more on future projection, see chapter 13).

Variations

- **Shame Letter Writing:** You can follow up this exercise with *Experiential Letter Writing* (page 44). Participants can write a letter to the part of themselves that carries shame or to someone they have felt shamed by or someone they have somehow shamed. They can share their letters with the group or in dyads or clusters, and they can read them to an empty chair or a role player.
- **Telehealth:** Display the options to the group using a whiteboard tool, a shared document, or another method that works for you. As you ask the criterion questions, group members can call out their answer and say a sentence or two about why they chose it. Or, if the group is large enough, you can use the initial questions as a warm-up and then move into breakout rooms for continued sharing.

Clinical Exercise

Passing Down the Pain Floor Check

This exercise helps clients get a basic sense of how unconscious and unprocessed pain gets passed down without their awareness. When they can't tolerate letting their pain, shame, and resentment surface and get some emotional literacy around it, they may want to get rid of it, to not feel it. They project it onto someone else, scapegoat others, transfer old pain into new relationships, and re-create painful relationship dynamics. This floor check provides a way into this unconsciousness that isn't blaming or overly diagnostic. The client can choose for themselves what they're ready to look at.

Goals

- Give participants a picture of how unprocessed, unhealed pain continues throughout their life and passes through generations.
- Provide an experiential, educational format for participants to reflect on and share how these forms of passing on pain are manifesting their lives.
- Create living case studies through which the group can become aware of the variety of ways in which generational pain can be passed along.

Steps

1. On separate sheets of paper, write the following ways in which pain is unconsciously passed on:
    - **Projection:** Projecting painful feelings that you don't want to experience onto people, places, and things other than yourself.
    - **Transference:** Layering features and expectations from a relationship in the past onto a relationship in the present.
    - **Reenactment dynamics:** Repeating and re-creating old painful relational dynamics in new relationships.
    - **Dysfunctional relationship patterns:** Patterns of relating that tend toward ineffective ways of solving conflicts and not communicating honestly and effectively. Or patterns where hurtful relational dynamics are rarely looked at, openly talked about, or resolved.
    - **Triangulating:** Talking about one person to another person without ever talking directly to the person being talked about.

- **Scapegoating:** When a couple or family is not dealing with their pain, they may assign problematic qualities to one of the members, who becomes a symptom bearer or an identified patient who wears or acts out unconscious family pain on behalf of the family members who can't see or own it.
- **Chronic negative sharing/forecasting:** Being consistently negative about life, critical of family members, and pessimistic about the future.
- **Rescuing/overprotecting:** Projecting your own unhealed pain onto another person and then attempting to rescue or fix in them what you unconsciously wish had been rescued (or still needs rescuing) in you.
- Other

2. Place the papers a couple of feet apart, scattered around the floor.
3. Ask criterion questions that help participants identify (1) how their family passed down unconscious pain from the previous generation, (2) how they are reenacting passed down pain, and (3) how they, themselves, might be passing down pain. Here are some options:
   - "Which way of passing down pain do you think you are doing right now in your life?"
   - "Which form of passing down pain have you done in the past but since become more aware of?"
   - "Walk over to a way that pain was passed down to you from your parents or grandparents that's really hurt you."
   - "Walk over to a form of passing down pain that you see your grandparents did with your parents, on either or both sides."
   - "Walk over to a way of passing down pain that's really impacted the way you are in relationships."
   - "Walk over to a way of passing down pain that describes a pattern you feel you're breaking."
   - "Walk over to a way of passing down pain that you might be doing with people in your present-day life, such as your children, friends, or coworkers."
4. If you want to extend the process, you can say, "Walk over to someone who said something that you identify with and tell them what it was."
5. When the group is saturated, you can sit down and share about the experience or move into another exercise, such as empty chair role plays, vignettes, or experiential letter writing.

Variations

- **Telehealth:** Display the options to the group using a whiteboard tool, a shared document, or another method that works for you. As you ask the criterion questions, group members can call out their answer and say a sentence or two about why they chose it. Or, if the group is large enough, you can use the initial questions as a warm-up and then move into breakout rooms for continued sharing.
- **One-to-One:** The client can use the *Passing Down the Pain* journaling page, then you can unpack together in session.

Journaling Page

Passing Down the Pain

Unprocessed, unhealed pain can pass from generation to generation. This can happen unintentionally and without awareness, like an invisible baton passing from hand to hand, from ghost to ghost. Read about the different ways that pain can become re-created and passed along with spouses, children, and grandchildren, then share your responses.

Ways That Pain Can Be Passed On

- **Projection:** Projecting painful feelings that you don't want to experience onto people, places, and things other than yourself.
- **Transference:** Layering features and expectations from a relationship in the past onto a relationship in the present.
- **Reenactment dynamics:** Repeating and re-creating old painful relational dynamics in new relationships.
- **Dysfunctional relationship patterns:** Patterns of relating that tend toward ineffective ways of solving conflicts and not communicating honestly and effectively. Or patterns where hurtful relational dynamics are rarely looked at, openly talked about, or resolved.
- **Triangulating:** Talking about one person to another person without ever talking directly to the person being talked about.
- **Scapegoating:** When a couple or family is not dealing with their pain, they may assign problematic qualities to one of the members, who becomes a symptom bearer or an identified patient who wears or acts out unconscious family pain on behalf of the family members who can't see or own it.
- **Chronic negative sharing/forecasting:** Being consistently negative about life, critical of family members, and pessimistic about the future.
- **Rescuing/overprotecting:** Projecting your own unhealed pain onto another person and then attempting to rescue or fix in them what you unconsciously wish had been rescued (or still needs rescuing) in you.
- Other: ______________________________

Questions

Which way of passing down pain do you think you are doing right now in your life?

Which form of passing down pain have you done in the past but since become more aware of?

In which way was pain passed down to you from your parents or grandparents that's really hurt you?

Which form of passing down pain did you see or hear about your grandparents doing with your parents, on either or both sides of your family?

Which form of passing down pain has really impacted the way you are in relationships?

Which form of passing down pain describes a pattern you feel you're breaking?

Which form of passing down pain might you be doing with people in your present-day life, such as your children, friends, or coworkers?

CHAPTER 5

The Attachment Timeline: Repairing Connection with the Self and Others

Misunderstandings are a normal part of long-term relationships. What determines whether or not these become the fuel for lasting and repeating relational problems is whether or not they were repaired. When the pain of disconnection is repaired, we become strong in the broken places—there is a step up in comfortable connection, both within the self and with others. We experience a sense of enhancement in our ability to connect with our inner world and communicate with others.

Unrepaired misunderstandings can do just the opposite: They can leave us feeling a need to withdraw from vulnerable, intimate connection in order to feel safe, or to shut down those inner states that feel too painful, which can translate into a feeling of disconnection from important parts of self.

All children long for a sustained rapport with those who raise them; it's built into our DNA. As parents, our evolutionary mandate is to nourish and protect our young until they can thrive on their own. As children, our biological drive is to stay close to our parents so that we will be fed, sheltered, and loved. When these powerful survival urges are thwarted from either end, we feel at risk.

Because maintaining an ongoing relationship with our attachment figures is so central to thriving, children who feel anxious in close connection may adopt strategies that require them to hide parts of themselves that might threaten the family bonds. Part of this is simply normal socialization. But when a child has to conceal much of who they are from those they want most to feel seen by, they can develop the habit of compartmentalizing or even hiding these parts from themselves as well. When they develop a self, based on an anxious need to garner approval and stay out of trouble, they may engage in what psychoanalysts refer to as false self-functioning.

Then years or decades later as an adult, the client who grew up in this way may wonder why they have trouble connecting in intimate and authentic ways with those they care about. They may also feel out of touch with their own inner aliveness. When asked how they feel, their lifelong habit of shutting down or camouflaging their innermost truths can leave them staring blankly into an inner world that feels inscrutable.

The attachment timeline helps clients come in touch with moments of rupture with attachment figures that went unrepaired and are still fueling a sense of disconnection and disappointment, as well as moments of comfortable connection when they felt seen, heard, or understood. Embodying these parts of self and/or attachment figures, talking to them and rekindling a lost sense of connection, provides an actual experience of repair that real life may not have allowed. It gives clients a pathway forward.

How the Attachment Timeline Helps

The attachment timeline is a remarkably efficient and enlightening process; it has become one of my most used processes in the mental health and addictions field. It helps clients:

- **Identify reenactment patterns:** The timeline tends to reveal how early trauma patterns continue to be re-created throughout the client's life, and reenactment patterns become clear. One client commented, "I can see how I re-created over and over and over again what happened in relationships when I was a kid."
- **Clarify who, where, and when:** The timeline allows the client to get a basic sense of how attachment trauma may have stretched out over their life and which parts of their life are relatively free of trauma. One client shared, "I didn't realize that this only happened a couple of times, because it felt like it kept happening. But really it was this one person and it happened two or three times." Another said, "I see that this was a painful relationship that hurt through all of my childhood. I was always on guard with this person. I hated the way they saw me and even made me see myself."
- **Reveal benefits of recovery:** Some clients can see how recovery helps them learn a language for emotions, which allows them to process rather than avoid pain, and to come to terms with challenging relationships or circumstances. They use their emotional literacy to share feelings and their emotional intelligence to form strategies to deal with problems. They feel resilient enough to take actions on their own behalf to make things better. One client commented, "It's interesting. Since I have been in recovery, it's not that bad things haven't happened, but I don't experience them as traumatic because I handle them differently. I reach out for support, and I process painful stuff as it happens; I don't shut down and hide like I used to."

This chapter includes a three-step attachment timeline process that can be done in tandem, broken up and done over several groups, or used one at a time as discrete processes. Here is a brief overview:

1. The *Attachment Timeline*, done on paper, can be a complete process in and of itself. It can be shared in group, one-to-one, or over telehealth. It can also focus attachment role plays or experiential letter writing according to age.
2. The *Experiential Attachment Timeline* allows the group members to connect with each other around common ages where they experienced pain so that they can share over common ground.

Clients can talk to each other from that age; it feels reparative to enter those inner states and ages with those who are also experiencing age-related issues.

3. *Walking the Attachment Timeline* allows clients to come up with an organic, embodied, experiential narrative. Potential role plays become developmentally focused—clients can do small role plays talking, for example, to a parent they had then from the age they were then. Or they can talk to the part of self they were then from the adult self they are now.

Clinical Exercise

Attachment Timeline

You may be surprised at how much information clients have forgotten about that emerges when you ask them to write down their painful patterns or moments on a timeline. This intervention helps clients see and understand issues that previously may have felt out of reach or hidden. It allows them to trace how unresolved trauma may have dogged their trail, how pain has been carried and repeated. It can also help them identify times when they did get the support they needed or break their silence, feel, and heal.

Goals

- Provide a visual context through which to identify the developmental progression of trauma.
- See where traumas may have clustered in life or where there was little to no trauma.
- Identify where development may have been arrested or gone off track.
- Bring to consciousness how trauma breeds trauma, connecting related traumas so that the client can see the full impact of a string of related traumas.
- Put life experiences back into a context and place traumatic patterns into real rather than imagined time.
- Focus attachment role plays or experiential letter writing.

Steps

1. Provide the participants with copies of the *Attachment Timeline* journaling page (or blank sheets of paper) and writing utensils.
2. Ask the participants to recall relational patterns or moments from their life and add these to their timeline. I recommend keeping your instructions vague so that they don't try to get it "right." You might say, "Jot down any moments in your life, relational dynamics, or events that felt impactful. This might include moments that hurt you, frightened you, felt traumatizing, or made you withdraw into yourself and shut down, as well as moments when you felt seen, heard, and understood. Take your time. There are no wrong answers; just add anything that comes to you."
3. Invite the group members to share their timelines. Sharing can be done in dyads or clusters or as a full group.
4. If the participants are warmed up for further work, you can move into focused role plays. Invite the clients to talk to themselves at any point along their development, using an empty chair or

a role player to represent them at that age. Doubling and role reversal can be used throughout the drama. Some clients may wish to talk to a future self (whether a feared one or a desired one) or trace their timeline back into the past—even before they were born—to understand intergenerational trauma.

Variations

- **Telehealth:** The group members can complete their timelines on their own paper or digitally and share them in the full group or in breakout groups. The process can be followed up on that day or another day with experiential letter writing, which can also be shared in the full group or in breakout groups. In either case, return to the larger group for sharing and closure.
- **One-to-One:** The client can create their timeline, then you can unpack together in session. It can also be followed by an empty chair role play.

Journaling Page

Attachment Timeline*

Next to the appropriate, approximate years, jot down anything in your life that felt impactful. This might include events, periods of time, or relational dynamics that felt deeply hurtful, frightening, or overwhelming, such as moments in which you felt frozen or became immobilized. It might also include moments when you felt seen, heard, and understood.

______ 80 ______

______ 75 ______

______ 70 ______

______ 65 ______

______ 60 ______

______ 55 ______

______ 50 ______

______ 45 ______

______ 40 ______

______ 35 ______

______ 30 ______

______ 25 ______

______ 20 ______

______ 15 ______

______ 10 ______

______ 5 ______

______ 0 ______

* Reprinted from *Relational Trauma Repair Therapist's Guide* (revised edition), © 2014 Tian Dayton.

Clinical Exercise

Experiential Attachment Timeline

It is a simple process to move the attachment timeline from page to stage and make it a powerful group experience. In this activity, participants become sociometrically aligned with each other according to the age they are drawn to—for example, the toddlers talk to each other, as do the adolescents, teens, young adults, and seniors. The participants can observe common threads as they share their struggles at particular ages with each other.

Goals

- Turn the attachment timeline into an experiential group process.
- Sociometrically align participants according to age so that they can heal each other through identification and sharing.
- Provide incremental moments of connection, healing, and repair through opening up and sharing over common ground.

Steps

1. Place large numbered cards on the floor in a timeline progression at five-year intervals, starting at 0 and ending at a high enough number to cover all ages in the group (such as 90).
2. Invite the group members to go to a place along the timeline where they feel they have unresolved issues. You can say, "Stand next to an age where you feel you still need to do some work" or "Walk over to an age where you feel stuck, where you have something that needs saying, or that you just feel you have some pull toward." Or you can say, "Walk over to an age where you had an experience or relational dynamic that caused you to shut down, withdraw, dissociate, or go into a defensive state in some way." Keep your questions vague enough that participants won't get hung up on finding the "right" answer. You might say, "Just go where you're feeling drawn; you can always change it."
3. Invite them to share with those nearest to them on the attachment timeline. This allows them to (1) begin to talk from that age and emotional and psychological space in time, (2) give that part of themselves a voice, and (3) receive identification and support. This will help to break the pain of isolation and helps to make the timeline a full exercise.

4. If the group wants to respond to more questions, you can choose from the following list or make up your own:
   - "At what age do you recall someone else's problems started to become yours?"
   - "At what age did something happen that you feel you are still stuck in?"
   - "At what age did you have an 'aha' moment or make a good decision that led to other good decisions?"
   - "What age would you never return to?"
   - "What age would you like to return to?"
5. If group members are warmed up to do so, you can put two chairs into the workspace and move into role play—for example, "Whom do you wish to talk to from any age that you would like to work with? Or do you wish to talk with a part of yourself at any age?"

Clinical Exercise

Walking the Attachment Timeline

Another way to use the timeline is to invite clients to walk it, one person at a time. The protagonist simply walks along the timeline and shares what comes up around periods in their life, creating a spontaneous, experiential, bottom-up narrative. This helps them become more aware of connections and patterns in their life. For example, a client who is recovering from drug addiction might see how they turned to drugs in order to manage what felt unmanageable during times in their life that felt overwhelming or traumatic.

Potential role plays emerge organically throughout this process. At any point along the timeline, a protagonist may wish to speak to themselves at an age they wish to explore (including a future age), a part of themselves, or other people from their life. Talking to the self at various points of development creates a connection between the adult self and the child self. The client learns to distinguish between a child or adolescent state of mind and an adult state of mind and develops the habit of the child self reaching out to the adult self so that the adult self can listen, translate the child self's powerful emotions into words, and place them within an adult framework rather than blurting them out in their triggered or unthought-through state.

In some cases, attachment wounds began before the client's own timeline. For example, a client might say, "I feel like I need to start way before my own birth because my parents were Holocaust survivors, and I feel like many of my issues were inherited because they brought so much unresolved pain into our family." Or the timeline may need to accommodate a future projection, such as, "I'm 28 but I'm standing on 50 because that's the age when my mother died by suicide and I'm afraid of it."

Goals

- Provide an embodied entry into the attachment timeline.
- Identify periods in the client's life when development may have been impacted by relational or other trauma.
- Warm clients up to developmental and attachment role plays.

Steps

1. Place large numbered cards on the floor in a timeline progression at five-year intervals, starting at 0 and ending at a high enough number to cover all ages in the group (such as 90).
2. Ask for volunteers, then invite the first protagonist to start at the beginning and narrate their walk through the various ages of their life, gaining a felt sense of where their pain may lie. They

can say things like "I am two and here I was told that I was . . ." or "Here I'm about four and I remember . . ."

3. If the protagonist passes an age where it looks like further investigation might be helpful, simply ask them, "Would you like to speak with yourself at this age?" or "Would you like to talk to that person you just mentioned?" Then let the protagonist choose a role player and bring them (or an empty chair) alongside the protagonist. After the role play has come to closure, let the protagonist continue to walk the timeline.
4. Invite the group to share, either after each person's walk or after multiple people have walked the timeline. The group can share about ways in which they identify and what was brought up for them while watching and witnessing.

CHAPTER 6

Revisiting and Repairing the Past: The Social Atom

Feeling trapped in a family system that is painful can be part of the residue of relational trauma that can resurface when clients become adults and create their own families. They can carry that feeling of being trapped—and all that goes with it, physiologically and emotionally—into their new relationships. The feelings they have stored around their early attachments get reactivated by the intense feelings of closeness as they partner and parent, and they can return to a feeling of being a choiceless, disempowered child all over again.

The interventions in this chapter help clients identify family of origin or intergenerational pain from the past that has been re-creating itself in the present. The social atom offers a living picture of the proxemics of a family system (or any system). Family dynamics can be incredibly complex, and nowhere in any kind of therapy can we embody those dynamics more clearly than in psychodrama. Clients can revisit, rather than avoid, their inner child's wounds, this time with witnesses and allies. Through focused social atoms, clients can *feel* in containment and safety. They can revisit and process childhood pain, see and work with times in life where complexes may have been set up, and then enrole more ideal forms of relationships so they can experience something different and template something new. They can *do*, *undo*, and *redo* the atom (Moreno, 1946/2019).

Social atoms are a remarkable contribution by psychodrama and sociometry to the mental health field. Murray Bowen, who created the much-used genogram, consulted with Moreno on the development of the genogram. While the genogram is linear, the social atom is based not only on whom the relationships in the client's life were with, but also on how those relationships felt. It is both a diagnostic tool and a relational map that can be used as a jumping-off point for focused, therapeutic work. It can also be used to create treatment plans.

I have adapted the social atom for focused use in the treatment of issues surrounding relational trauma. The social atom is flexible and fluid, and it allows for the proxemics of any relational network to be revealed. I use it in treatment of relational trauma to give clients a way to talk about the family they grew up in or any relational network or moment in time they wish to explore: they can revisit their past, focus on their present, or even imagine scenes they want to experience in the future. It helps the client get both a visual picture and a visceral experience of their position in a system. Social atoms are spontaneous, live representations of constellations of relationships that can begin on paper and then be embodied on stage as family sculptures or psychodramas.

From Page to Stage

Social atoms can be used in a variety of ways in working with adult relational trauma. Using the social atom as a family or relational map, the client can embody all of the characters they grew up around, know today, or imagine in their future. They can move their social atom from a piece of paper into a role play or sculpt the scene on stage, placing role players to represent and reveal power dynamics, distance and closeness, or family factions (for example, covert and overt alliances, or over-close, overlapped, or distant pairs or clusters). I ask clients to choose someone to represent themselves and act as a stand-in in a scene so the client can see from outside how they looked when inside that situation.

The client (the adult self) can talk to the child they were (represented in that scene by the stand-in), then they can reverse roles and talk as that child self back to the adult self. They can become that child, that disgruntled teen, that young adult trying to individuate but scared of the cost of doing so. Those selves can tell the adult self how it feels to be trapped inside a moment, or a person, or a relational dynamic. Then the client can reverse back out again and heal and un-trap themselves.

After a social atom has been used to explore proxemics that have been painful, it can be "repaired" by moving the role players into more desired positions, reflecting new and more satisfying proxemics and allowing the client to experience what it feels like to be in a network that feels more supportive or loving. Clients are also free to choose more "ideal" versions of those on their social atom, which we refer to as "reformed auxiliary egos" in psychodrama, giving the client an experience of what they longed to have. In this way they "do, undo, and redo" their social atom/sculpture in therapy.

Types of Social Atoms

Social atoms can be done for painful times or for times in life when a client felt great, made a good choice, felt secure and loved, and so forth. In treatment centers, I like to do a social atom upon entering treatment reflecting the network of using that got someone into treatment. Then during treatment, I use family of origin atoms (see the *Basic Social Atom* exercise, page 84) and the *Frozen Moment Social Atom* (page 96). To help clients build resilience and consolidate life and recovery gains, I have them do atoms of moments when they felt wonderful about themselves, their life, a relationship, or a direction in which they were heading (see the *Resilience Social Atom*, page 233). As part of an aftercare plan, I ask clients to make an atom of their support network, of how they intend to organize their recovery life, or both.

Frozen Moments

When I began being known as someone who works with trauma, something unusual began to happen. At conference after conference, protagonists would emerge from the group, we'd structure their drama as I normally did—and they would sometimes freeze. It took me a while to realize that while in my own mind I was a psychodramatist just doing my work, others saw me as a trauma expert. They wanted me to heal what they saw as their trauma.

I believe they were reacting to the word *trauma* itself, and that word was causing them anxiety and the thought that they had to bring their worst moment to the stage. So they were often bringing highly charged moments or model scenes from their past in which they had felt frozen, and they were freezing again in the face of them. Once they froze, it took a large part of the psychodrama just to help them warm up enough to do trauma work.

I wasn't sure how best to handle this, but in a spontaneous moment of trying to make clients' entry into the work easier, I asked them to do a social atom of a moment when they froze in their tracks, when they were speechless, shut down, or collapsed. Immediately they just got it and began diagramming and sharing such moments. From there the work was simple—for example: "What do you want to say to that part of you that froze? Now reverse roles and talk *as* that part *back* to your more mature, adult self."

This simple shift created connection with frozen parts of these individuals that they themselves felt in charge of, that they had in a sense titrated and already begun to manage within themselves, that resonated with the felt sense of the actual experience. Rather than feeling blindsided, clients owned their withdrawn or shut-down inner state—and from here the work flowed once again. Calling something a "frozen moment" became a user-friendly shorthand in working with relational trauma. It allowed the client to be in charge of what they were working on.

When a client is locked in the freeze stress response, they are effectively losing a connection with the feeling part of themselves and they may withdraw or dissociate. They can have trouble accessing and describing what they are feeling to someone else and even to themselves. As Gabor Maté (2010), summarizing Peter Levine, puts it, "Trauma is not what happens to us, but what we hold inside in the absence of an empathetic witness" (p. xii).

The term *frozen moment* intentionally avoids the use of the words *trauma* or *PTSD*, as these are not helpful to clients in terms of healing what hurt them. And perhaps most important of all, *frozen* goes straight to a body awareness. I simply ask questions like, "When did you freeze? Brace up? Feel collapsed, shut down, withdraw, or become speechless? What inner state of frozenness is still living inside of your nervous system now, today, that causes you to act out, shut down, withdraw, or self-medicate when it gets triggered?" This offers a much less daunting way into trauma work.

I almost never re-create an actual trauma scene, as to do so can be shocking to the protagonist. I particularly don't intentionally amp up feelings around trauma because it can overwhelm an already overwhelmed client and cause them to slide back into defenses such as placating, numbing, bracing, or running away or hiding. Encountering the full scene at once can overwhelm their capacity to cope just as it did when the scene took place originally, and it's not necessary or even advisable for healing.

Clinical Exercise

Basic Social Atom

The social atom is a diagram or map of the client's relationships. The client begins by placing themselves on the page with a symbol. Then they add symbols representing individuals, groups, or institutions to whom they are emotionally related, placing and sizing each symbol to reflect how they feel about that person or entity. For example, the client might show that someone is overbearing by making that person's symbol quite large and close to their own, or reflect relational distance by making it far away on the page. The client can reveal support, antipathy, cliques, covert and overt alliances, and isolates through their diagram. The study of these atoms and the interrelations represented on them is important in understanding both how the client's relational environment has shaped them and how they can shape their relational environment.

Social atoms can be done for virtually any moment or circumstance in life. They can also represent a model scene—one that isn't actual but a sort of composite of the basic dynamics in a relational network. The variations section of this exercise lists some ideas for moments and themes that clients may wish to explore through a social atom.

The safest way to do the social atom is to invite the group members to draw their atoms on paper and then share them. This, in and of itself, is a very complete process. The next level is to do simple two-character role plays talking to the self at the time of the atom and/or anyone represented in the atom. Sculpting the social atom, which is described in the next exercise, requires more experience and training on the part of the therapist.

Goals

- Create a map of a client's relational world.
- Reveal the proxemics of any relational network and the client's place within them.
- Create a map of any moment in time (past, present, or future) that will benefit from investigation and exploration.

Steps

1. Provide the participants with copies of the *Social Atom Template* (or blank pieces of paper) and writing utensils.
2. Explain that the participants will be creating a social atom, which is a map of their relationships with others. You can specify a moment in time or a type of network that you would like them to

diagram (e.g., their family of origin or their current support network), or you can invite them to explore any network or time that they feel drawn to.

3. Go over the symbols and what they represent: circle for female, triangle for male, diamond for another gender, square for an institution or group, and a symbol with a dashed line for someone who is deceased.
4. Say, "First, locate yourself on the paper anywhere that feels right to you."
5. Say, "Now locate your important relationships. You can place them as close to or distant from yourself as you feel them to be, and in the size or proportion that feels right. You may include parents, siblings, pets, in-laws, grandparents, friends, institutions, and so on. Write their name in or next to their symbol." Remind the participants that these atoms are only a current reflection; they are always subject to change and can be done for as many moments in time as one can imagine.
6. Once the participants feel that their atoms are finished, invite them to share, either in the full group or in dyads or clusters. Or, if clients feel warmed up for role plays, invite them to do so: "If you want to talk to anyone from your atom—including yourself—choose a role player to represent them or use an empty chair." Drawing and sharing the social atom is a complete process. If you add role plays, once they are finished, move into sharing and deroling as outlined in the *Basic Role Play* (page 35).

Variations

- **Entering or Leaving Treatment Atom:** Upon entering treatment, ask clients to do a social atom of their life just before treatment, perhaps the lifestyle that got them into treatment. Upon leaving treatment, ask clients to do a social atom of the support network that they are setting up post-treatment, including relationships, twelve-step programs, and ongoing therapy.
- **Family of Origin Atom:** This is a basic snapshot of the nature of the client's family network of relationships. It can be done for any point in time, and several can be done over the course of therapy.
- **Frozen Moment Atom:** See the *Frozen Moment Social Atom* exercise (page 96).
- **Two Different Worlds:** Use this when addiction is part of a family system. Sometimes the family dynamics change when the addicted person is using compared to when they are sober. Invite the client to create one atom for when they are sober and another for when they are using. Closeness or distance can be different on each atom. You can also ask an addicted person to do an atom of their own relational network when they are using and another one when they are sober. This allows both the addicted person and the family members to understand why living with addiction can be so disorienting and disequilibrating.

- **Before and After Trauma Atom:** If a client is working with a traumatic event, they can draw a social atom of life before the traumatic event and another atom of life after it. Life can feel different after something traumatic occurs. Relationships—both with the self and with those around us—can change. Reconnecting with the self the client was before a traumatic thing happened can be important in healing certain types of trauma.
- **Developmental Atom:** Clients can make developmental social atoms representing various stages of life—child, adolescent, teenager, young adult, householder, elder, future self, and so on—in order to examine any stage along the way when development was impaired or their life took a different path. This helps them to recapture something that was lost along the way or to project and explore their wishes and goals. While sharing, they can speak from the present day or reverse roles and share as the age represented on the atom.
- **Parent-Child Atom:** This is an age correspondence atom. If a client feels that their child is having a particularly difficult time, it may be useful for that client to do a social atom of their own life at the current age of their child. This can help the parent to see if any unresolved pain from that period in their life might be getting confused or enmeshed with their child's pain.
- **Status Nascendi Atom:** Invite the client to do a social atom of a time in their life when they sense that a complex may have begun to set in ("status nascendi" in psychodrama parlance). You might ask, "Where do you think this complex or feeling about yourself had its origin? Draw a social atom of that period of time and those people from your life who were a part of your relational influences then."
- **Reformed Atom:** I recommend doing a reformed version of any social atom so the client can gain a felt sense of how they would have liked the family or constellation of relationships to feel. This can bring up feelings of loss because the client sees what never got a chance to happen, but in doing so, they open a door for things to be different. Simply say to the client, "Now draw your atom the way you wish it had been" or "Sculpt your atom the way you wish it had been, physically moving role players around or choosing 'reformed' auxiliaries to interact with." You can even invite the client to draw an atom of the way they wish their life could be, either as a way of gaining a felt sense of how it might feel so they can move toward it or as a way to "have" it and let it go, relinquishing a controlled vision of how they feel their life should look so they can, as Joseph Campbell would say, have the life that is waiting for them (Osbon, 1991).
- **Telehealth:** Give the group members time to complete their atoms on their own paper or digitally. Then invite them to share, either in the full group or in breakout groups. Return to the large group for continued sharing and closure.
- **One-to-One:** The client can use the *Social Atom* journaling page, then you can unpack together in session.

Client Handout

Social Atom Example

Key

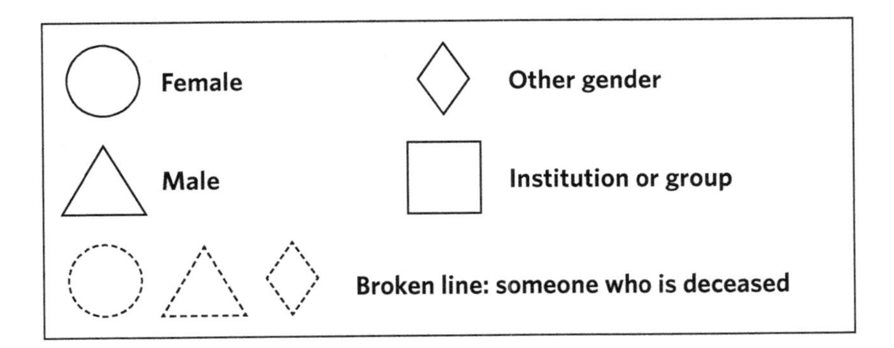

Diagram

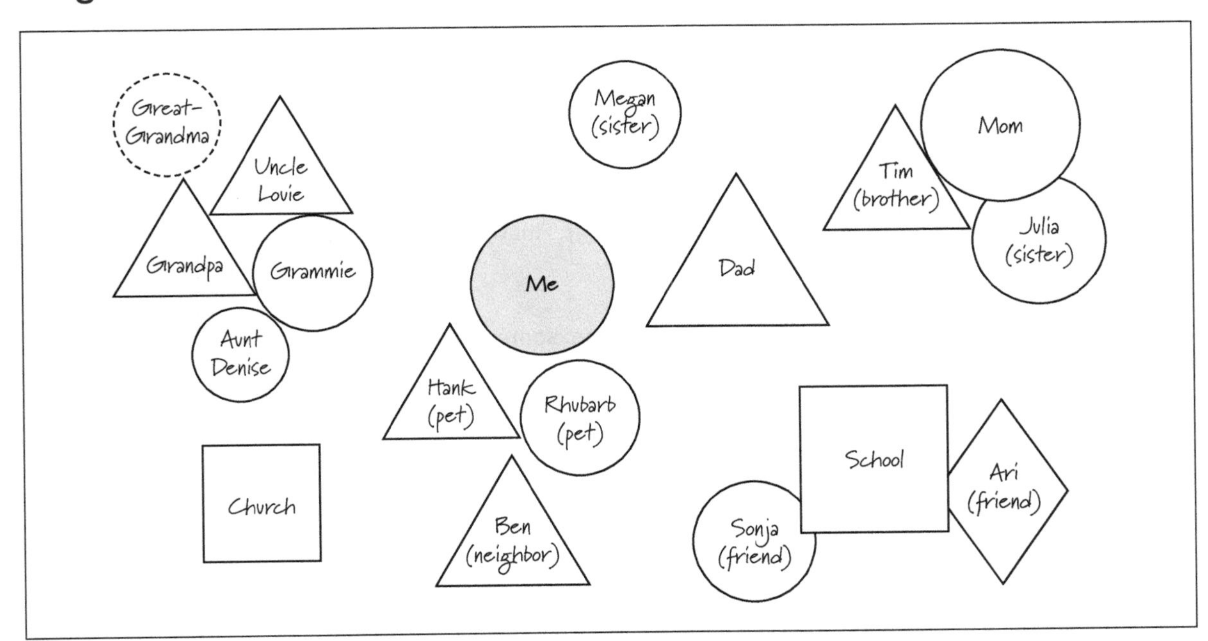

Narrative

"This is how my family looked while I was growing up. My mom and my sister Julia are overlapped—they act like clones of each other. My brother hangs in there, too. My other sister is floating out there, sort of on her own. I am next to Dad and our family dogs. Grammie is great; so are my aunt and uncle. I like school and church. I play with Ben a lot—he's my age and lives next door."

Journaling Page

Social Atom

A social atom is a map of your relationships with other people, pets, groups, institutions, and so on. It shows your relational network at a particular moment in time, whether that's right now, or when you were a child, or any other time that you wish to explore (it could even be the future). Diagramming your relationships in this way will help you better understand how your relational environment has shaped you—and how you can shape your relational environment today.

Use the key below when creating your social atom. First, draw a symbol to represent yourself, placing this symbol anywhere in your diagram that feels right to you. Then enter the relationships that were present at that time. You can place them as close to or distant from yourself as you feel them to be, and in the size or proportion that feels right. Once your social atom feels complete, reflect on the questions that follow.

Key

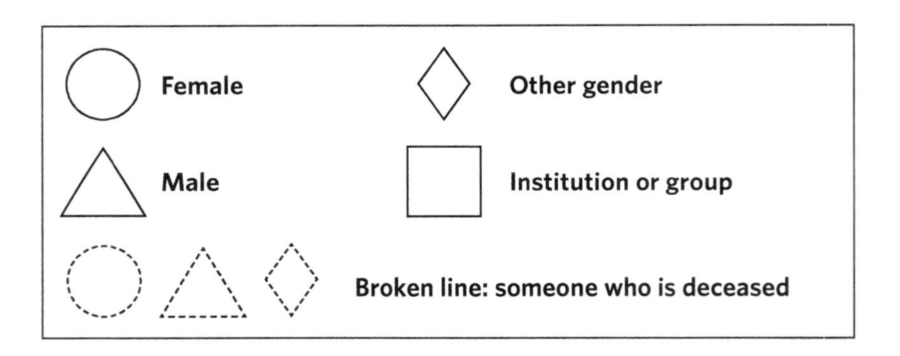

Diagram: Social Atom

Questions

What moment in time does your social atom represent?

Of the people or entities in your atom, whom do you feel close to? Describe.

Whom do you feel distant from? Describe.

Whom do you feel anxious around or tension with? Describe.

Is anyone enmeshed (lacking true autonomy due to unclear boundaries or because one person expects the other to think, feel, and behave in certain ways)? Describe.

Are there overt or covert alliances between people? Are there "sides" or "factions" within the family or group? Describe.

Are there abusive relationships? Are some people trauma-bonded? Describe.

Do people talk directly to each other, or do they tend to pair off and talk about each other instead (triangulation)?

Is there a scapegoat—someone who is unfairly blamed for others' problems or who has become a "symptom bearer" wearing denied family pain on "behalf " of the family? Describe.

Is there a "little parent" ("parentified child")—a child who was pushed into taking care of others (like their siblings or parents) and expected to act like an adult? Describe.

Are any of the children "silent partners" of the parents, serving as their parent's confidant and filling in for a deficit in the parents' relationship with each other? Describe.

Is there anything else that is represented in your social atom, or that came to mind as you were reflecting on it, that you'd like to share more about?

As you look at this social atom from the outside, from a more mature and distanced place, what would you like to say to the you that is inside the social atom?

Clinical Exercise

Sculpting the Social Atom

Any moment or relational circumstance can be "sculpted" so that the relational dynamics within the situation can be embodied, concretized, and dealt with in real time. Sculpting a social atom creates a living representation of the relational proxemics in the client's life at a particular moment.

Space is part of the therapeutic process in psychodrama, as role players can be positioned to reflect distance and closeness, relative size, or power dynamics—the proxemics—that are or were a part of any grouping. Sculptures can be still or go live. They can be done to reveal dynamics in the protagonist's life, and they can also be redone by placing role players as protagonists wished they would have been, allowing the protagonist to template new possibilities or gain a felt sense of experiencing what they have longed for. I always ask the protagonist to choose someone to represent themselves as a stand-in, so that they can reverse in and out of the sculpture to take a breather, gain perspective, or get the visceral feeling of untrapping themselves from a system they may feel stuck in. Role reversal also trains spontaneity and creativity as protagonists shift from seeing the world one way to seeing it another way, as they shift their view.

Goals

- Provide a visual and embodied, concretized snapshot of the client's place within their relational network.
- Give the client a chance to talk to themselves, then reverse roles and actually experience standing inside any phase or constellation of a relational network that shaped or impacted them.
- Give the client a chance to reshape their own relational experience and feel it in a new way.

Steps

1. Have the protagonist create a social atom on paper, as described in the *Basic Social Atom* exercise.
2. Using the social atom as a map, "sculpt" the scene with role players: Allow the protagonist to choose a role player to represent themselves (their stand-in) and then more role players to represent all the people, institutions, parts of the self, and so on that the protagonist wishes to include in their sculpture. They need not enrole every aspect of their social atom but encourage them to fully represent whatever they wish to work with. Setting up the sculpture is part of the protagonist's warm-up and should be done, as much as possible, by the protagonist themselves: "Sculpt it as you see it; the stage is yours."

3. As they are setting up their sculpture, the protagonist should locate themselves and the role players in whatever size, shape, and relative distance feels appropriate and accurate. In other words, the proxemics or the unspoken (or even unconscious) but very impactful relational dynamics that shaped the situation may make themselves evident by how and where they are represented on the stage. The protagonist might also reverse roles and say something as that person. This allows the protagonist to give the role players some insight and training as to the role that they are portraying. It also lets the protagonist use fewer words and explanations to get the character's essence across.

Note: Steps 4 through 8 will guide you in using the social atom in titrated stages. After any of these steps, you can choose to either continue on to the next one or stop the experience there and move into sharing as a group. The process can end at any of these steps and still be very impactful.

4. Once the sculpture is set up, invite the protagonist to stand outside their sculpture with you, look at themselves in this situation, and share about how it feels to see the whole system or moment at once.
5. Invite the protagonist to mill around their sculpture and to double for any role, including themselves, saying what they imagine is going on inside of all those represented that was not spoken out loud. Group members can also be invited to double.
6. Invite the protagonist to talk to themselves inside the sculpture.
7. The protagonist can reverse roles with themselves inside the sculpture, thus entering the moment and becoming themselves at that moment. They can talk to themselves outside the sculpture—for example, "What would you like to say to your adult or witnessing self?"—and they can reverse in and out of that dialogue if it seems indicated.
8. While they are inside the sculpture, the protagonist can also talk to any role player in it and use doubling and role reversal. Group members can also jump in and double for the protagonist or the protagonist in role reversal.
9. Have the protagonist end the scene from the role of the adult or witnessing self—for example, "What do you want to tell yourself inside this scene from your more mature self of today?"
10. Invite the protagonist to reconstruct the scene, moment, or period of time as they wish it had been. They can stand inside the repaired sculpture and talk to their adult, witnessing self outside of it, then reverse back to their adult, witnessing self and say what they want to say to the self now in this new, restructured system. This moment of repair often brings up a lot of feelings for the protagonist, as they feel what never got a chance to happen.

Variations

- **Soliloquy (Walk and Talk):** This technique can be done during any moment or scene, but it is especially helpful as a safety valve if the protagonist begins to flood or freeze. Invite them to walk around with you inside the sculpture and soliloquize in the first person about how they are feeling. This gives them a breather from the heat of the action while keeping them a part of the scene. Even in a slow stroll, the body relaxes and the limbic mind-body begins to flow. It is a lovely in-between place in trauma work. It provides a little distance and a sense of safety, but the client is still in the affective moment, moving, feeling, and adding words to express what is happening on the inside. They can also reverse roles with the adult self outside the sculpture and soliloquize from a greater distance.
- **Talking from the Adult to the Child Self:** If the sculpture involves a younger self, you can encourage the client to explore how their adult self can better care for this younger self by prompting: "Younger self, tell your self of today what you want or need from them going forward." Then ask them to reverse roles. This can facilitate a running dialogue between the adult and child selves, through role reversal. Speaking as both selves allows the adult self to translate feelings and messages from the child self into mature language so that the adult self can communicate with the adult world in a way that is more likely to be listened to and achieve healthy relating.

Clinical Exercise

Frozen Moment Social Atom

This intervention allows the client to take ownership of their own forgotten experience that lives wordlessly within them. It provides a safer way for them to identify a moment that they shut down around. Identifying the moment as "frozen" allows them to feel like a coinvestigator in exploring it. You can invite the protagonist to simply share about their moment, without moving it into a sculpture or scene. Or you can guide them to a variety of role play possibilities, the simplest one being talking to the part of them that froze. They can talk *to* and *as* that self—this helps them to not become overwhelmed by a full scene.

It may be helpful to show your clients a sample social atom; you can find one in the *Basic Social Atom* exercise (page 84).

Goals

- Create a smooth entry into trauma work.
- Examine significant moments or model scenes that have had long-term impact.
- Bring the then and there into the here and now—allow the client to feel feelings that went unfelt, say words that went unsaid, and move the mind-body out of its frozenness into expression.
- Clarify the seed of possible relational reenactments.

Steps

1. Provide writing utensils and copies of the *Social Atom* journaling page (page 88) or blank pieces of paper to the participants.
2. Say, "Draw a social atom of a time in your life when you felt frozen in place, hurt, or as though you didn't get a chance to say what you wanted to say or do what you wanted to do. It can be a moment, a relational dynamic, or a sort of snapshot or model scene of a period in your life."
3. Go over the symbols and what they represent: circle for female, triangle for male, diamond for another gender, square for an institution or group, and a symbol with a dashed line for someone who is deceased.
4. Say, "First, locate yourself on the paper anywhere that feels right to you."
5. Say, "Now locate your important relationships. You can place them as close to or distant from yourself as you feel them to be, and in the size or proportion that feels right. You may include parents, siblings, pets, in-laws, grandparents, friends, institutions, and so on. Write their name in

or next to their symbol." Remind the participants that these atoms are only a current reflection; they are always subject to change and can be done for as many moments in time as one can imagine.

6. Once the participants feel that their atoms are finished, invite them to share, either in the full group or in dyads or clusters.
7. At this point, the frozen self is in view so that the work is already focused and warmed up. Invite whoever is warmed up to talk to their frozen aspect of self to do so using an empty chair or a role player and proceed with the drama as usual.
8. Allow the role play to proceed as usual, using doubling, role reversal, role reversal interview, or soliloquy.
9. Several clients can do a role play with a frozen aspect or part of self, and sharing can happen after one protagonist has completed their work or after a few have done shorter role plays. The important thing is not to waste the warm-up—do not interrupt it with talking or questioning, but simply let the work flow.
10. You can also invite the clients to revise their frozen moment by creating a second social atom representing the way they wish that moment had been. This allows for inner repair and templating future possibilities. Ask questions like:
    - "How do you feel when you look at your revised frozen moment? Do you feel any sadness that it wasn't this way?"
    - "Is there anything you wish you could have felt safe enough to say to those involved or to your loved ones—maybe how important they were to you or how much you loved or needed them?"
    - "How do you think your life today might be different had you had more moments of repair?"
    - "Does anything sit differently inside of you when you change it around?"

Variations

- **Sculpting the Frozen Moment Social Atom:** The frozen moment can also lead to sculptures, as described in *Sculpting the Social Atom*.
- **Telehealth:** Give the group members time to complete their atoms on their own paper or digitally. Then invite them to share, either in the full group or in breakout groups.
- **One-to-One:** The client can complete their atom, then do a role play talking to that part of self using an empty chair and the techniques listed in the *Basic Role Play* exercise (page 35).

CHAPTER 7

Taming the Wild Beast: Working with Anger

There are many ways that anger—especially unconscious, denied, or unprocessed anger—can leak out sideways. If anger isn't processed, it can fuel other problems, like depression, a desire to self-medicate, or the sabotaging of relationships. By processing their anger, the client feels, owns, and translates those feelings of anger into coherent words so that they can process and examine it, understand it more carefully, and parse out the many sources and manifestations of their anger. They don't pin it on one or two people, places, or things and make their anger about everything but themselves. They process it so that they can get beyond it, because they recognize that staying stuck in it only hurts them.

If there's historical anger that has remained hidden, it can be triggered by and complicate a situation in the present. When this piece of historical anger is denied, the present-day situation can become mired in blame and projection. The client looks for an object in the present to "hold" their unconscious anger from the past; they make their uncomfortable or even rageful feelings about the wrong person, at the wrong place, and at the wrong time, which can make the present conflict very difficult to work through.

People also use anger to protect their feelings of vulnerability, which keeps them from letting their more tender sides emerge or processing the emotions that would help them to own their part of a problem, listen as someone else owns their part, and make the kinds of changes that might move the situation forward. When someone keeps cycling around in old, unconscious anger from the past that they're making about someone or something outside of the self in the present, other emotions associated with the grief process—like sadness, hurt, and a feeling of falling apart—never emerge. They're living with one foot in the past, trying to work something out in the present, and they can't separate one from the other.

The Rage State

Rage can hijack our brains. It can take us over, obliterating reason and blowing past ordinary boundaries. Our attention narrows and becomes locked onto the target of our anger; soon we can pay attention to nothing else. As our body and mind churn around, that lingering arousal keeps us primed for more anger. Our focus narrows, and we become less aware of what is happening around us, such as what someone else is saying to us.

A certain level of arousal is vital for efficient remembering, and there is an optimal level of arousal that benefits memory. However, when arousal exceeds that optimal level, it makes it more difficult for new memories to be formed. This is why it is difficult for clients to remember the details of their angry outbursts or explosive arguments. As Dr. Norman Rosenthal (2002) explains, during rage attacks, "those parts of the brain that are central to feeling and expressing anger, such as the amygdala and the hypothalamus, commandeer the rest of the brain. In this wholesale takeover, the cerebral cortex is overwhelmed and restraint and reasoning are impossible" (p. 210).

Thus, extreme anger can override both the client's ability to make good choices in the heat of the moment and their ability to later recall what they did say and do. They often don't remember what they were like while raging and minimize their effect on others. This makes it much harder for them to repair the hurt. They're not able to own their part because they don't remember it fully. And without having all the information about what happened, they may be confused and unsure how to resolve the problem. Although rage, as Rosenthal (2002) writes, "may be adaptive as a response to severe threat, in most situations it destroys much more than it accomplishes" (p. 210).

Trapped in Rage

Just as anger has a physiological preparation phase during which our resources are mobilized for a fight, it also has a wind-down phase. We start to relax back toward our resting state when the target of our anger is no longer accessible or an immediate threat. It is difficult to relax from an angry state, however. The adrenaline-caused arousal that occurs during anger lasts a very long time (many hours, and sometimes days) before we return to our resting state. This cool-down period also lowers our anger threshold—we are more likely to get very angry in response to minor irritations that normally would not bother us. This can become a self-perpetuating cycle of rage that is difficult to escape.

Chronic rage might also be an indicator of depression, PTSD, or C-PTSD. It's been estimated that 40 percent of those suffering from rage attacks also suffer from clinical depression (Fava & Rosenbaum, 1999). Sudden angry outbursts can be a part of both PTSD and unresolved grief. As Rosenthal (2002) notes:

> Dr. Martin Teicher and colleagues at Harvard have found that adults who were abused as children, whether verbally, physically, or sexually, show brain-wave changes over the temporal lobe of the cerebral cortex. These changes resemble those seen in people with documented seizures in the temporal lobe, which surrounds the limbic-system structures. Teicher suggests that early traumatic experiences might kindle seizure-type activity in this area, resulting in a storm of electrical activity in the emotional part of the cerebral cortex. . . . The end result could be a brain that is cocked and all too ready to fire off a limbic storm. (p. 213)

Given this relationship between trauma and rage, helping clients process their anger is an essential part of trauma treatment.

The exercises in this chapter involve the body and allow feelings to be stimulated so that what happened then and there can be brought into the here and now to be refelt, reunderstood, and reprocessed. They will help clients understand the many ways that anger might be manifesting, gain insight into what historical anger might be getting triggered and layered onto the present situation, and access embodied and experiential ways of processing anger in a relational context. This therapy is psychoeducational, so that clients can understand their own relational trauma and begin to feel and heal. They can learn to feel their anger, name it, regulate, and reflect on why they're feeling it. By identifying anger before it takes over and using it as information about the self, they can manage it more effectively.

Clinical Exercise

Anger Floor Check

This exercise generally works very smoothly, but one of my early memories of it that has lasted was when I first used it in a men's program. I observed how ready and willing they were to own and talk about the ways in which their anger was manifesting. They found such relief in seeing that they weren't alone in how they manifested anger and no one was condemning them. I hardly did a thing but watch as they clustered around their various manifestations of anger, talking buoyantly and intimately about this challenging subject. They helped each other, laughed, patted each other on the back, and hugged. I created the exercise to help clients understand that anger can come out in many, many ways, some quite unconscious. It definitely does the job.

Goals

- Help clients broaden their concept of the many ways in which anger may manifest.
- Provide a sociometric exercise for the exploration of anger.

Steps

1. On separate pieces of paper write, or have the group write, the many manifestations of anger. You can draw from the following list. Be sure to include the "Other" card; you can also leave a blank piece of paper for any write-in that the group may spontaneously wish to use.

    - Cynicism
    - Negativity
    - Criticism
    - Sarcasm
    - Digging in one's heels
    - Passive aggression
    - Whining
    - Rage
    - Acting-out behaviors
    - Violence
    - Stonewalling
    - Withdrawal
    - Shunning
    - Coldness
    - Resentment
    - Self-medication
    - Tight jaw
    - Clenched fists
    - Opening and closing fists
    - Red face
    - Increased blood pressure
    - Other

2. Place the papers a couple of feet apart, scattered around the floor.
3. Invite the group members to stand on or near the manifestation of anger that they identify as their go-to—the one that they experience most often.

4. Invite the group members to share with each other, saying a sentence or two about why they are standing where they are standing.
5. Repeat this process with a few other criterion questions. You can draw from the following list, create your own questions, or invite the group members to suggest questions that they wish to explore.
   - "Which manifestation of anger do you avoid?"
   - "Which manifestation of anger did your family avoid?"
   - "Which manifestation of anger do you have the most trouble containing?"
   - "Which manifestation of anger goes straight to you acting out in some way?"
   - "Which manifestation of anger did your family get stuck in a lot?"
   - "Which manifestation of anger do you have trouble tolerating in others?"
   - "Which form of anger have you become more aware of in yourself recently and are learning to cope with in healthy ways?"
6. Once the group is saturated, say, "Walk over to someone who shared something that you identified with or that moved you, stand next to them, and share with them what moved you."
7. Invite the group to sit down and share about the experience as a whole. Or, if they are warmed up for further work, you can move into role plays or experiential letter writing. Group members may wish to talk to a manifestation of anger, a person whom they are angry with, or a part of self that feels angry or that they are angry with.

Variations

- **Telehealth:** Display the options to the group using a whiteboard tool, a shared document, or another method that works for you. As you ask the criterion questions, group members can call out their answer and say a sentence or two about why they chose it. Or, if the group is large enough, you can use the initial questions as a warm-up and then move into breakout rooms for continued sharing.

Clinical Exercise

Anger Map

When I first devised the *Anger Map*, I was amazed at how well it worked. People wanted to dive in and analyze themselves and their own anger, and they seemed to know just how to do it. What they came up with in terms of self-reflection was better and more courageous than anything I came up with in analyzing them. It was self-directed—I wasn't telling them who they were or what they were like. In seven minutes, a group of any size had insights and "aha" moments all at the same time, rather than one by one. And they felt proud to share—there was an acceptance around anger that I wasn't used to seeing. Likely this was because they could begin to see where their anger came from and because the exercise helped to reduce shame and isolation.

Goals

- Provide a safe and contained way of talking about how anger from the past may be getting triggered in the present.
- Help clients become aware of what triggers them into states of feeling old anger intruding into the present.

Steps

1. Provide the participants with copies of the *Anger Map* journaling page (or blank pieces of paper) and writing utensils.
2. Invite them to fill in their anger map: "In the center of the circle, write down the situation that's triggering you right now. On the jutting lines, jot down any times when you felt similarly angry, or any moments, scenes, or dynamics from your past that get triggered when you're angry like this."
3. Invite them to share their anger maps, either in the full group or in clusters.
4. Doing and sharing the anger map may be sufficient. Or, if the group members are warmed up, they can do role plays talking to someone they have anger toward, including themselves, from any time in their life.

Variations

- **Telehealth:** Give the group members time to complete their anger maps on their own paper or digitally. Then invite them to share, either in the full group or in breakout groups.
- **One-to-One:** The client can use the *Anger Map* journaling page, then you can unpack together in session.

Journaling Page

Anger Map

When you're carrying unprocessed anger from your past, you may tend to layer that anger onto situations in your present, without being consciously aware that you're doing so. You might try to make your anger about anything or everything else—another person, place, thing, or circumstance in your present-day life. Tracing your anger back to its origins in the past will help you understand and process it. Rather than staying stuck in the past, you'll be able to move on in the present.

Use the template to create your anger map. In the center of the circle, write down the situation that's triggering you right now. On the jutting lines, jot down any times when you felt similarly angry or any moments, scenes, or dynamics from your past that also get triggered when you're angry like this. Then answer the questions that follow.

Diagram: Anger Map

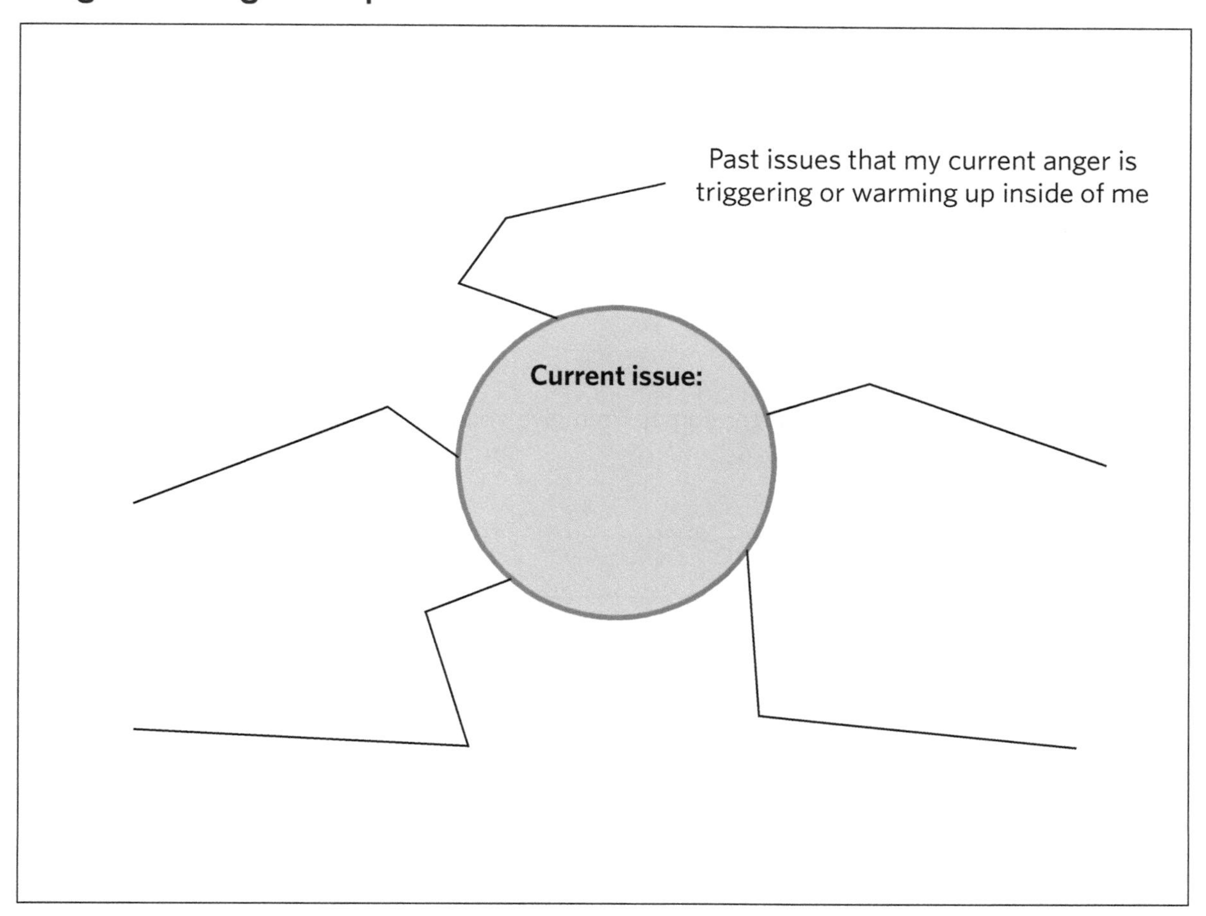

Questions

What did you notice as you created your anger map? Describe any connections, insights, feelings, or questions that this process brought up for you.

Does understanding where your anger comes from give you any new ideas that could help you in the future? If so, please describe.

Clinical Exercise

Anger Spectrogram

This exercise gives group members a sense of control around their anger by helping them figure out to what extent they experience anger and its manifestations in any given situation. Just bringing up the subject of anger in a communal space with nothing bad happening is also part of the healing.

Goals

- Help clients gain a sense of regulation around anger.
- Parse out how anger is experienced differently for each client.

Steps

1. Designate an area in the workspace and explain to the participants that each end of this area represents an extreme—for example, one end represents 0 percent and the opposite end represents 100 percent. Next, draw an imaginary line bisecting the area, representing the midpoint (50 percent).
2. Ask a criterion question that explores the participants' experience of anger, and invite them to move to whatever point along the continuum best describes their response. For example:
    - "How much anger do you feel you carry around with you?"
    - "How triggered do you get around other people's anger?"
    - "How much shame do you feel around your anger?"
    - "How much do you beat yourself up when you get angry?"
    - "How easily are you triggered into an angry state?"
    - "How much hurt do you think is underneath your anger?"
    - "How depressed do you feel around your anger?"
    - "How overtly aggressive do you become?"
    - "How passive-aggressive do you become?"
    - "How vulnerable do feel opening up about your anger?"
3. Allow people to share, either with the full group or in dyads or clusters with the people nearest to them (those they are sociometrically aligned with). Invite them to share a sentence or two about why they're standing where they're standing.

4. After you have explored as many questions as you wished to or the group has reached its saturation point, you can invite them to return to their seats and continue to share. You can also begin a role play, such as the *Anger Role Play* (page 109). You can also follow up with the *Anger Floor Check* (page 102) because it helps the group members begin to understand how their anger manifests.

Variations

- **Telehealth:** You can simply ask the criterion questions and invite the group members to rate their degree of intensity by holding up one to five fingers (with one being the least intense and five being top intensity) or by holding their arm sideways across the screen in a lower or higher position. You can also create the spectrogram using an interactive whiteboard tool: Draw a line and label the two endpoints and the midpoint, then invite the group members to add a dot or other mark along the line to represent their answer.

Clinical Exercise

Anger Role Play

This exercise can be done after any process in this chapter or as a stand-alone role play. The protagonist is invited to speak to an angry part of the self or to someone that they feel anger toward. This fosters greater understanding, empathy, and self-regulation.

Goals

- Help the client gain a sense of separateness from and empathy for their angry parts.
- Bring more understanding and regulation to the client's angry parts.
- Help the client gain a better sense of what old anger from yesterday might be fueling overreactions today.

Steps

1. After the group has warmed up through one of the processes in this chapter, place two chairs in the center of the stage area.
2. Invite anyone who's warmed up to choose an angry part of themselves that they want to talk to or someone toward whom they have anger that they want to express. The protagonist can use the empty chair or choose a role player to represent that person or part.
3. Or the protagonist can reverse roles and show the group how this part or person sits and what they would say as a form of role training.
4. Then ask the protagonist, "What would you like to say to this person or this part of yourself?"
5. Allow the role play to develop, following the lead of the protagonist. Use doubling, role reversal, and role reversal interview wherever appropriate.
6. When the role play seems to be drawing to a natural close, invite the protagonist to say the last thing they need to say to themselves or the other person.
7. Have the group members return to their seats for deroling and sharing. Ask the role players to say, "I am [their own name], I am no longer [the name of the character]." Then ask them to share how they felt while playing the role. "Playing [name of character or part of protagonist] I felt..." They can also share any identification from their own life.
8. Invite the other group members to share as well, like this: "What came up for me from my own life while witnessing your drama was . . ."

Variations

- **Telehealth:** These empty chair role plays can be directed through the "window" if a client has two chairs so that they can reverse roles back and forth. The group or therapist can double, and role reversal interview can be used effectively as well.
- **One-to-One:** The client can use the empty chair technique for this role play.

Clinical Exercise

Giving My Body a Voice

This is an activity that can be done with paper, pen, and colors, and it can also lead into a floor check. The idea is to give clients a creative way to become aware of and talk about how emotion manifests in their bodies when they are experiencing certain feeling states.

Goals

- Help clients identify how emotions are experienced in the body.
- Provide a way for clients to process emotions that are being held by or experienced in the body.
- Create bottom-up emotional literacy.

Steps

1. Provide the participants with copies of the *Emotions Anatomy* journaling page and coloring utensils.
2. Invite the group to use their colors to visually show how they are experiencing emotions and sensations in their bodies. Encourage them to use the colors and techniques (e.g., scribbling, intense or light color, bubbles, jagged lines, dots) that correspond to their inner experience.
3. Invite them to also write words on the body part, giving that part a voice.
4. After giving them time to journal, invite them to share, either in the full group or in dyads or clusters. Ask any of the following questions and let group members share as they are moved to:
   - "What part of your body do you hold anger (or grief, fear, etc.) in, and how does it feel inside of you?"
   - "Does this feeling have a sensation, such as numb, pins and needles, tight, loose, intense sensation, dead, adrenalized, collapsed, balanced/calm, breathless, weary, or energized? Share about how that feels."
   - "Does this feeling have a color, texture, or sound? If so, describe it."
   - "If this part of you had a voice, what would it like to say?"
5. From there, you can continue sharing as a full group or begin a role play, if participants are warmed up to do so. They may wish to talk to an emotion, a part of their body, or a person or part of self that they hold strong emotion toward.
6. The group can share after each role play or after several have been done.

Variations

- **Telehealth:** Share the journaling page electronically for the participants to print out, fill in digitally, or simply reference as they draw on their own paper. Then invite them to share, either in the full group or in breakout groups.
- **One-to-One:** The client can use the journaling page, then you can unpack together in session.

Journaling Page

Emotions Anatomy

Emotions, especially intense ones, can cause a variety of body sensations. Some might seem obvious to you, like when you feel embarrassed and you immediately feel your face flush. Other times, the connection may be more subtle—for example, depression can slow the digestive process, causing nausea, changes in appetite, or other digestive problems. This activity will help you identify where and how you feel emotions in your body.

First, in the diagram, use your colors to visually show how you are experiencing emotions and sensations in your body. Feel free to use different colors and techniques—such as scribbling, intense or light color, bubbles, jagged lines, or dots—to represent your inner experience. You can also write words on the body part, giving that part a voice. Some emotions and sensations you may wish to include in your diagram are listed below.

When your diagram is complete, reflect on the questions that follow.

Emotions

- Anger
- Rage
- Sadness
- Grief
- Fear
- Anxiety
- Calm
- Joy

Sensations

- Frozen
- Numb
- Pins and needles
- Tight
- Loose
- Intense sensation
- Dead
- Adrenalized
- Collapsed
- Balanced
- Breathless
- Weary
- Energized

Diagram: Emotions Anatomy

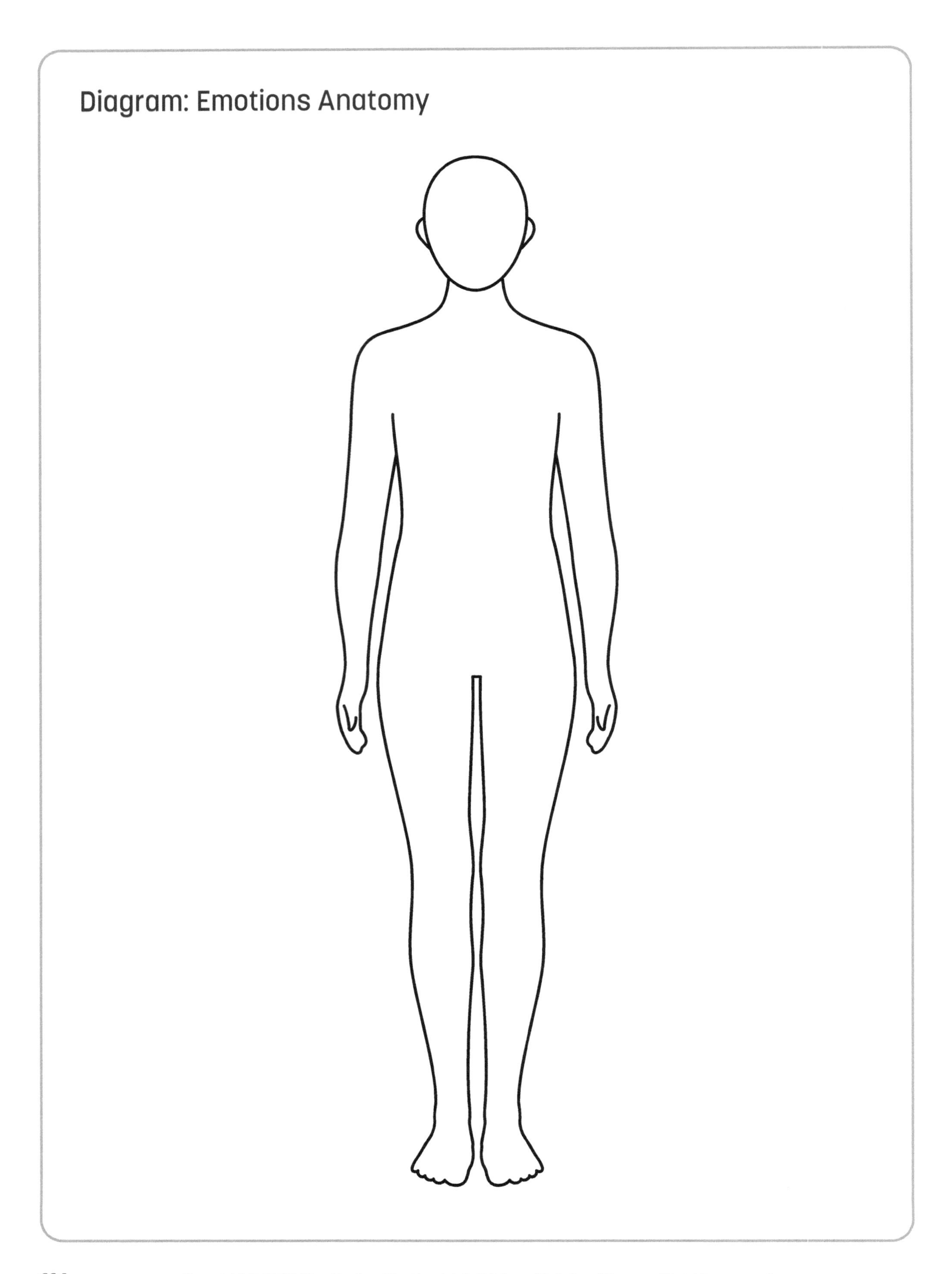

Questions

What part of your body do you hold anger or rage in, and how does it feel inside of you? Does this feeling have a sensation? Does it have a color, texture, or sound? What would this part of your body like to say or do?

What part of your body do you hold sadness, weariness, or grief in, and how does it feel inside of you? Does it have a sensation? A color, texture, or sound? What would this part of your body like to say or do?

What part of your body do you hold fear or anxiety in, and how does it feel inside of you? Does it have a sensation? A color, texture, or sound? What would this part of your body like to say or do?

Where in your body do you feel calm, at peace, or energized, and how does that feel inside of you? If this part of your body could talk, what would it like the world to know about you? What would it like to say or do?

Clinical Exercise

Emotions Anatomy Floor Check

Becoming comfortable identifying disequilibrating body states and talking about them is an important part of healing trauma. Developing emotional literacy through translating problematic inner states into words, making them conscious, reflecting on them, and talking about them allows a client to manage difficult feelings and sensations rather than act them out unconsciously, or self-harm or self-medicate over them. It is part of developing a recovery-oriented skill set.

Goals

- Allow the body's inner states and emotions to become embodied, experiential, and vocal.
- Allow clients to become comfortable identifying, articulating, and sharing about how emotion manifests for them in their bodies.
- Allow group members to connect with each other around vulnerable inner states, share, and take in sharing and support.

Steps

1. On separate pieces of paper, write inner body states such as frozen, numb, pins and needles, tight, loose, intense sensation, dead, adrenalized, collapsed, balanced/calm, breathless, weary, and energized. Have one paper marked "other" so clients can choose their own emotion/sensation; you may also leave a few pieces of paper blank for the group members to write in their own words.
2. Place the papers a couple of feet apart from each other, scattered around the floor.
3. Ask the participants to stand on or near the state that best describes their experience of the moment.
4. Say, "Whenever you are warmed up, share a sentence or two about why you are standing where you're standing."
5. At this point you can vary the criterion questions. For example:
    - "Which state do you avoid, or self-medicate or self-injure around?"
    - "Which state do you fear will become bigger if you let yourself feel it?"
    - "Which state do you want to experience more of? How can you take steps toward that?"

- "Which state do you have trouble tolerating in someone else?"
- If you want to build resilience, you might ask, "Which state used to drag you down but now you have learned how to manage it better?"

6. If you'd like to extend the process, you can say, "Place your hand on the shoulder of someone who shared something with which you identified. Now tell them why you chose them."
7. Role plays may emerge at any point in this process.
8. Or invite the group to sit down and share about the entire process and what came up throughout.

Variations

- **Telehealth:** Display the options to the group using a whiteboard tool, a shared document, or another method that works for you. As you ask the criterion questions, group members can call out their answer and say a sentence or two about why they chose it.

CHAPTER 8

Accessing Inner States: Working with Anxiety and Depression

Relational traumatic stress may express itself through anxiety, depression, or both. Clients can become mired in these states, overwhelmed by worry, fear, pessimism, and grief. I have had the most success in helping clients climb out from these pits by adapting the same experiential and embodied processes that I use throughout this book. Spectrograms, locograms, and floor checks provide ways for clients to safely explore, feel, and learn to regulate their feelings.

Group therapy can be especially powerful for those with depression and anxiety. The nature of these inner states can make the client feel alienated, as if they are uniquely unlovable, incapable, or "wrong" in some way; it can be such a profound moment for them to see that they are not alone in this experience. Working with these issues experientially and in a group is healing in and of itself: The group members' support and sharing normalizes their feelings, reduces their anxiety, and pulls them out of isolation. Withheld emotion can shift and be witnessed in this mutually supportive environment.

Once clients are given this support to face their depression or anxiety, they can enter the work of tracing it back to the experiences and situations where it began. Often there is an original model scene or episode that can benefit from being identified, talked about in group, or drawn in a social atom. In this way, clients can safely enter the work of deconditioning their anxiety or processing the kinds of anger, sadness, or grief that might be underneath their depression.

Depression

Many researchers believe that early trauma causes subtle changes in brain function that contribute to symptoms of depression and anxiety. The key brain regions involved in the stress response may be altered at the chemical or cellular level. Profound early losses, such as the death of a parent or the withdrawal of a loved one's affection, may resonate throughout life, causing depression (Harvard Health Publishing, 2022).

Later losses or disappointments may continue to trigger depression unless the person gains a conscious understanding of the source.

The past and present can mix together and become a roiling cocktail of emotional and physiological pain. Physiological sensations such as head pounding, body aches, queasiness, or nervousness can trigger disturbing thoughts, which trigger more sensations, which trigger more thoughts. This can cause the types of inner states that people try to manage with drugs, alcohol, and other forms of self-medication. Once someone is caught up in this depression cycle, it can be difficult to get back out.

I have the best results in healing depression when I take a multilayered approach. I use floor checks as the foundation of the group process and psychodrama to address the relational anger, sadness, and grief that might be fueling depression. Mobilizing all of these feelings—through crying, grieving, and even expressing rage—tends to get depression to move. The experience of actually getting angry with the person they hold resentment toward can help the client become more open to experiencing the sadness that may also be contributing to their depression.

I also focus on lifestyle adjustments that can alleviate depression. I ask that clients incorporate walking, preferably outdoors and with a friend with whom they can share genuine feelings, to get the serotonin flowing. Research shows that adding 45 minutes of walking three times per week is as effective as medication in managing depression and there are few, if any, side effects (Babyak et al., 2000). Then I make sure that clients aren't overeating foods that depress the system, such as white flour, fast foods, and white sugar. I encourage those who smoke to quit and ask that clients not self-medicate with drugs or alcohol, since these substances prevent them from feeling or healing their feelings.

Anxiety

Children of relational trauma may not learn to modulate their deep sense of connection with another human being; rather, they vibrate along the extremes. Intimacy and social relationship can become fear-bound for the traumatized person. Relationships can be full of stimuli reminiscent of early relationship trauma, which can trigger fear and anxiety. Then the instinctual fight, flight, or freeze response kicks in, which can lead to defensive relational responses like projection, transference, fighting, blaming, withdrawing, or stonewalling.

Peter Levine and Maggie Phillips (2012) remind us that anxiety is much more than a word—it is an active, full-body experience that we must invite into and work with in therapy if we're going to make progress in shifting it. Porges (personal communication, 2021) also discusses the full-body changes that people experience when they're in interchanges that cause them to feel anxious or braced for danger and the way the nervous system recalibrates in order to manage these painful encounters. This recalibration can become a part of how they live in the world if the body stores it.

Deconditioning Anxiety

Fortunately, fears can be deconditioned, and the exercises in this chapter do just that, assuming that the stimulus of the fear is lessened. Research has demonstrated how stimulating the prefrontal cortex can gradually work toward lessening—or even, in some cases, distinguishing—the fear response by mimicking the brain's own "safety signal." According to Dr. Gregory Quirk, "Repeated exposure to traumatic reminders without any adverse consequences causes fear responses to gradually disappear. Such reduction of fear appears to be an active rather than passive process. It doesn't erase the fear association from memory, but generates a new memory for safety" (National Institutes of Health, 2002).

When a client learns through therapy to reexperience, recalibrate, and reframe painful interactions from childhood so that they can see them differently as adults, they can lessen their tendency to re-create painful interactions, or at least step out of their piece in creating them. They can handle these moments differently and have new life experiences that decondition their fear.

For example, if fear is enrolled in an empty chair or by a role player, the client can talk back to it, talk as it, then reverse roles and talk back again. You can interview the client in role reversal, asking questions like, "Is there something wrong here in the moment? If so, what is it? Is it real right now, or is it your ruminating that is giving you pain in this moment?" The fear will loosen its grip as the protagonist gets underneath it. Psychodrama allows clients to play with these things that plague them, toss them into the air, and get new input through doubles and role players. The client's perspective naturally shifts as they interact with and question their fear.

Bringing the body into the work, through either role play or sociometrics that offer here-and-now group interactions, is a crucial part of the healing process. Adult children of relational trauma have often learned to recalibrate or upregulate their nervous systems vis-à-vis another human being during triggering relational interactions. So they need to have new experiences of interacting in order to learn how to relate in calmer, less anxious ways. And this needs to be learned in relationship, not in the clients' heads or through words. They need new sets of interactions—and sociometrics, floor checks, and role plays give them experiences in doing just that.

Emotional Sobriety

The term *emotional sobriety* was introduced by Bill Wilson, the founder of Alcoholics Anonymous. He felt that in order to lead full, happy, and balanced lives, people must become sober not only from addictive behaviors, but also emotionally. Certainly, the subsequent science on emotional self-regulation and coregulation supports this point of view. When our emotions are out of control, so is our thinking. And when feeling and thinking come into balance, behavior follows. Emotional sobriety, in my mind, includes the ability to:

- **Self-regulate and coregulate,** keeping feelings, thoughts, and behavior in a balanced range rather than cycling between extremes and acting out.
- **Self-soothe** and find healthy ways to feel good and keep the limbic system in balance.
- **Pay attention to the body** and take care of it through good nutrition, sleep, rest, downtime, pleasure, exercise, and sunlight.

- **Use the thinking mind** to process and make sense of emotions, bring them into balance, and draw meaning from experience.
- **Live in the present** rather than being preoccupied with what happened in the past.
- **Live with both social and intimate connection** rather than avoiding relationships out of fear.

The exercises in this chapter, and throughout this book, serve at some level the idea of emotional sobriety or regulation. Embodied therapy activates the emotional fascia of relational dynamics and events, and through exploring, playing, testing, releasing, and understanding, clients can untangle themselves from the convoluted and painful stranglehold that inner frozenness can have on them. This release allows for a new kind of energy to flow through the mind and body, one that can help the client to live life more fully.

Clinical Exercise

Anxiety Spectrogram

Some people feel overwhelmed when their anxiety is triggered; some shut it down, withdraw, or numb out; some move immediately to anger or blame; and some act out through frenetic or self-medicating behaviors. This exercise helps clients develop the ability to experience, breathe through, and tolerate anxious feelings so that they become less destabilizing. As part of that learning, clients start to get a sense of regulation, identifying the level of anxiety they may experience and how it may be showing up for them.

Goals

- Gain a sense of whether anxiety is a problem for a particular client.
- Help the client develop a sense of regulation around the feeling of anxiety.

Steps

1. Designate an area in the workspace and explain to the participants that each end of this area represents an extreme—for example, one end represents 0 percent and the opposite end represents 100 percent. Next, draw an imaginary line bisecting the area, representing the midpoint (50 percent).
2. Ask a criterion question that explores the participants' experience of anxiety, and invite them to move to whatever point along the continuum best describes their response to the question. For example:
    - How flooded or overwhelmed do you feel when scared or anxious?
    - How helpless or immobilized do you feel?
    - How much do social or political issues trigger anxiety or fear in you?
    - How controlling do you get when you feel anxious?
    - How much body disequilibration do you experience (shortness of breath, tingling limbs, tightness, sweating, etc.)?
    - How much reactivity do you feel or act out when your anxiety or fear gets triggered?
    - How much do you try to get rid of the feeling through some kind of defense (projection, blaming, raging, denial, self-medicating, etc.)?

3. For each criterion question, allow people to share, either with the full group or in dyads or clusters with the people nearest to them (those they are sociometrically aligned with). Invite them to share a sentence or two about why they're standing where they're standing.
4. You can also ask, "Did anyone say something that particularly resonated with you? Or is there someone you feel you could learn something from? If so, walk over to that person, place your hand on their shoulder, and share why you choose them."
5. After you have explored as many questions as you wished to or the group has reached its saturation point, you can invite them to return to their seats and continue to share. You can also begin a role play.

Variations

- **Telehealth:** You can simply ask the criterion questions and invite the group members to rate their degree of intensity by holding up one to five fingers (with one being the least intense and five being top intensity) or by holding their arm sideways across the screen in a lower or higher position. You can also create the spectrogram using an interactive whiteboard tool: Draw a line and label the two endpoints and the midpoint, then invite the group members to add a dot or other mark along the line to represent their answer.

Clinical Exercise

Fear and Anxiety Floor Check

This exercise helps clients discern the ways in which their own anxiety and fear might manifest. By parsing out how they feel or act when they're scared, triggered, or anxious, they can start to develop some emotional literacy and intelligence around it so they can begin to regulate it. They can also take some steps in deconditioning the fear response by being triggered in a safe environment where they can share and get some understanding and support. They can see that something bad isn't necessarily happening when they feel anxious, that their urge to blame or act out can be tempered and traded for a more functional response like talking about their anxiety or fear in a vulnerable way. This helps to separate the past from the present, reducing reenactment and re-creation of old pain in new relationships.

The key to the process is the continuous choosing and re-choosing that trains clients to think (and feel!) on their feet and to use their spontaneity to make novel choices related to themselves and others.

Goals

- Help the group members broaden their concept of the many ways in which fear and anxiety manifest.
- Give the group a chance to get safely triggered and to develop new ways of behaving when triggered (e.g., talking rather than acting out).

Steps

1. On separate pieces of paper, write the manifestations of fear or anxiety. You can draw from the following list:
    - Constantly feeling overwhelmed or under pressure
    - Fear of retribution or punishment if life works out
    - Caretaking too much
    - Talking too much
    - Sleep issues
    - Heart pounding or chest tightness
    - Queasiness

- Tremors or shivers
- Headaches, muscle aches, or other body aches
- Hypervigilance—always waiting for the other shoe to drop
- Fear of panic attacks
- Irrational fears or free-floating anxiety
- Overcontrolling other people, places, and things
- Phobias (social anxiety, agoraphobia, fear of animals, etc.)
- Guilt
- Chronic regrets or feeling you have missed out
- Transference
- Projection
- Blaming
- Withdrawing or shutting down
- Other

2. Place the papers a couple of feet apart, scattered around the floor.
3. Invite the group members to stand on or near the manifestation of anxiety that they identify with the most.
4. Invite the group members to share with each other, saying a sentence or two about why they are standing where they are standing.
5. Invite them to make another choice and repeat the sharing. Most people have more than one way that anxiety manifests.
6. Repeat this process with a few other criterion questions. You can draw from the following list, create your own questions, or invite the group members to suggest questions that they wish to explore.
    - Which form of anxiety is your go-to—the one that shows up the most in your life or relationships?
    - Which type of anxiety do you have the hardest time coping with or fear the most?
    - Which form of anxiety creates problems for you in relationships?
    - Which form of anxiety do you have the hardest time dealing with in someone else?
    - Which manifestation of anxiety did your family get stuck in a lot?
    - Which form of anxiety was a problem for you, but you have learned to cope successfully with it?

7. Once the group is saturated, say, "Walk over to someone who shared something that you identified with or that moved you, stand next to them, and share with them what moved you."
8. Invite the group to sit down and share about the experience as a whole. Or, if they are warmed up for further work, you can move into role plays; group members may wish to talk to an anxious or scared part of themselves or someone with whom they felt or feel those feelings.

Variations

- **Telehealth:** Display the options to the group using a whiteboard tool, a shared document, or another method that works for you. As you ask the criterion questions, group members can call out their answer and say a sentence or two about why they chose it. Or, if the group is large enough, you can use the initial questions as a warm-up and then move into breakout rooms for continued sharing.
- **One-to-One:** The client can talk to an anxious part of self in an empty chair role play.

Clinical Exercise

Depression Floor Check

Experiential therapy offers a direct route to feeling the sadness and anger that might be part of depression. It helps clients connect with parts of themselves that they may feel disconnected from in a supportive, communal setting that is normalizing. It can kick in a grief process that can help feelings to move and be felt rather than foreclosed on. Becoming active in experiencing blocked emotion in both the mind and the body—and embodying parts of self or others who are associated with hurt—can help clients process their emotions. When they understand that depression can manifest in many ways, they can see how depression influences their own behavior.

Goals

- Open up the subject in an experiential format and educate clients on the range of symptoms that can be part of depression.
- Provide a format through which clients can choose for themselves which symptoms they identify with and hear about how symptoms manifest for others.
- Encourage connection, sharing, and support around facing difficult personal issues.
- Allow clients to actually experience, rather than only talk about, feelings of anger, rage, sadness, hurt, and so on that may be part of depression.

Steps

1. On separate pieces of paper, write the following symptoms of depression:
    - Blocked anger or rage
    - Blocked sadness
    - Isolation—feeling disconnected from the self and others
    - Irrational guilt
    - Persistent sad, anxious, or "empty" mood
    - Hopelessness or pessimism
    - Feelings of guilt, worthlessness, or helplessness
    - Loss of interest or pleasure in hobbies and activities you once enjoyed (this can include sex)
    - Decreased energy, tiredness, being "slowed down"

- Difficulty concentrating, remembering, or making decisions
- Insomnia, early-morning awakening, or oversleeping
- Changes in appetite or weight (in either direction)
- Thoughts of death or self-harming
- Restlessness, irritability
- Persistent physical symptoms that do not respond to treatment, such as headaches, digestive disorders, or chronic pain
- Self-medicating behaviors
- Other

2. Place the papers a couple of feet apart, scattered around the floor.
3. Invite the group members to stand on or near a manifestation of depression that draws them, one that they experience in their life.
4. Invite the group members to share with each other, saying a sentence or two about why they are standing where they are standing.
5. Repeat this process with a few other criterion questions. You can draw from the following list, create your own questions, or invite the group members to suggest questions that they wish to explore.
    - "Which manifestation do you struggle with the most?"
    - "What do you feel someone close to you struggles with that affects you?"
    - "Which manifestation have you been successful in dealing with—that is, you used to struggle with it more before than you do now?"
    - "Which symptom seemed to be the most present in your family of origin?"
    - "Which manifestation do you feel you inherited from the dynamics in your family of origin?"
    - "Which manifestation do you feel you have because of social or institutional issues (e.g., racial or gender oppression, war, or state violence)?"
    - "Which manifestation do you feel most hopeful about?"
    - "Which manifestation do you feel most hopeless about?"
6. Once the group is saturated, say, "Walk over to someone who shared something that you identified with or that moved you, stand next to them, and share with them what moved you."

You can also use this resilience-building prompt: "Walk over to someone from whom you feel you could learn something and ask them for help."

7. Invite the group to sit down and share about the experience as a whole. Or, if they are warmed up for further work, you can move into role plays; group members may wish to talk to a part of themselves or another person.

Variations

- **Telehealth:** Display the options to the group using a whiteboard tool, a shared document, or another method that works for you. As you ask the criterion questions, group members can call out their answer and say a sentence or two about why they chose it. Or, if the group is large enough, you can use the initial questions as a warm-up and then move into breakout rooms for continued sharing.

Clinical Exercise

Anxiety and Depression Floor Clock

Depression and anxiety can emerge or become more intense at different times of the day. This floor check helps clients explore their moods and inner states in relationship to the daily cycle. It allows them to identify patterns and possible causalities; they can then use this information to better anticipate, tolerate, and treat their manifestations of anxiety or depression. Doing this exercise in a group has the added benefits of normalizing these emotions and helping clients move from isolation into connection.

Goals

- Concretize and bring awareness to times of the day that the client is likely to feel depressed, anxious, or overwhelmed.
- Give clients a sociometric opportunity to identify their own patterns and make positive connections with others.
- Break patterns of isolation through getting honest, opening up, and sharing.

Steps

1. On separate pieces of paper, write the numbers 1 through 12.
2. Lay the numbers on the floor in the shape of a clock.
3. Invite the group members to stand on or near the time of day that they are most likely to feel down or stressed out.
4. Invite the group members to share with each other, saying a sentence or two about why they are standing where they are standing.
5. Invite the group members to choose another time of day that is a problem for them and share again.
6. You can repeat this process with other criterion questions—for example:
    - "What time of day do you feel overwhelmed?"
    - "What time of day goes fairly smoothly?"
    - "Is there a time of day when your body feels symptomatic in some way, such as queasy, tingly, lethargic, or tight?"
    - "Is there a time of day when you feel desperate?"

- "Is there a time of day when you feel relieved?"
- "What time of day are you more likely to feel hopeful, content, relaxed, or focused?"
- "When do you usually go to sleep? When do you usually wake up?"

7. Once the group is saturated, say, "Walk over to someone who shared something that you identified with or that moved you, stand next to them, and share with them what moved you."
8. Invite the group to sit down and share about the experience as a whole, or you can move into another activity.

Variations

- **Telehealth:** Display a clockface to the group. As you ask the criterion questions, group members can call out their answer and say a sentence or two about why they chose it. Or you can set up breakout rooms and cluster the clock numbers into four (midnight to 3:00 a.m., 3:00 a.m. to 6:00 a.m., etc.). For two or three selected questions, give the participants time to join and share in their chosen breakout group before bringing them back to the main room. You can also use the *Anxiety and Depression Clock* journaling page: You can call out one question at a time and invite the group members to share their responses. If they might benefit from further sharing, they can do so in breakout rooms or they can continue the process of working through one question at a time in breakout rooms.
- **One-to-One:** The client can use the *Anxiety and Depression Clock* journaling page, then you can unpack together in session.

Journaling Page

Anxiety and Depression Clock

Depression and anxiety can emerge or become more intense at different times of the day. This exercise will help you explore the relationship between the daily cycle and your symptoms of depression or anxiety. You may notice patterns—for example, maybe you tend to feel more down in the evenings, or you often feel stressed as you get ready for work. Understanding this can help you anticipate your mood, tolerate intense feelings as they occur, and even take steps to alleviate your depression or anxiety, such as changing parts of your routine to make difficult moments of your day easier.

Reflect on the following questions. Mark your answers on the accompanying clockface by drawing, coloring, or writing, and journal a sentence or two about each answer.

Diagram: Anxiety and Depression Clock

Questions

What time of day do you feel overwhelmed?

What time of day goes fairly smoothly?

Is there a time of day when your body feels symptomatic in some way (e.g., queasy, tingly, lethargic, tight)?

Is there a time of day when you feel desperate? Are you able to feel more regulated if you use deep, rhythmic breathing to bring calm to yourself?

Is there a time of day when you feel relieved?

What time of day are you most likely to feel down?

What time of day are you most likely to feel stressed out?

____

____

____

What time of day are you more likely to feel hopeful, content, relaxed, or focused?

____

____

____

When do you usually go to sleep? When do you usually wake up?

____

____

____

Are there any other times that are significant for you (e.g., work, school, appointments, activities, time with family or friends)?

____

____

____

What is one thing that you can do in order to make a difficult or stressful part of your day less so?

____

____

____

What is one thing you can do to make a feeling of calm, peace, or hopefulness expand into more of your day?

____

____

____

Clinical Exercise

Anxiety and Depression Floor Calendar

Depression and anxiety can emerge more intensely at different times of the week. This exercise introduces awareness around these times in a group setting so feelings can be normalized and the group members can support each other through their sharing and witnessing. Clients can also begin to identify patterns in their weekly experience; they can then use this information to better anticipate, tolerate, and treat their symptoms of anxiety or depression.

Goals

- Concretize days or times of the week that the client is most at risk for becoming depressed or overwhelmed.
- Offer a sociometric way of processing depression, anxiety, and stress.

Steps

1. On separate pieces of paper, write the seven days of the week.
2. Lay the days on the floor in a straight line to form a week-long calendar.
3. Invite the group members to stand on or near the day of the week when they are most likely to feel depressed, anxious, or overwhelmed.
4. Invite the group members to share with each other, saying a sentence or two about why they are standing where they are standing.
5. Invite the group members to choose another day that is a problem for them and share again.
6. You can repeat this process with other criterion questions. For example:
   - "On which day do you tend to feel overwhelmed?"
   - "Which day goes fairly smoothly?"
   - "Are there days when your body feels symptomatic in some way, such as queasy, tingly, lethargic, or tight?"
   - "Are there days when you feel desperate?"
   - "On which day are you more likely to feel hopeful, content, relaxed, or focused?"

7. Once the group is saturated, say, "Walk over to someone who shared something that you identified with or that moved you, stand next to them, and share with them what moved you."
8. Invite the group to sit down and share about the experience as a whole, or you can move into another activity.

Variations

- **Telehealth:** Display the days of the week to the group using a whiteboard tool, a shared document, or another method that works for you. As you ask the criterion questions, group members can call out their answer and say a sentence or two about why they chose it. You can also use the *Anxiety and Depression Calendar* journaling page: You can call out one question at a time and invite the group members to share their responses. If they might benefit from further sharing, they can do so in breakout rooms or they can continue the process of working through one question at a time in breakout rooms.
- **One-to-One:** The client can use the *Anxiety and Depression Calendar* journaling page, then you can unpack together in session.

Journaling Page

Anxiety and Depression Calendar

Depression and anxiety can emerge or become more intense at different times of the week. This exercise will help you explore the relationship between the weekly cycle and your symptoms of depression or anxiety. You may notice patterns—for example, maybe you tend to feel more down on the weekends when there is less structure, or maybe you feel more stressed on Mondays as you go back to work. Understanding this can help you anticipate your mood, tolerate intense feelings as they occur, and even take steps to alleviate your depression or anxiety, such as changing parts of your routine to make difficult days easier. You can also track your symptoms over the course of a month to look for any week-to-week changes that reflect an overall pattern of functioning.

Reflect on the following questions. Mark your answers on the accompanying calendar by drawing, coloring, or writing, and journal a bit about each answer.

Diagram: Anxiety and Depression Calendar

Monday	Tuesday	Wednesday	Thursday	Friday	Saturday	Sunday

Questions

On which day of the week do you tend to feel overwhelmed?

Which day goes fairly smoothly?

Are there days when your body feels symptomatic in some way (e.g., queasy, tingly, lethargic, tight)?

Are there days when you feel desperate? Are you able to feel more regulated if you use deep, rhythmic breathing to bring calm to yourself?

On which day are you most likely to feel down?

On which day are you more likely to feel hopeful, content, relaxed, or focused?

Are there any other parts of the week that are significant (e.g., weekends/days off from work or school, appointments, activities, time with family or friends)?

____

____

____

What is one thing that you can do in order to make a difficult or stressful part of your week less so?

____

____

____

Are you aware of how your exercise, eating, or using/self-medicating patterns may be affecting your mood on days that you find challenging? If so, what are the patterns, and how can you make changes that will improve your overall well-being?

____

____

____

Are you aware of changes you have already made that have changed your days for the better? (For example: adding exercise, twelve-step programs, therapy, mindfulness/meditation, or leisure or social activities that bring you pleasure, or making positive adjustments in your eating or sleep habits.) If so, how can you continue to add these activities to your life?

____

____

____

CHAPTER 9

The Intergenerational Path of Trauma and Addiction

When clients' inner pain feels like too much to deal with on their own, they may try to manage it with drugs, alcohol, food, sex, money, and so on. For a while, these behaviors help them numb out the needy, anxious parts of themselves that hurt. But eventually their "solution" becomes a new problem—it spirals out of control and they become addicted. And the trauma for those close to them can spiral out of control, too.

Living in addiction's wake can be deeply wounding, and those wounds can last a lifetime. Watching a loved one, perhaps a person they depend on, disappear into the addiction and become someone they no longer recognize, and witnessing their loved one's life falling apart, is extraordinarily painful. And those closest to the person with an addiction, especially those who live with them, aren't just watching this happen—they're feeling it, hearing it, and living smack in the middle of the strange, warped, devasting chaos and pain that addiction creates. They may also be experiencing this sober, with nothing to dull their pain.

In this way, the children of people with addictions are also put at risk, and these children may eventually reach for ways of managing their trauma that lead in some way to addiction. Thus, the wheel of trauma and addiction makes a predictable turn through the generations. Even if the child doesn't develop an addiction of their own, they may have relational trauma that is being passed down through the generations and that needs to be healed to break the chain of dysfunction.

Growing Up with Addiction

The cycle of trauma and addiction is well-supported by research, including the CDC-Kaiser Permanente adverse childhood experiences (ACE) study, a cornerstone in trauma research. Drs. Robert Anda and Vincent Felitti, the principal investigators, sought to understand what sorts of early life experiences led to an unusually high number of doctor visits in adulthood, reasoning that if they could understand causal factors, they could shape strategies toward better health.

Even though they weren't looking for it, growing up with the adverse childhood experience of parental substance abuse popped up again and again as one of the most statistically significant drivers of physical and mental health issues in adulthood. People with high ACE scores have an increased risk of lung disease, liver disease, stroke, and diabetes; their risk of cancer and heart disease is nearly twice that of people with lower scores. They are also more likely to experience depression, and the likelihood of suicide increases twelvefold (Anda et al., 2005).

Adverse experiences in childhood can also shape one's relationship to addictive substances. People with high ACE scores are two to four times more likely to start using alcohol or drugs at an early age. The chance that they will develop an alcohol use disorder increases sevenfold, and those with a score of 5 or higher are up to 10 times more likely to develop an addiction compared to people who haven't experienced childhood trauma. Those with high ACE scores are more likely to experience chronic pain and to misuse their prescription medication, another common path to addiction (Anda et al., 2005). The discovery that drugs and alcohol help to manage and numb emotional, physiological, and psychological pain becomes a slippery slope that all too often leads to abuse.

And addiction doesn't ride alone; ACEs tend to cluster. Once a home environment becomes disordered, such as when an adult develops an addiction, the risk of children in the home witnessing or experiencing emotional, physical, or sexual abuse rises dramatically (Anda et al., 2005). After all, alcohol and drugs reduce inhibition and alter one's state of mind. Inebriated people may violate their own sense of what is right, and later they may not even remember what they did. But the children they hurt do remember and carry that pain, confusion, and resentment.

The Wheel of Intergenerational Trauma and Addiction

A parent is addicted to a substance or behavior that consumes their thoughts, feelings, and behavior.

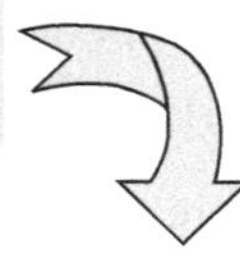

Their child becomes traumatized by the parent's distorted thinking; dismissive, neglectful, erratic, or abusive behavior; and/or denial, secrecy, or compensatory/confusing behavior.

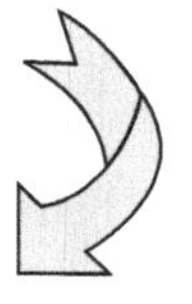

The child develops their sense of self and relationships with an attachment figure who creates chaos, pain, and instability. They may be parentified (turned into a little partner).

As an adolescent/teen, they discover that substances (alcohol and/or drugs) or behaviors (e.g., overeating, exercise, internet use, work, sex, shopping) help manage their anxiety and pain.

They become an adult reenacting patterns of addiction and dysfunctional relating. They partner and parent re-creating these patterns.

Intergenerational Pain, Intergenerational Healing

Anda and Brown (2010) explain why ongoing traumatic experiences—such as growing up with addiction, abuse, or neglect in the home—can have such tenacious effects: "For an epidemic of influenza, a hurricane, earthquake, or tornado, the worst is quickly over; treatment and recovery efforts can begin. In contrast, the chronic disaster that results from ACEs is insidious and constantly rolling out from generation to generation" (p. 2). If the effects of toxic stress are not understood, so that children can receive some sort of understanding and support from home, school, and community, these children simply "vanish from view . . . and randomly reappear—as if they are new entities—in all of your service systems later in childhood, adolescence, and adulthood as clients with behavioral, learning, social, criminal, and chronic health problems" (Anda & Brown, 2010, p. 3).

These are the kids who get sick more often, who get into trouble, who are labeled "at risk." Understanding two things could make a world of difference, not only for these children but for all of us: First, how can we reduce the impact of adverse childhood experiences in our children's lives? And second, how can we work through the effects of our own adverse childhood experiences so that we can stop re-creating our own unprocessed historical pain in our children's lives? This could turn around the intergenerational impact of addiction and relational trauma.

Addiction and Grief

Adult children of addiction and relational trauma need to mourn all that happened and all that never got a chance to happen when they were young. They need to shed the tears that could never safely come out before. They need to mourn everything that left them wounded and traumatized—the broken promises, abuse, neglect, and lost years.

Children of parents with an addiction can become anxious and hypervigilant. And when nothing they can do can make them feel safe, they feel helpless and despairing. In the absence of an apology or resolution, the child may feel shame and hurt. They may feel very alone and resourceless because the person they are supposed to go to for comfort and reassurance is the one causing them pain.

These feelings of hurt and fear can become part of the child's developing psyche, part of their lessons on relationship, part of who they are on the inside. If they don't unearth, understand, and process that pain, they are at risk of passing it down to the next generation through the same (or similar) projections, transferences, and reenactment dynamics. Or they self-medicate it, and the wheel of trauma and addiction makes another sinister turn through another heart, another mind, another generation.

Treatment and Recovery

Often, treatment programs are hesitant to address powerful issues of trauma or grief because they are legitimately concerned that doing so could undermine sobriety. However, not addressing trauma issues can also lead to relapse. Because the client has relied on a substance to manage their emotions, they may have trouble facing their unmedicated pain in recovery. They may need support in dealing with their addiction and their trauma simultaneously.

Recovering from addiction means that someone who has been self-medicating their emotional, psychological, and physiological pain is suddenly being asked to live without that substance or behavior. They're giving up what they have been using to manage their hurting inner world. So they're left with raw pain that can become overwhelming in its intensity. Those early losses that went ungrieved—that were numbed through self-medication rather than felt, understood, and integrated—now surface. And the pile-on from their own addiction, of more relational and life problems that grew out of their use and abuse, emerges as well. The client has a whole lot of pain to heal.

Their trauma issues may be complex and thorny. They may need to grieve the life they have lost through addiction, the lost time that they could have devoted to getting their life in order, or the pain that they have caused those they love. And they may well be grieving these losses with a weakened or underdeveloped set of psychological and emotional tools. Adults with addictions have often been medicating their wounds that stretch out from childhood, so their grief is developmental, stretched out over the timelines of their lives. Their feelings may reach back for years, even decades, making the painful past and the dysfunctional present feel all mixed up together.

Those who are in recovery for addiction, codependency, or PTSD can be especially vulnerable to becoming symptomatic around current life losses that carry painful histories. When a current loss triggers emotional states from previous losses, mourning can become what is known in the vernacular as "complicated"—that is, unconscious, unresolved pain from past losses gets stirred up and seeps into the current loss, making the client's feelings more intense and confusing than they might otherwise be. Soldiers, for example, are more likely to develop PTSD if they have previous histories of traumatization, such as within their family or community (van der Kolk, 1985).

The client may need to sort through the confusion and summon the strength to live through the pain that previously felt like too much to tolerate. But by processing and understanding it, they take steps toward building a life they never dreamed was possible. They can learn to work with past and present trauma and loss, rather than falling back into the addictive substance or behavior. The exercises in this chapter point the way to recovery by building self-awareness, resilience, and connection. For additional support in working with the grief that is so often a part of recovery, see chapter 10.

Clinical Exercise

Addiction and Relational Trauma Spectrogram

This spectrogram starts to bring awareness and regulation around the extent to which addiction and relational trauma have impacted a client's life. It brings up some of the feelings that clients may have trouble talking about so that they can share these with the identification and support of their fellow group members. The fact that they can immediately share the feelings that are getting triggered or warmed up inside of them helps to make the exercise healing. And as they share, they feel witnessed and held by the energy of the group, which allows them to expand their own internal container.

Goals

- Create awareness as to how much growing up with addiction and dysfunctional family patterns have impacted the client's inner world and relational habits.
- Allow group members to see hidden emotions and thoughts to come to the surface.

Steps

1. Designate an area in the workspace and explain to the participants that each end of this area represents an extreme—for example, one end represents 0 percent and the opposite end represents 100 percent. Next, draw an imaginary line bisecting the area, representing the midpoint (50 percent).
2. Ask a criterion question that explores the participants' experience of self-medication or living with or growing up with addiction and relational trauma, and invite them to move to whatever point along the continuum best describes their response to the question. For example:
    - How much sadness do you feel relative to this?
    - How much anger do you feel relative to this?
    - How much shame do you feel relative to this?
    - How much loss do you feel relative to this?
    - How much confusion do you feel relative to this?
    - How derailed do you feel your life has been by addiction?
    - How much regret about the past do you feel relative to this?
    - How much anxiety about the future do you feel?
    - How vulnerable do you feel opening up about your self-medication?

- How much hope do you feel?
- How much strength or personal growth do you feel?
- How much faith do you have?

3. Allow people to share, either with the full group or in dyads or clusters with the people nearest to them (those they are sociometrically aligned with). Invite them to share a sentence or two about why they're standing where they're standing.
4. You can also ask, "Did anyone say something that particularly resonated with you? Or is there someone you feel you could learn something from? If so, walk over to that person, place your hand on their shoulder, and share why you choose them."
5. After you have explored as many questions as you wished to or the group has reached its saturation point, you can invite them to return to their seats and continue to share. You can also begin a role play; participants may wish to talk to another person, a part of themselves, a feeling or concept (e.g., hope, despair, recovery), or the addictive substance or behavior itself (e.g., alcohol, food, the internet, money).

Variations

- **Telehealth:** You can simply ask the criterion questions and invite the group members to rate their degree of intensity by holding up one to five fingers (with one being the least intense and five being top intensity) or by holding their arm sideways across the screen in a lower or higher position. You can also create the spectrogram using an interactive whiteboard tool: Draw a line and label the two endpoints and the midpoint, then invite the group members to add a dot or other mark along the line to represent their answer.

Clinical Exercise

Process Addictions Floor Check

Over the past two decades, what people think of as addiction has broadened considerably. With an increasing body of research connecting the brain's dopamine production with behaviors such as sex, eating, work, and internet use, we have a growing understanding of how we can stimulate and manipulate these pleasure chemicals with behaviors. This floor check is a way to bring awareness around the various ways that people might be self-medicating C-PTSD pain, beyond using drugs and alcohol.

Goals

- Help clients understand how unresolved trauma manifests in other addictions and process disorders.
- Gain awareness of the extent to which substances or behaviors are being used to self-medicate.
- Allow for open and honest sharing about compulsive behaviors.
- Help clients become aware of any secondary addictions that may have affected their family dynamic and influenced their own addiction.

Steps

1. On separate pieces of paper, write examples of process addictions or other forms of self-medication that clients may fall into, such as:
   - Food
   - Sex/porn
   - Spending/debting
   - Frenetic activity/adrenaline
   - Cigarettes
   - Work
   - Exercise
   - Technology/internet
   - Other
2. Place the papers a couple of feet apart, scattered around the floor.
3. Ask the group members to stand on or near a form of self-medication that they currently use or that they believe they could fall into.
4. Invite the group members to share with each other, saying a sentence or two about why they are standing where they are standing.
5. Next, invite the group members to stand on or near a form of self-medication that they feel was present in their family of origin, either in a particular person or in their family as a whole, that

created problems. (This may well be the same form of self-medication currently used by the client, which would illustrate the intergenerational nature of addiction.) Invite them to share again.

6. Ask the participants to stand on or near a form of self-medication that they feel they may once have slipped into, or could slip into, and share how they found their way through it, or how they keep themselves from going there.
7. Invite them to walk over to someone who shared something that made sense to them, or someone they feel they could learn something from, and ask that person for their insight, support, or advice.
8. At this point the group may be ready to sit down and share about the experience so far or move into another process. Clients may wish to use role play or experiential letter writing to talk to the form of self-medication that they are using or abusing.

Variations

- **Telehealth:** Display the options to the group using a whiteboard tool, a shared document, or another method that works for you. As you ask the criterion questions, group members can call out their answer and say a sentence or two about why they chose it. Or, if the group is large enough, you can use the initial questions as a warm-up and then move into breakout rooms for continued sharing. You can also use the *Process Addictions* journaling page: You can call out one question at a time and invite the group members to share their responses. If they might benefit from further sharing, they can do so in breakout rooms or they can continue the process of working through one question at a time in breakout rooms.
- **One-to-One:** The client can use the *Process Addictions* journaling page, then you can unpack together in session.

Journaling Page

Process Addictions

Over the past two decades, our definition of addiction has expanded. While alcohol and drug use are still the first examples that come to mind for many people, research shows that behaviors like sex, eating, work, and internet use also stimulate the production of "pleasure chemicals" in the brain and can therefore become addictive. This activity will help you identify ways that you might be self-medicating your pain with substances or behaviors besides drugs and alcohol, so that you can better understand how these secondary addictions may be impacting your life.

Read through the list of self-medicating behaviors and substances, and reflect on the questions that follow.

Self-Medicating Behaviors and Substances

- Food
- Sex/porn
- Spending/debting
- Frenetic activity/adrenaline
- Cigarettes
- Work
- Exercise
- Technology/internet
- Other: ____________________

Questions

Which forms of self-medication do you currently use or believe you could fall into?

____

Which forms of self-medication were present in your family of origin, either in a particular person or in your family as a whole, that created problems? Describe these behaviors and how they affected you and your family members. Are there forms of self-medication that you feel you learned from your family of origin?

____

____

____

____

____

____

Is there a form of self-medication that you slipped into in the past but no longer struggle with as much? If so, how did you find your way through it?

Is there a form of self-medication that you feel you could slip into but haven't yet? If so, how do you keep yourself from going there?

Choose a form of self-medication that you would like to speak to or talk back to. What would you like to say to it?

Clinical Exercise

Twelve-Step Floor Check

Twelve-step programs offer a network of support for people in recovery from addictions of all kinds, as well as their children, partners, and other loved ones. This is a no-cost, peer-led community with worldwide meetings available most, if not all, days of the week. The combination of therapy and a twelve-step program constitutes a recovery safety net. While some people immediately see the usefulness of twelve-step programs, others resist or find it difficult to engage with them. This exercise is a nonthreatening way to introduce twelve-step concepts into the therapeutic process. You might also invite group members who have already embraced the steps to share a bit of what they have learned with the group.

Goals

- Provide an experiential approach to working the steps.
- Motivate group members to work the steps and offer an experiential way to work through blocks to doing so.
- Introduce twelve-step concepts in a low-stress, supportive, and even playful way.

Steps

1. On separate pieces of paper, write down the twelve steps, along with their respective numbers:*
    1. We admitted we were powerless over alcohol—that our lives had become unmanageable.
    2. Came to believe that a Power greater than ourselves could restore us to sanity.
    3. Made a decision to turn our will and our lives over to the care of God as we understood Him.
    4. Made a searching and fearless moral inventory of ourselves.
    5. Admitted to God, to ourselves, and to another human being the exact nature of our wrongs.
    6. Were entirely ready to have God remove all these defects of character.
    7. Humbly asked Him to remove our shortcomings.
    8. Made a list of all persons we had harmed, and became willing to make amends to them all.
    9. Made direct amends to such people wherever possible, except when to do so would injure them or others.

---

* This is the original twelve-step doctrine of Alcoholics Anonymous (https://www.aa.org/the-twelve-steps); it is also applied to other addictions.

10. Continued to take personal inventory and when we were wrong promptly admitted it.
11. Sought through prayer and meditation to improve our conscious contact with God as we understood Him, praying only for knowledge of His will for us and the power to carry that out.
12. Having had a spiritual awakening as the result of these Steps, we tried to carry this message to alcoholics, and to practice these principles in all our affairs.

2. Place the papers a couple of feet apart, scattered around the floor.
3. Ask a few criterion questions. With each question, invite the group members to stand on or near the step that best represents their answer, then invite them to share a sentence or two about why they are standing where they are standing. You may have them share with the full group, with those standing on the same step, or a combination of these. Possible questions include:
   - "Which step are you currently working on?"
   - "Which step do you feel blocked around?"
   - "Which step do you anticipate with pleasure?"
   - "Which step confuses you or makes you feel vulnerable?"
   - "Which step do you feel you have made progress in?"
   - "Which step, if any, do you feel is out of reach for you?"
4. At any point you might say, "Walk over to someone who shared something that you identified with or that moved you, stand next to them, and share with them what moved you" or "Walk over to someone from whom you feel you could learn something and ask them for help."
5. Invite the group to sit down and share about the experience as a whole. Or, if they are warmed up for further work, you can move into role plays: They can do role plays for anything that "comes up" for them as an issue around any step, enrolling a group member or using an empty chair to embody and talk to it. You might also invite them to journal and then share about whichever step or issue they feel warmed up to; it may be helpful to play some soft sound or music in the background.

Variations

- **Telehealth:** Display the steps to the group using a whiteboard tool, a shared document, or another method that works for you. As you ask the criterion questions, group members can call out their answer and say a sentence or two about why they chose it. Or, if the group is large enough, you can use the initial questions as a warm-up and then move into breakout rooms for continued sharing. You can also use the *Twelve Steps of Recovery* journaling page: You can call out one question at a time and invite the group members to share their responses. If they might benefit from further sharing, they can do so in breakout rooms or they can continue the process of working through one question at a time in breakout rooms.

- **One-to-One:** The client can use the *Twelve Steps of Recovery* journaling page, then you can unpack together in session.

Journaling Page

Twelve Steps

Twelve-step programs offer a network of support for people in recovery from addictions of all kinds, as well as their children, partners, and other loved ones. Twelve-step meetings have no dues or fees and are available most, if not all, days of the week. Whether you're already participating in a twelve-step program or you're wondering if this approach would be helpful for you, this journaling page will help you understand the twelve steps, identify where you are in this process, and explore issues that might be helping or hindering your progress.

Read through the twelve steps and reflect on the questions that follow.

The Twelve Steps

1. We admitted we were powerless over alcohol—that our lives had become unmanageable.
2. Came to believe that a Power greater than ourselves could restore us to sanity.
3. Made a decision to turn our will and our lives over to the care of God as we understood Him.
4. Made a searching and fearless moral inventory of ourselves.
5. Admitted to God, to ourselves, and to another human being the exact nature of our wrongs.
6. Were entirely ready to have God remove all these defects of character.
7. Humbly asked Him to remove our shortcomings.
8. Made a list of all persons we had harmed, and became willing to make amends to them all.
9. Made direct amends to such people wherever possible, except when to do so would injure them or others.
10. Continued to take personal inventory and when we were wrong promptly admitted it.
11. Sought through prayer and meditation to improve our conscious contact with God as we understood Him, praying only for knowledge of His will for us and the power to carry that out.
12. Having had a spiritual awakening as the result of these Steps, we tried to carry this message to alcoholics, and to practice these principles in all our affairs.

Questions

Which step are you currently working on? Write a few sentences about that.

Which step do you feel blocked around? Describe the resistance you're feeling or the obstacles you're facing.

Which step do you anticipate with pleasure? Why?

Which step confuses you or makes you feel vulnerable? Why?

Which step do you feel you have made progress in? Why?

Which step, if any, do you feel is out of reach for you? Why?

Clinical Exercise

Relapse Triggers Floor Check

More and more, relapse is seen as part of the recovery process. Developing an awareness around which circumstances or emotional states might trigger the urge to use or abuse can help clients come out of denial and talk about what might become an issue before it actually mushrooms into one. Listening as others share vulnerably about what triggers them can also make it easier for group members to come forward rather than hide their fears and concerns.

Goals

- Help group members concretize where they feel they are in their recovery process.
- Create group cohesion and provide a warm-up or group check-in.

Steps

1. On separate sheets of paper, write the following relapse triggers:
    - Somatic issues (e.g., poor sleep, chronic pain)
    - Skipping meetings
    - Seeing or hearing something triggering in a TV show, movie, song, etc.
    - Feeling depressed
    - Feeling anxious
    - Relationship issues (feeling left out, rejected, misunderstood, etc.)
    - Anniversary of a significant emotional event (e.g., getting sober, divorce, death, job loss)
    - Disappointment or discouragement in recovery
    - Skipping self-care (e.g., not getting enough rest, poor nutrition)
    - Lack of an inner, spiritual life
    - Not having a sober social life; spending time with people who are using
    - Other
2. Place the papers a couple of feet apart, scattered around the floor.
3. Ask a few criterion questions. With each question, invite the group members to stand on or near the trigger that best represents their answer, then invite them to share a sentence or two about

why they are standing where they are standing. You may have them share with the full group, with those standing on the same trigger, or a combination of these. Possible questions include:

- "Where is your growing edge?"
- "Where do you feel you're screwing up?"
- "Which trigger makes you anxious to consider?"
- "Which trigger are you developing the ability to manage better?"
- "Where do you feel proud of yourself?"
- "Where do you feel ashamed of yourself?"
- "Which trigger makes you angry?"

4. At any point you might say, "Walk over to someone who shared something that you identified with or that moved you, stand next to them, and share with them what moved you" or "Walk over to someone from whom you feel you could learn something and ask them for help."
5. Invite the group to sit down and share about the experience as a whole. Or, if they are warmed up for further work, you can move into role plays.

Variations

- **Relapse—The Progressive Process:** This is a floor check on relapse that I developed using Terry Gorski's stages of the progressive process of relapse. You can find it in *The Living Stage* (Dayton, 2005, pp. 404–405).
- **Telehealth:** Display the options to the group using a whiteboard tool, a shared document, or another method that works for you. As you ask the criterion questions, group members can call out their answer and say a sentence or two about why they chose it. Or, if the group is large enough, you can use the initial questions as a warm-up and then move into breakout rooms for continued sharing. You can also use the *Relapse Triggers* journaling page: You can call out one question at a time and invite the group members to share their responses. If they might benefit from further sharing, they can do so in breakout rooms or they can continue the process of working through one question at a time in breakout rooms.
- **One-to-One:** The client can use the *Relapse Triggers* journaling page, then you can unpack together in session.

Journaling Page

Relapse Triggers

More and more, relapse is seen as part of the recovery process. If you've ever relapsed, you're certainly not alone! When you understand your triggers, you can think and talk about what might become an issue before it actually mushrooms into one. It gives you an opportunity to take care of yourself during difficult moments so you're less likely to use or abuse.

Read through the list of relapse triggers that many people experience, then reflect on the questions that follow.

Relapse Triggers

- Somatic issues (e.g., poor sleep, chronic pain)
- Skipping meetings
- Seeing or hearing something triggering in a TV show, movie, song, etc.
- Feeling depressed
- Feeling anxious
- Relationship issues (feeling left out, rejected, misunderstood, etc.)
- Anniversary of a significant emotional event (e.g., getting sober, divorce, death, job loss)
- Disappointment or discouragement in recovery
- Skipping self-care (e.g., not getting enough rest, poor nutrition)
- Lack of an inner, spiritual life
- Not having a sober social life; spending time with people who are using
- Other: ______________________________

Questions

Where is your growing edge—which trigger do you feel hopeful about working on? Describe the work you are doing or plan to do.

Where do you feel you're screwing up? Explain why this trigger is difficult for you.

Which trigger makes you anxious to consider? Why?

Which trigger are you developing the ability to manage better? Describe your progress.

Where do you feel proud of yourself? Describe your accomplishments in this area.

Where do you feel ashamed of yourself? What would you like to improve in this area?

Which trigger makes you angry? Why?

Clinical Exercise

Recovery Locogram

This experiential check-in is designed for groups in recovery. People tend to be engaged, honest, and spontaneous when checking in like this. They can banter back and forth a bit, double for each other, or make a couple of choices as part of the process. I find that this is an easy way to move through group members' resistance to participating or opening up around what can be a difficult topic.

Goals

- Help group members concretize where they feel they are in their recovery process.
- Create group cohesion, break the ice in engaging in any group process, and provide a warm-up or group check-in.
- Provide a way for the clients, particularly those in the early stages of recovery, to track themselves.
- Identify those who need extra support in their recovery and help them get honest about it.

Steps

1. With the first criterion question, it's helpful to ask the group members to check in about how they are feeling about their recovery process. Designate four areas on the floor to represent possible responses—for example:
    - "I feel very solid in my recovery"
    - "I'm feeling pretty good, but not great"
    - "I'm feeling shaky in my recovery"
    - Other
2. Invite the group members to move to the area that best represents where they feel they are at this moment. If they feel ambivalent or between responses, they may want to stand between those areas.
3. Invite them to share a sentence or two about why they are standing where they are standing. Group members may spontaneously double for each other if this seems useful to the process.
4. If you feel that the group wants to make another choice, you might say something like, "Has anything changed for you since you shared just now? If so, change places and share from where you are right now."

5. You can invite further sharing by saying, "Walk over to someone who shared something with which you identify and place your hand on their shoulder. Now share with them why you chose them or how you identify."
6. Once the group is saturated, you may ask them to return to their seats for sharing or move into other processes.

Variations

- **Recovery Feelings Locogram:** You can invite the group to explore their feelings by using designations such as:
  - "I'm feeling numb or emotionally constricted inside"
  - "I have rumblings of strong feelings but I'm not sure what they're all about"
  - "I'm feeling able to put words to my feelings and express them clearly"
  - Other

  With these possible responses, you can ask, "Where are you right now?" "Where do you feel you're making some progress?" "Where do you get lost?" "Where do you feel better about yourself today than you felt before?"

- **Lifelong Healing Locogram:** Label the areas with different aspects of life in recovery, such as:
  - Going to meetings
  - Having a sober social life
  - Taking care of my body (eating well, exercising, rest)
  - Other

  With these possible responses, you can ask, "In which area do you feel that you're doing what you need to do for your self-care?" "Which area needs improvement?" "Is there an area that brings up anxiety?" "Is there an area where you have hope or a sense of pride?"

- **Telehealth:** Display the options to the group using a whiteboard tool, a shared document, or another method that works for you. As you ask the criterion questions, group members can call out their answer and say a sentence or two about why they chose it. You can also create the locogram using an interactive whiteboard tool: Draw a large square, divide it into four sections, label the sections, then invite the group members to add a dot or other mark on the diagram to represent their answer and then share about why they are located at that point. You can extend the process by inviting the group to double for anyone who said something that they intuitively "got."

CHAPTER 10

Reawakening Feeling: Working with the Grief of Trauma

There are few losses that hurt more than the loss of love. This is the kind of loss that is part of relational trauma, and it needs to be mourned, honored, taken out of hiding, and given the space, time, and attention that it needs to heal.

Clients often avoid grief because it hurts to revisit pain, especially the kind of childhood pain that felt unsurvivable. But once they let themselves feel it, it moves faster and feels better than they expected. It actually feels good to finally stop pushing away the pain of their inner child. It helps them make sense of things that felt senseless. It takes what was tight and turgid inside of them and gives it breath. It lets them befriend a set of emotions that may have felt like the enemy, and it allows their nervous system to relax.

Another very important benefit is that once the client understands their childhood pain, they know what's happening when it gets triggered by something in their current life. Eventually, they learn to hit the pause button and give their inner child some understanding so they don't make everyone else the target of their denied pain.

Disenfranchised Loss and Pain

Our society gives us ways of dealing with the profound changes in our lives as a result of death. There are funerals and black arm bands that signal to the world that we hurt, that we need the support of those around us and time and space to grieve our loss. But the kinds of losses that the adult child of relational trauma or addiction faces are not clear, and there aren't any rituals to deal with them. These kinds of losses that society doesn't recognize are referred to as *disenfranchised losses*. Examples include loss of self, loss of safety, divorce or breakup, abortion, miscarriage, infertility, job loss, retirement, moving, injury, changes in a relationship due to addiction, developmental issues in children, or mental illness.

Because these losses go unacknowledged by others, they can get buried and thrown out of conscious awareness. Traumatized adult clients—who have often experienced multiple adverse childhood events and deep wounds—may act out pain that they do not properly see themselves, not necessarily because they refuse to acknowledge the loss itself, but because their feelings surrounding the loss are so confusing and difficult to find and feel. They don't know that they have a right to their pain and that they need support.

Bringing disenfranchised or hidden losses to the surface so that they can be felt and processed is so important for long-term resilience and mental and physical health. When a client can't, doesn't, or won't process their loss, parts of themselves or their family can carry hidden pain. When they do process the loss, they can find these parts again, both inside themselves and inside others, and process the pain they may be holding.

Why Adult Children of Relational Trauma Need to Mourn

As we explored in the previous chapter, when a parent is addicted, neglectful, or abusive, their child can become anxious and hypervigilant. In the absence of an apology or resolution, the child may come to feel shame and hurt. If they don't know how to help themselves feel safe, they can fall into helplessness and despair, then grow frustrated and angry. And they feel very alone and resourceless because the very person they are supposed to go to for comfort and reassurance is the one causing their pain and fear.

If the adult child avoids or cannot move through some sort of mourning process for this experience, they may:

- Stay stuck in anger, pain, and resentment.
- Remain numb, getting stuck in the first stage of the grief process and losing access to important parts of their inner, feeling world.
- Have trouble engaging comfortably in intimacy.
- Be hypervigilant and unconsciously preoccupied with pain that stems from previous relationships that they have not processed and understood.
- Project or transfer unfelt, unresolved grief onto other relationships or situations, placing unfelt and unacknowledged feelings of hurt, pain, and resentment where they do not belong.
- Lose access to parts of themselves.
- Carry deep fears of subsequent abandonment, betrayal, or disillusionment.

Experiential group processes that allow clients to grieve and feel their pain are powerful tools for recovery from relational trauma. After years of their losses going unrecognized—by society, by their family, and even by themselves—clients discover a community that sees and shares in their hurt. They have the opportunity to feel the group members' support and caring, and to experience healing in relationship to others. They have access to a safe place where they can mourn all that happened, and all that never got a chance to happen, when they were young.

Stages of Loss Experienced in Dysfunctional Family Systems

To more effectively treat the kinds of losses experienced by adult children of relational trauma, I have come up with my own stages of loss, informed by the work of John Bowlby (1982), Elisabeth Kübler-Ross (2014), and Rachel Naomi Remen (2006) and my own clinical work in the addictions field. I prefer addressing the stages with floor checks (see the *Stages of Loss Floor Check*, page 174) because this provides more opportunity for movement, grounding, choice, and connection. Additionally, because these stages do not necessarily occur in order, the floor check format allows each client to tailor their own process.

These stages of grieving loss offer a map of the emotional terrain that clients who live with relational trauma find themselves traversing. The client may or may not identify or deal with these feelings and behaviors. The dysfunction in the family may involve addiction, abuse, neglect, or any other form of relational trauma.

- **Numbness/shock:** The trauma of living with a dysfunctional family member is deeply disturbing and frightening. The family is initially shocked; then, over time, they become numb, inured to the pain.
- **Denial/enabling:** The family tries to "change the channel," to hide their pain and shame from themselves, each other, and the world. They make excuses for the dysfunctional family member's behavior or absence: "Mom has the flu again"; "Dad is tinkering in his garage"; "We're fine—nothing's wrong."
- **Hypervigilance/anxiety:** As the problem gets worse, the family becomes hypervigilant, constantly preoccupied with the dysfunctional person's behavior or state. Family members scan them for signs of danger, slipping, secrecy, lying, using/abusing, or dysfunctional behavior.
- **Avoidance/withdrawal/factioning:** Because the family cannot grieve openly and together, they may avoid subjects, people, places, or activities that are now painful, avoid or withdraw from each other, or separate into factions (Collins-Stuckert, personal communication, 2022).
- **Yearning/returning:** The family is trapped in a repetitive pattern of yearning for the dysfunctional person to return to normal—"Will Mom remember my birthday?" "Will Dad be sober for parents' night?"—and then losing them to their substance or behavior again. Grief is ongoing; there is no clear beginning, middle, and end.
- **Helplessness/despair/hopelessness:** Family members feel that nothing they can do will make things better. They come to feel hopeless and despairing of ever returning to normal again.
- **Anger/blaming/mistrust:** These feelings become internalized by each family member, then they act them out in their relationships. Anger and resentment get projected around the family and create free-floating pain and scapegoats.

- **Chaos/cathexis:** Family factions form. Some people gain power while others become marginalized; some act out, others placate. Bonds become dysfunctional, traumatic bonding and codependency develop, and there can be a preoccupation with a person or the family that borders on obsessive.
- **Intervention/mobilization:** Something in the environment intervenes on the family dysfunction directly or indirectly—for example, a child acting out, a DUI, getting fired, or a family member reaching out for help. There is a dawning of recognition of the dysfunction in the family and the need for help.
- **Reorganization/recovery/decathexis:** Family members begin a process of decathexis and recovery from the dysfunction. They learn both intrapersonal and interpersonal strategies for dealing with it.
- **Acceptance/gratitude/posttraumatic growth:** Family members realize that they, too, are involved in the dysfunction and that they need to take individual responsibility for an extended process of recovery. The recovery process itself becomes a new design for living, and they come to appreciate their deepened and more meaningful experience of life.

These stages do not necessarily occur in order. The client may find themselves cycling through these stages over and over again, hovering between stages, and even zig-zagging among them or skipping over some.

Although mourning can feel messy and dark at moments, it is also a time-honored path toward the light. The vulnerability we feel, along with the depth of emotion that is connected with mourning, brings us in touch with our own and others' humanity. It softens our hearts and opens our minds. And it gives us confidence that we can face what life deals us. The interventions in this chapter will help you guide clients through the grief process and toward these silver linings.

Clinical Exercise

Types of Grief Floor Check

The types of losses experienced by adult children of relational trauma often go unrecognized by others and even by themselves. This floor check introduces the many forms of grief, both conscious and unconscious, so the group members can gain awareness of the impact that their family dysfunction has had on their lives. It gives them the opportunity to share in a supportive community that allows for identification and relational healing.

Goals

- Provide a grief "grid" that can be used to cover many categories of grief, ranging from the personal to social (e.g., race, gender).
- Help clients understand that grief can manifest in many ways, including unexpected ways.
- Engage group members and allow them to bond and support each other.
- Provide experiential, embodied psychoeducation on the subject of grief.
- Act as a warm-up to further and more in-depth embodied work on grief.

Steps

1. On separate sheets of paper, write the following types of grief most commonly experienced around life loss and loss to death:
    - Normal grief
    - Anticipatory grief
    - Parental inner child grief
    - Age correspondence reaction
    - Complicated grief
    - Inhibited grief
    - Cumulative grief
    - Collective grief
2. Place the papers a couple of feet apart, scattered around the floor.
3. Ask the participants to stand on or near the type of grief that they feel they may be experiencing right now, then invite them to share about why they are standing where they are standing.

4. Repeat the process with additional criterion questions. Possible questions include:
    - "Which type of grief do you feel you might be experiencing that you didn't know you were in or that surprises you as a way that grief might show up in your life?"
    - "Did your family of origin have a hard time with or get stuck in any of these types of grief? If so, which one?"
    - "Which form of grief do you feel somewhat stuck in?"
    - "Which form of grief do you feel that you have moved through successfully?"
5. Say, "Walk over to someone who shared something that you identified with or that moved you, stand next to them, and share with them what moved you" or "Walk over to someone from whom you feel you could learn something and ask them for help."
6. Invite the group to sit down and share about the experience as a whole. Or, if they are warmed up for further work, you can move into role plays or experiential letter writing. They may wish to talk to another person, a part of the self, a former self, a group, an abstract idea, the self they feel they "should" be, the self they feel they actually are, the self they would like to become, or anything they wish to explore through role play.

Variations

- **Telehealth:** Display the options to the group using a whiteboard tool, a shared document, or another method that works for you. As you ask the criterion questions, group members can call out their answer and say a sentence or two about why they chose it. Or, if the group is large enough, you can use the initial questions as a warm-up and then move into breakout rooms for continued sharing. You can also use the *Types of Grief* journaling page: You can call out one question at a time and invite the group members to share their responses. If they might benefit from further sharing, they can do so in breakout rooms or they can continue the process of working through one question at a time in breakout rooms.
- **One-to-One:** The client can use the *Types of Grief* journaling page, then you can unpack together in session.

Journaling Page

Types of Grief

Grief can take many forms, both conscious and unconscious. Identifying the types of grief that you've experienced in the past, as well as those you may be feeling now, will allow you to better understand and process the difficult emotions, thoughts, and physical symptoms that come with grief. This journaling page will help you to do just that. Read through the descriptions of the different types of grief, then reflect on the questions that follow.

Types of Grief

- **Normal grief:** This is the mix of responses that people typically experience after a loss; it can involve shock, anguish, sorrow, anger, relief, guilt, regret, anxiety, fear, loneliness, overwhelm, crying, difficulty concentrating, intrusive thoughts, changes in appetite, sleep issues, and more. Normal grief tends to run its own course and lessen over time, although the duration and intensity may vary from person to person and also according to the timing, nature, and intensity of the loss itself.
- **Anticipatory grief:** You feel grief in anticipation of what *could* happen—you grieve in advance. You may get sad before something bad happens to prepare yourself for the worst (which you've learned to expect) so it won't hurt as much if and when it actually happens. You may have learned this kind of grief as a child.
- **Parental inner child grief:** This happens to parents who don't want to repeat the past but don't fully understand how to identify and validate the grief of their own inner child. You feel that you are giving to your child what you never got. If you're a parent and you haven't done your own "work" and processed your own childhood wounds, the neediness of your child can act as a trigger for your own unmet childhood needs. You need to attend to the wounds of your inner child so that you can gain some relief and healing, and stop feeling as if you are giving from an empty well.
- **Age correspondence reaction:** This is another grief reaction that can happen to parents, and understanding it can be very liberating. When your child hits the age of a time in *your* life when *you* were traumatized, your unconscious pain from that time may get triggered. Then you will tend to make your pain from the past about your present. As the parent, you may go to one extreme or the other: You may experience extra worry and anxiety for your child and want to overprotect them because the child in you felt underprotected and unsafe. Or you may want to distance from your child because the child in you wants to go numb and avoid feeling that old wound.

- **Complicated grief:** Complicated grief may begin as normal grief, but it doesn't resolve itself over time and instead becomes prolonged or chronic. This can occur when the nature of the loss is sudden, violent, or hidden (such as incarceration, relational trauma, or addiction), or when you are ambivalent about the loss. If you haven't grieved these previous losses, you may have trouble openly grieving subsequent losses. Warning signs of this kind of complex mourning can include self-medication, sexual acting out, self-harming behaviors, chronic and disabling feelings of guilt or worthlessness, suicidal thoughts, violence, or radical lifestyle changes. The age correspondence reaction may be seen as a form of complicated grief.
- **Inhibited grief:** When you do not let your grief show—whether it's because you want to keep it private or because you have hidden it even from yourself—that grief becomes inhibited. When you cannot allow yourself to openly grieve, your body may do it for you. You may have physical symptoms like muscle stiffness, back pain, migraines, or illnesses that are directly connected to deep, emotional stress. Or you may act out or self-medicate.
- **Cumulative grief:** This develops when losses accumulate: A loss occurs and then, before you've had enough time to process and heal from that loss, you experience another one (and perhaps even more losses after that). The difficult emotions brought up by each loss can become tangled up together, making your grief feel even more confusing and painful.
- **Collective grief:** This occurs when a community collectively experiences loss. Examples include war or veteran-related issues; violence and oppression related to race, gender, and other social categories; the death of a public figure; or the effects of a natural disaster.

Questions

Which forms of grief are you experiencing right now? Describe how you are feeling—what emotions, thoughts, or physical sensations are part of your grief?

____

____

____

____

____

____

Which forms of grief were present in your family of origin? How did this grief affect you and your family members?

Have you experienced collective grief in any of the communities that you are a part of? Describe this, including aspects that may have differed from other forms of grief that you've experienced.

Are there any forms of grief that you have been able to move through in the past, or that you feel hopeful about being able to move through in the future? What strengths and resources have helped you, or could help you, in this?

Clinical Exercise

Stages of Loss Floor Check

Please read the section "Stages of Loss Experienced in Dysfunctional Family Systems" (page 167), which describes the stages in more detail. What I like about doing these stages as a floor check is that participants gain a felt sense of how the stages can overlap, repeat, and leapfrog—they don't necessarily follow a strict order. Seeing how messy grief can be can actually make it less messy, as the client becomes more comfortable and finds it easier to open up about and process their feelings.

Goals

- Offer an experiential way to heal grief.
- Bring clients to an awareness of the many stages that one can pass through while grieving.
- Help those overwhelmed by unconscious grief gain the perspective that there is a beginning, middle, and end to intense grief.
- Engage group members and allow them to bond and support each other.
- Provide a list of symptoms for use with individuals and families who have experienced relational trauma from addiction or dysfunction.

Steps

1. On separate sheets of paper, write the following stages of loss:
    - Numbness/shock
    - Denial/enabling
    - Hypervigilance/anxiety
    - Avoidance/withdrawal/factioning
    - Yearning/returning
    - Helplessness/despair/hopelessness
    - Anger/blaming/mistrust
    - Chaos/cathexis
    - Intervention/mobilization
    - Reorganization/recovery/decathexis
    - Acceptance/gratitude/posttraumatic growth
2. Place the papers a couple of feet apart, scattered around the floor.
3. Ask the participants to stand on or near the stage that best describes their experience at this moment, then invite them to share a sentence or two about why they are standing where they are standing. You may have them share with the full group, with those standing on the same trigger, or a combination of these.

4. Repeat the process with additional criterion questions. Possible questions include:
    - "Which stage do you avoid going into or shut down around because it makes you feel too vulnerable?"
    - "Which stage do you feel stuck in?"
    - "Did your family of origin have a hard time with or get stuck in any stage of grief? If so, which one?"
    - "Which stage do you have trouble tolerating when someone else is going through it?"
    - "Which stage do you feel that you have moved through successfully?"
5. Say, "Walk over to someone who shared something that you identified with or that moved you, stand next to them, and share with them what moved you" or "Walk over to someone from whom you feel you could learn something and ask them for help."
6. Invite the group to sit down and share about the experience as a whole. Or, if they are warmed up for further work, you can move into role plays or experiential letter writing. They may wish to talk to another person, a part of the self, a moment or period in their life, or something else (like a sense of safety or willingness to trust others) that they have lost.

Variations

- **Telehealth:** Display the stages to the group using a whiteboard tool, a shared document, or another method that works for you. As you ask the criterion questions, group members can call out their answer and say a sentence or two about why they chose it. Or, if the group is large enough, you can use the initial questions as a warm-up and then move into breakout rooms for continued sharing. You can also use the *Stages of Loss* journaling page: You can call out one question at a time and invite the group members to share their responses. If they might benefit from further sharing, they can do so in breakout rooms or they can continue the process of working through one question at a time in breakout rooms.
- **One-to-One:** The client can use the *Stages of Loss* journaling page, then you can unpack together in session.

Journaling Page

Stages of Loss

In families where there is dysfunction—such as addiction, abuse, or neglect—the family members tend to move through stages of grief. Each person's grief process is unique, and the stages don't necessarily occur in order; you might repeat, skip, cycle through, or hover between stages. However you move through the stages, learning more about them will help you better understand your experience and identify where you may need support.

As you read through the descriptions of the stages of loss, answer the questions that follow each stage. On the scale, make a mark representing how much or how little you're experiencing that stage right now. Then, in response to the prompts, describe how each stage may or may not be showing up in your life today.

1. **Numbness/shock:** The trauma of living with a dysfunctional family member is deeply disturbing and frightening. The family is initially shocked; then, over time, they become numb, inured to the pain.
    - To what extent are you experiencing this stage now?

      0% ———————— **50%** ———————— **100%**
    - How has this stage affected you?
        - Do you feel there are parts of you that went underground, got tight and constricted, or shut down for self-protection?
        - Did you shut down parts of yourself that, when triggered, make you lash out in anger and blame, or try to numb the pain, or withdraw from relationships?

2. **Denial/enabling:** The family tries to "change the channel," to hide their pain and shame from themselves, each other, and the world. They make excuses for the dysfunctional family member's behavior or absence: "Mom has the flu again"; "Dad is tinkering in his garage"; "We're fine—nothing's wrong."
   - To what extent are you experiencing this stage now?

     0% ——————— **50%** ——————— **100%**
   - How has this stage affected you?
     - Did you or your family members rewrite reality to make it more palatable?
     - Did you feel gaslighted? Did someone say or imply, "This isn't really happening; you're seeing it all wrong"?
     - Did you or your family members flat-out lie or deny what was going on because it was too painful or overwhelming to deal with?

3. **Hypervigilance/anxiety:** As the problem gets worse, the family becomes hypervigilant, constantly preoccupied with the dysfunctional person's behavior or state. Family members scan them for signs of danger, slipping, secrecy, lying, using/abusing, or dysfunctional behavior.
    - To what extent are you experiencing this stage now?

      0% ——————— **50%** ——————— **100%**
    - How has this stage affected you?
        - Did you feel anxious a lot? Were you and your family members always walking on eggshells or waiting for the other shoe to drop?
        - Did you pay close attention to the dysfunctional person or to your family, trying to gauge their mood, detect their behavior, or predict when there would be trouble?
        - Did you or your family engage in denial or wishful or magical thinking, trying to make the problem "go away?"

4. **Avoidance/withdrawal/factioning:** Because the family cannot grieve openly and together, they may avoid subjects, people, places, or activities that are now painful, avoid or withdraw from each other, or separate into factions (Collins-Stuckert, personal communication, 2022).
   - To what extent are you experiencing this stage now?

     0% ———————— **50%** ———————— **100%**

   - How has this stage affected you?
     - Did you or your family members avoid talking about reality because it was too disturbing or hard to talk about?
     - Did you or your family members stop going certain places or doing certain things in an attempt to avoid triggering emotions or behaviors?
     - Did your family members withdraw and isolate from each other or take sides for a sense of security or power?

5. **Yearning/returning:** The family is trapped in a repetitive pattern of yearning for the dysfunctional person to return to normal—"Will Mom remember my birthday?" "Will Dad be sober for parents' night?"—and then losing them to their substance or behavior again. Grief is ongoing; there is no clear beginning, middle, and end.

   - To what extent are you experiencing this stage now?

     0% ———————— **50%** ———————— **100%**

   - How has this stage affected you?
     - Did you alternate between wishing that the dysfunctional person would change their behavior and feeling sad all over again when the change didn't last?
     - When things were going well, did you expect that something would happen to make that end?
     - Did you have fantasies of getting rid of the dysfunctional person or scapegoat so the family could find relief?

6. **Helplessness/despair/hopelessness:** Family members feel that nothing they can do will make things better. They come to feel hopeless and despairing of ever returning to normal again.

   - To what extent are you experiencing this stage now?

     0% ———————— **50%** ———————— **100%**

   - How has this stage affected you?
     - Do you carry a sense of failure inside yourself or disappointment in others that stems from a feeling of living on a sinking ship, believing there was nothing you could do to mend the family or keep them from falling apart?
     - Do you still feel stuck in the middle of a family in free fall?
     - Do you feel you don't deserve for your life to feel good if others are in pain?

7. **Anger/blaming/mistrust:** These feelings become internalized by each family member, then they act them out in their relationships. Anger and resentment get projected around the family and create free-floating pain and scapegoats.

   - To what extent are you experiencing this stage now?

     0% ———————————— **50%** ———————————— **100%**

   - How has this stage affected you?
     - Do you have sudden bouts of anger in which you get negative and blame others?
     - Do you find it difficult to sit with your pain without making it about other people?
     - Do you have trouble trusting that people will be who they say they are, that they won't let you down, or that things will go well?
     - Did your family have scapegoats who were unfairly blamed or symptom bearers who "acted out" or "wore" the unacknowledged pain of the parents or family?

8. **Chaos/cathexis:** Family factions form. Some people gain power while others become marginalized; some act out, others placate. Bonds become dysfunctional, traumatic bonding and codependency develop, and there can be a preoccupation with a person or the family that borders on obsessive.
   - To what extent are you experiencing this stage now?

     0% ———————— **50%** ———————— **100%**

   - How has this stage affected you?
     - Do you feel that you grew up in a chaotic atmosphere?
     - Do you find it difficult to set and maintain your own boundaries or to respect the boundaries of others?
     - Do you tend to get fused or overly close with people, then become disengaged when that feels like too much?

9. **Intervention/mobilization:** Something in the environment intervenes on the family dysfunction directly or indirectly—for example, a child acting out, a DUI, getting fired, or a family member reaching out for help. There is a dawning of recognition of the dysfunction in the family and the need for help.

   - To what extent are you experiencing this stage now?

     0% ———————————— **50%** ———————————— **100%**

   - How has this stage affected you?
     - Have you come to realize that something needs to change and that you will need to mobilize and take actions, either to make your own personal changes or changes in your family system?
     - Do you feel blocked at taking steps to get your life working?
     - Do you feel like a chronic failure?

10. **Reorganization/recovery/decathexis:** Family members begin a process of decathexis and recovery from the dysfunction. They learn both intrapersonal and interpersonal strategies for dealing with it.

- To what extent are you experiencing this stage now?

  0% ———————— **50%** ———————— **100%**

- How has this stage affected you?
  - Do you have a sense of personal space and agency?
  - Are you taking steps to change how you deal with your family members and how you live your own life?
  - Are you better able to set your own boundaries and respect those of others?

11. **Acceptance/gratitude/posttraumatic growth:** Family members realize that they, too, are involved in the dysfunction and that they need to take individual responsibility for an extended process of recovery. The recovery process itself becomes a new design for living, and they come to appreciate their deepened and more meaningful experience of life.

    - To what extent are you experiencing this stage now?

      0% ———————— **50%** ———————— **100%**

    - How has this stage affected you?
        - Are you proud of the way you've been able to work through pain from the past so that you can avoid passing it on to others?
        - Do you experience gratitude for the inherent goodness of life and relationships?
        - Can you name and measure areas in which you have really grown on the inside and changed the way you live and relate on the outside?

Clinical Exercise

Grief Spectrogram

Both trauma and grief are on a continuum, and clients will vary considerably as to how they experience the same traumatic episode or relational dynamic. Consequently, the level of grief, sadness, anger, disruption, and so on will depend upon the individual. This spectrogram helps clients to identify and understand their experiences of grief. The use of a grief spectrogram is an adaptation developed by Ronny Halpren, MSW, bereavement coordinator for the Carbini Hospice in New York City.

Goals

- Help clients access their experiences and symptoms of grief.
- Allow for identification, support, and bonding among group members.
- Provide a safe context in which clients can open up and be vulnerable about their grief.

Steps

1. Designate an area in the workspace and explain to the participants that each end of this area represents an extreme—for example, one end represents 0 percent and the opposite end represents 100 percent. Next, draw an imaginary line bisecting the area, representing the midpoint (50 percent).
2. Ask a criterion question that explores the participants' experience of grief, and invite them to move to whatever point along the continuum best describes their response to the question. Grief is complicated and messy, so reassure them that they are free to change their minds and move around as the sharing progresses. Possible questions include:
    - "How much unresolved emotion do you feel surrounding this loss?"
    - "How much yearning do you feel?"
    - "How much sadness, depression, or regret do you feel?"
    - "How much anger or resentment do you feel?"
    - "How much self-recrimination, shame, or embarrassment do you feel?"
    - "How blocked are you from getting in touch with your genuine feelings involved in this issue?"
    - "How much has grief disrupted your daily routine?"

- "How much trouble are you having organizing yourself?"
- "How much is your sleep affected?"
- "How tired do you feel?"
- "How uninterested in your life do you feel?"
- "How much fear of the future do you feel?"
- "How much hope do you feel about your life and the future?"
- "How much do you feel your grief has contributed to your becoming a deeper person?"
- "How much old, unresolved grief is being activated and remembered as a result of this current issue?"
- "How vulnerable do feel when you're experiencing grief-related feelings?"

3. After each question, allow people to share, either with the full group or in dyads or clusters with the people nearest to them (those they are sociometrically aligned with). I sometimes let the group choose how they would like to share by simply asking, "Would you like to share in the large group or subgroups on this one?" Invite them to share a sentence or two about why they're standing where they're standing.
4. You can also ask, "Did anyone say something that particularly resonated with you?" or "Is there someone you feel you could learn something from?" and invite them to "Walk over to that person, place your hand on their shoulder, and share why you choose them."
5. After you have explored as many questions as you wished to or the group has reached its saturation point, you can invite them to return to their seats and continue to share. You can also move into a role play or experiential letter writing.

Variations

- **Telehealth:** You can simply ask the criterion questions and invite the group members to rate their degree of intensity by holding up one to five fingers (with one being the least intense and five being top intensity) or by holding their arm sideways across the screen in a lower or higher position. You can also create the spectrogram using an interactive whiteboard tool: Draw a line and label the two endpoints and the midpoint, then invite the group members to add a dot or other mark along the line to represent their answer.

Clinical Exercise

Disenfranchised Losses Floor Check

There are many losses in life that go unnamed and ungrieved. By this I am not saying that a full grief process is necessary for each and every loss, simply that it is important for the client to acknowledge their loss and feel all their feelings around it rather than trying to make it go away by pretending it isn't there. When losses that deserve time and attention go unseen and unmourned, they are referred to in the grief vernacular as *disenfranchised*. These losses live in unmarked graves within people and family systems who often avoid discussing them. The pain becomes covert rather than overt—that is, unexamined feelings surrounding the loss still affect the client, who may not be aware of the way in which they are impacting their life and relationships.

This floor check helps clients identify, honor, and begin to process their disenfranchised losses. They also get to receive the identification and support of their fellow group members. This process works well as a warm-up to the next exercise, the *Loss Map*; clients will begin to understand that feelings related to previous losses can resurface when a new loss occurs, and the *Loss Map* gives them a safe entry into these complicating losses.

Goals

- Help clients understand the types of losses that often go unrecognized and unmourned.
- Help clients identify and begin to mourn these types of losses in a supportive container.

Steps

1. On separate sheets of paper, write the following types of disenfranchised losses:
    - Loss of a connection to the self
    - The grief of the inner child who lives inside of the adult
    - Loss of safety in family relationships
    - Loss of an unencumbered childhood
    - Divorce or breakup
    - Loss of a trusted and dependable loved one (e.g., due to addiction or illness)
    - Parental estrangement, abandonment, or visitation changes
    - Socially stigmatized death (e.g., AIDS, suicide, murder, DUI, overdose)
    - Death of a pet

- Infertility, miscarriage, or abortion
- Disabling condition or other health issue
- Brain injury, dementia, or cognitive deficit
- Mental health issue
- Moving or loss of a home
- Job loss or retirement
- Other

2. Place the papers a couple of feet apart, scattered around the floor.
3. Ask criterion questions and invite the participants to stand on or near the type of loss that represents their response. Possible questions include:
    - "Which type of loss is pulling you now?"
    - "Which type of loss do you feel you most need to work on?"
    - "What is a kind of loss that you feel your family experienced (either family of origin or progenitive)?"
    - "Is there a type of loss that you feel you have come a long way in working through?"
    - "Which type of loss have you denied?"
    - "Which type of loss did your family deny?"
    - "Which type of loss do you keep hidden or have trouble talking about?"
    - "Which type of loss makes you feel like a victim?"
4. After each question, invite the group members to share a sentence or two about why they are standing where they are standing. You may have them share with the full group, with those standing on the same type of loss, or a combination of these.
5. Say, "Walk over to someone who shared something that you identified with or that moved you, stand next to them, and share with them what moved you" or "Walk over to someone from whom you feel you could learn something and ask them for help."
6. Invite the group to sit down and share about the experience as a whole. Or, if they are warmed up for further work, you can move into a role play, the following *Loss Map* exercise, or another process.

Variations

- **Telehealth:** Display the options to the group using a whiteboard tool, a shared document, or another method that works for you. As you ask the criterion questions, group members can call out their answer and say a sentence or two about why they chose it. Or, if the group is large enough, you can use the initial questions as a warm-up and then move into breakout rooms for continued sharing. You can also use the *Disenfranchised Losses* journaling page: You can call out one question at a time and invite the group members to share their responses. If they might benefit from further sharing, they can do so in breakout rooms or they can continue the process of working through one question at a time in breakout rooms.

- **One-to-One:** The client can use the *Disenfranchised Losses* journaling page, then you can unpack together in session.

Journaling Page

Disenfranchised Losses

Our society provides ways of dealing with the death of a loved one; there are rituals, like funerals and mourning clothes, that encourage others to recognize our loss, share in our sorrow, and give us their help and support. But there are many other kinds of losses that go unacknowledged by society, including a divorce or breakup, estrangement, loss of safety, and loss of self. These are known as *disenfranchised losses*. When you experience these kinds of losses, you may be given little to no support. Your pain may then become covert rather than overt—that is, your unexamined feelings surrounding the loss still affect you, but you may not be aware of the way in which they are impacting your life and relationships.

This journaling page will help you identify, honor, and begin to process your disenfranchised losses. Read through the examples of losses that often go unacknowledged by society, then reflect on the questions that follow.

Disenfranchised Losses

- Loss of a connection to the self
- The grief of the inner child who lives inside of the adult
- Loss of safety in family relationships
- Loss of an unencumbered childhood
- Divorce or breakup
- Loss of a trusted and dependable loved one (e.g., due to addiction or illness)
- Parental estrangement, abandonment, or visitation changes
- Socially stigmatized death (e.g., AIDS, suicide, murder, DUI, overdose)
- Death of a pet
- Infertility, miscarriage, or abortion
- Disabling condition or other health issue
- Brain injury, dementia, or cognitive deficit
- Mental health issue
- Moving or loss of a home
- Job loss or retirement
- Other: ______________________________

Questions

Which type of loss drew your attention as you read through the list? Why?

Which type of loss do you feel you most need to work on? Describe what you feel you need to do related to this loss.

Which types of losses has your family experienced (either your family of origin or your progenitive family)?

Is there a type of loss that you feel you have come a long way in working through? Describe the work you have done.

Which types of loss have you denied? Maybe you didn't think of it as a loss before now. Describe how this has affected you.

Which types of loss did your family deny? Describe what this was like for you.

Which types of loss do you keep hidden or have trouble talking about? Why?

Which types of loss make you feel like a victim? How do you mourn—or try not to mourn—this loss?

Clinical Exercise

Loss Map

This exercise works well as a follow-up to the previous activity, the *Disenfranchised Losses Floor Check*. Clients may have begun to identify the disenfranchised losses that they have experienced and to realize that their feelings around past losses can resurface when a new loss occurs, making their grief feel even more overwhelming and complicated. This activity helps them explore this relationship further by actually mapping their losses.

Goals

- Help clients understand how a current loss brings up past losses.
- Offer a safe entry into sharing about and grieving past losses that a current loss might be triggering.

Steps

1. Provide the participants with copies of the *Loss Map* journaling page (or blank pieces of paper) and writing utensils.
2. Invite them to fill in their loss map: "In the center of the circle, write down the loss that you are currently experiencing or feeling grief around. On the jutting lines, write down any other losses that this current loss warms up in you or brings to mind."
3. Invite them to share their loss maps, either in the full group or in breakout groups.
4. Afterward, you might move into role plays or experiential letter writing; participants may wish to talk to another person, a part of the self, a moment or period in their life, or something else (like a sense of safety or willingness to trust others) that they have lost.

Variations

- **Telehealth:** Give the group members time to complete their loss maps on their own paper or digitally. Then invite them to share, either in the full group or in breakout groups.
- **One-to-One:** The client can use the *Loss Map* journaling page, then you can unpack together in session.

Journaling Page

Loss Map

When you haven't been able to fully grieve the losses that occurred in your past, that grief can become triggered when another loss occurs in the present. All your feelings related to those past losses bleed into your feelings around the present loss, making your grief—which is already an intense experience—feel even more complicated and overwhelming. This activity will help you map how past losses might be affecting your life and relationships today, so that you can begin to process and move through your grief.

Use the template to create your loss map. In the center of the circle, write down the loss that you are currently experiencing or feeling grief around. On the jutting lines, write down any other losses that this current loss warms up in you or brings to mind. Then answer the questions that follow.

Diagram: Loss Map

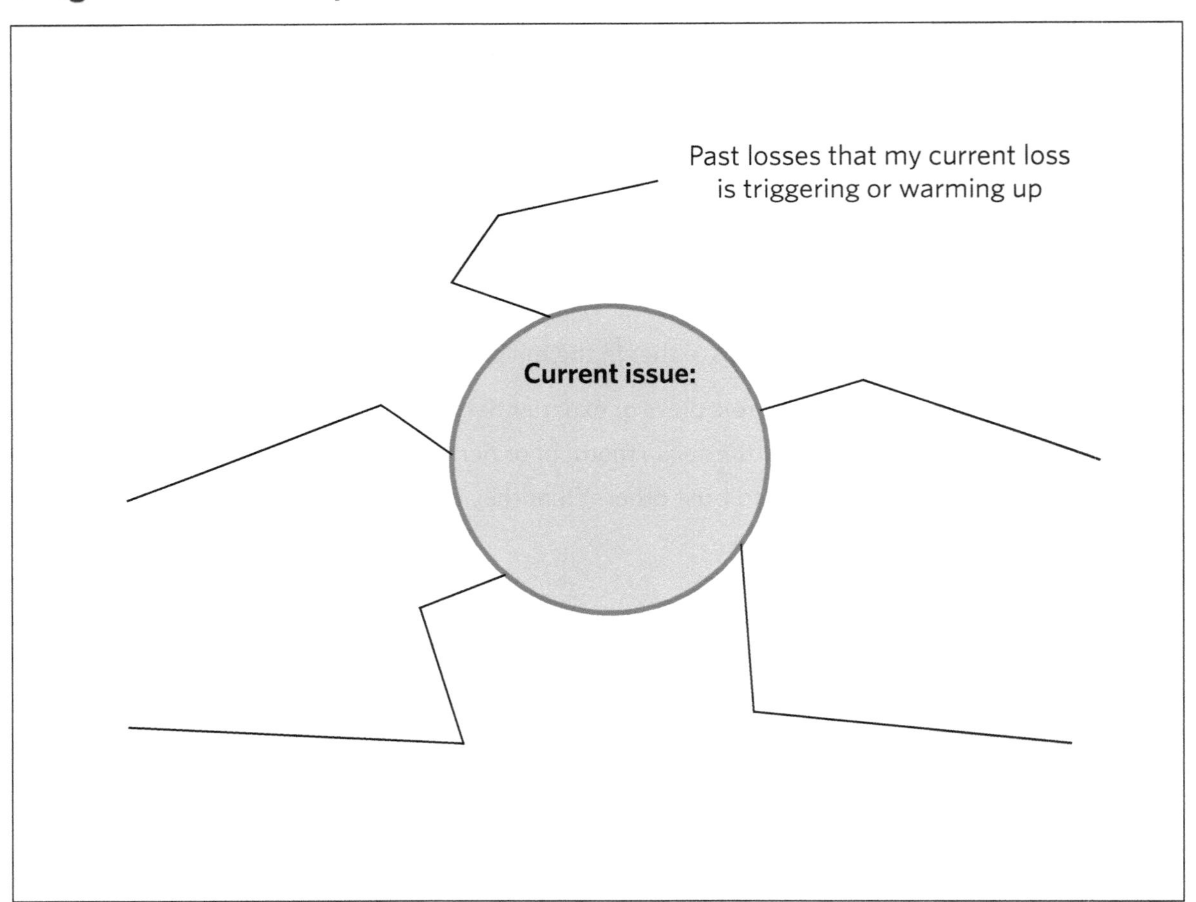

Questions

What did you notice as you created your loss map? Describe any connections, insights, feelings, or questions that this process brought up for you.

How is the loss that you are currently experiencing or grieving similar to your past losses? How is it different from those earlier losses?

What do you feel you need in order to better understand or move forward through your grief? What are some steps you can take now to get the support you need?

CHAPTER 11

Forgiveness: Giving Oneself the Gifts of Humility and Choice

Sometimes clients feel that if they forgive, they are leaving themselves vulnerable to being hurt all over again. Or they see forgiveness as giving up the hope of ever righting the wrong or getting retribution—they fear letting go of the wish of finally getting what they always wanted. They may worry that forgiving means that they condone someone else's bad actions, that they wish to continue having a relationship with the person who hurt them, or that they are relinquishing their right to continued feelings about an issue.

In fact, forgiveness should empower the client and give them choices. It allows them to call something by its right name. Rather than denying the impact of someone's behavior, for example, the client is looking at it for what it was and deciding how they want to deal with it, either in their relationship with that person or, more importantly, as it still lives inside of them. Forgiveness is a recognition within the self of a wish or a need to place a particular issue into a different internal context. It motivates the client to do the kind of work that allows them to move forward and reclaim their own life. They can work through the resentments from the past that have been preoccupying them and getting in the way of comfortable relating.

Self-Forgiveness

Clients sometimes struggle the hardest with self-forgiveness. Feelings of shame and self-loathing can make them want to retreat into emotional isolation, to hide the parts of themselves that they're ashamed of. But when a client can't forgive themselves, they burden those they love twice: once because they did something hurtful to them and again because they're so absorbed with own self-recrimination that they don't allow for a better relationship to develop with the person they have hurt. It's important for the client to realize that no one is benefiting from their holding an inner grudge. Instead, they're keeping themselves, and often others who care about them, glued to pain from the past.

It takes humility to admit that we have been wrong or cruel. And it takes humility to forgive ourselves.

Secular and Spiritual Approaches to Forgiveness

Dr. Ken Hart (1999) identifies two different approaches to forgiveness that have been used in Alcoholics Anonymous programs: secular and spiritual.

The secular approach aims to speed up the growth of empathy and compassion so that people in recovery can better understand the imperfections and flaws of those who have hurt them. In psychodrama, we do this through role reversal, giving clients the opportunity to stand in the shoes of another person. Usually, they come to realize that they were never the real problem, just the tragic target of someone else's unfelt, unprocessed pain. Then they can see that the sense of "badness" they carry around—the thought of "something must be wrong with me or I wouldn't be treated this way"—is not and probably was never true. This awareness can be a great burden lifted; it allows the client to see their hurt differently and to take it less personally. It can also develop some empathic awareness, both for themselves and for the person who hurt them.

In the spiritual approach to forgiveness, people in recovery who have harmed others are encouraged to apologize for their wrongdoing, thereby making an attempt at restitution. Hart (1999) feels that because asking forgiveness for something we have shame and regret around requires humility, having faith in a higher power or some higher purpose helps. It allows us to transcend the ego that might normally resist admitting mistakes and owning wrongdoing. In recovering from addiction, Hart observes that both approaches to forgiveness can help clients move through the kind of self-recrimination that might lead to relapse or keep them from fully embracing recovery.

These two approaches to forgiveness—gaining empathy when we're the hurt party and making amends when we're the offending party—are useful cornerstones in a practical approach to forgiveness. I believe the real purpose of forgiveness is to free the self, to free our inner being from conflict and pain. After all, when we can't forgive, we're essentially carrying someone else's pain for them. It doesn't hurt them; it hurts us. When clients realize this, they can begin to forgive and move forward.

Clinical Exercise

Forgiveness Myths Floor Check

When I began working with forgiveness using embodied and experiential forms of therapy, all sorts of conflicting feelings surfaced for clients. They felt angry, as if they were condoning someone else's bad actions. They worried that forgiveness meant they had to maintain a relationship with that person. They *wanted* to forgive but they felt *blocked.* And then I realized that working with blocks was indeed the path forward in healing. I began to pick out and name the most common blocks, which I call "myths." Once clients realize that these myths are not true, they are motivated to accept and move through their conflicting emotions rather than hold on to them.

Goals

- Provide an action format for working with forgiveness.
- Provide a way of bringing forgiveness into an embodied process.

Steps

1. On separate sheets of paper, write the following forgiveness myths:
    - If I forgive this person, my relationship with them will definitely improve.
    - If I forgive, I'll no longer feel angry at that person for what happened.
    - If I forgive, I forgo my right to have hurt feelings.
    - If I forgive this person, it means I want to continue to have a relationship with them.
    - If I forgive this person, I'm condoning their behavior and letting them off the hook.
    - If I haven't forgotten, I haven't really forgiven.
    - I only need to forgive once.
    - I forgive for the sake of the other person.
    - Other
2. Place the papers a couple of feet apart, scattered around the floor.
3. Ask the participants to stand on or near the myth that they most identify with, then invite them to share a sentence or two about why they are standing where they are standing. You may have them share with the full group, with those standing on the same myth, or a combination of these.

4. Repeat this process with additional criterion questions—for example:
   - "Which myth do you feel stuck in, or which myth is blocking you in your recovery?"
   - "Which myth did you learn from your family or do you carry from childhood?"
   - "Which myth makes you feel bad for some reason?"
   - "Which myth did you buy into previously, but you've since busted it?"
   - "Which myth are you making progress in working through?"
5. Say, "Walk over to someone who shared something that you identified with or that moved you, stand next to them, and share with them what moved you" or "Walk over to someone from whom you feel you could learn something and ask them for help."
6. When the group is saturated, invite them to sit down and share about the experience as a whole. Or, if they are warmed up for further work, you can move into role plays or experiential letter writing using one of the final three exercises in this chapter: *Forgiving Another Person* (page 207), *Asking for Another Person's Forgiveness* (page 208), or *Granting Forgiveness to the Self* (page 209).

Variations

- **Telehealth:** Display the options to the group using a whiteboard tool, a shared document, or another method that works for you. As you ask the criterion questions, group members can call out their answer and say a sentence or two about why they chose it. Or, if the group is large enough, you can use the initial questions as a warm-up and then move into breakout rooms for continued sharing. You can also use the *Forgiveness Myths* journaling page: You can call out one question at a time and invite the group members to share their responses. If they might benefit from further sharing, they can do so in breakout rooms or they can continue the process of working through one question at a time in breakout rooms.
- **One-to-One:** The client can use the *Forgiveness Myths* journaling page, then you can unpack together in session.

Journaling Page

Forgiveness Myths

There are many myths around forgiveness that we absorb from our parents, families, and society in general. These myths might discourage you from forgiving yourself or others, when in reality, contemplating forgiveness can motivate you to work through the feelings that block it. Truly, the purpose of forgiveness is to free yourself so that you can let go of the pain that preoccupies you when you are filled with anger and resentment. Read through this list of common forgiveness myths, then reflect on the questions that follow.

Forgiveness Myths

- If I forgive this person, my relationship with them will definitely improve.
- If I forgive, I'll no longer feel angry at that person for what happened.
- If I forgive, I forgo my right to have hurt feelings.
- If I forgive this person, it means I want to continue to have a relationship with them.
- If I forgive this person, I'm condoning their behavior and letting them off the hook.
- If I haven't forgotten, I haven't really forgiven.
- I only need to forgive once.
- I forgive for the sake of the other person.
- Other: ______________________________

Questions

Which myth do you feel stuck in, or which myth is blocking you in your recovery? Describe why this myth is so powerful or difficult to counter.

____

____

____

____

____

Which myths did you learn from your family or do you carry from childhood? How have these myths affected your life?

Which myth makes you feel bad for some reason? Why do you think this is the case?

Are there any myths that you previously bought into, but were later able to bust? What helped you do so?

Which myth are you making progress in working through? What next steps do you plan to take to move through the issues surrounding this myth?

Clinical Exercise

Forgiveness Spectrogram

This exercise is meant to flush out some of the complicated and complex emotions that come up around the notion of forgiving someone who has hurt the client or forgiving themselves for hurting someone else. It offers a way to bring some awareness and regulation around each feeling, to really look at how much or how little they're experiencing it. And it gives space to put some language around these emotions so they can be reflected on and communicated.

Goals

- Bring regulation to difficult feelings.
- Provide an experiential format for dealing with forgiveness issues.

Steps

1. Invite the group members to think of a forgiveness issue that has come up—this might be in relation to forgiving themselves, forgiving someone else, or hoping for another person's forgiveness.
2. Designate an area in the workspace and explain to the participants that each end of this area represents an extreme—for example, one end represents 0 percent and the opposite end represents 100 percent. Next, draw an imaginary line bisecting the area, representing the midpoint (50 percent).
3. Ask a criterion question that explores the participants' forgiveness issues, and invite them to move to whatever point along the continuum best describes their response to the question. Possible questions include:
    - "How blocked are you from getting in touch with your genuine feelings involved in this issue?"
    - "How much do you feel this issue is affecting your inner peace today?"
    - "How much fear are you feeling at the thought of honestly addressing your feelings around this issue?"
    - "How much anger or resentment are you feeling associated with this issue?"
    - "How much hurt or sadness are you feeling associated with this issue?"
    - "How much self-recrimination, guilt, or shame do you feel around this issue?"

- "How much hope do you have that you can work through your feelings surrounding this issue?"
- "How vulnerable do feel at the thought of forgiving someone?"
- "How vulnerable do feel at the thought of forgiving yourself?"
- "How undeserving of others' forgiveness do you feel?"
- "How much of your energy do you feel is being absorbed by this issue?"
- "How much do you feel this issue impacts your relationships today?"
- "How much do you feel this issue has impacted your ability to move into future relationships comfortably?"

4. After each question, allow people to share, either with the full group or in dyads or clusters with the people nearest to them (those they are sociometrically aligned with). Invite them to share a sentence or two about why they're standing where they're standing.
5. You can also ask, "Did anyone say something that particularly resonated with you? Or is there someone you feel you could learn something from? If so, walk over to that person, place your hand on their shoulder, and share why you choose them."
6. After you have explored as many questions as you wished to or the group has reached its saturation point, you can invite them to return to their seats and continue to share. You can also move into a role play or experiential letter writing using one of the next three exercises (*Forgiving Another Person*, *Asking for Another Person's Forgiveness*, or *Granting Forgiveness to the Self*).

Variations

- **Telehealth:** You can simply ask the criterion questions and invite the group members to rate their degree of intensity by holding up one to five fingers (with one being the least intense and five being top intensity) or by holding their arm sideways across the screen in a lower or higher position. You can also create the spectrogram using an interactive whiteboard tool: Draw a line and label the two endpoints and the midpoint, then invite the group members to add a dot or other mark along the line to represent their answer.

Clinical Exercise

Forgiving Another Person

These next three embodied processes—*Forgiving Another Person*, *Asking for Another Person's Forgiveness*, and *Granting Forgiveness to the Self*—are where the gold is in terms of relational forgiveness. Having prepared the group through the warming-up and identifying process of the previous exercises, these role plays are where some deep, embodied change and understanding can take place. They can also be done through experiential letter writing. Prepare yourself for grief and anger to pour forward as clients bare their hearts to those they have hurt or who have hurt them. Forgiveness gives them a way of working through this pain.

Goals

- Concretize the relationship that involves forgiveness issues.
- Help clients work through issues that may be blocking forgiveness.

Steps

1. Ask the group members to think of and share about someone they are having trouble forgiving or would like to forgive.
2. Invite whoever feels warmed up to choose another group member to play that person, or they can use an empty chair.
3. Ask the protagonist, "What would you like to say to this person?" Allow the scene to unfold and work with it using any techniques that might be appropriate, including role reversal.
4. When the scene seems to be coming toward resolution, bring it to closure by saying, "Say the last things you need to say for now."
5. Have the role players return to their seats for deroling and sharing. Or you can do several role plays, one right after the other, and move into sharing after this.

Variations

- **Telehealth:** You can do this role play over telehealth, or you can use the same prompt for experiential letter writing.
- **One-to-One:** The client can use the empty chair technique.

Clinical Exercise

Asking for Another Person's Forgiveness

It takes humility for a client to own something they feel shame or regret around and ask for forgiveness for their behavior. But it is relieving and an important part of "keeping their side of the street clean." Once the client gets good at this, it becomes easier for them to own their wrongdoing. It also motivates them to choose better actions that they won't later regret and have to ask forgiveness for—it's self-regulating.

Goals

- Get square with the self so that clients can stop carrying unspoken shame and guilt.
- Concretize a forgiveness issue and work through the blocks within the self that may be keeping a client from making amends.

Steps

1. Ask the group members to think of and share about someone they feel a need to make amends to.
2. Invite whoever feels warmed up to choose another group member to play that person, or they can use an empty chair.
3. Ask the protagonist, "What would you like to say to this person?" Let the scene progress and allow the protagonist to really sink into all the emotions that come up around asking for someone's forgiveness. You can use role reversal, doubling, and whatever other techniques feel appropriate.
4. When the scene seems to be coming toward resolution, bring it to closure by saying, "Say the last things you need to say for now."
5. Have the role players return to their seats for deroling and sharing. Or you can do several role plays, one right after the other, and move into sharing after this.

Variations

- **Telehealth:** You can do this role play over telehealth, or you can use the same prompt for experiential letter writing.
- **One-to-One:** The client can use the empty chair technique.

Clinical Exercise

Granting Forgiveness to the Self

People sometimes have a harder time forgiving themselves than forgiving others. Feelings of shame, unworthiness, and guilt can make them feel that forgiving themselves is somehow not okay. If they can't forgive themselves, their self-recrimination can turn into anger toward someone they've hurt; in this case, forgiving themselves is better for that person too. When the client can forgive themselves, in a humble way, and they're not using self-forgiveness as a way to cancel someone's pain, then forgiving themselves is healthy and helpful for both themselves and others.

Goals

- Give the client a concrete way of experiencing self-forgiveness.
- Free the self.

Steps

1. Ask the protagonist to choose someone to play the self they want to forgive.
2. Invite the protagonist to begin the scene by telling that part of themselves why they want to forgive them, or why they are having trouble forgiving them, or to say anything they wish to say to that part of themselves.
3. Let the scene progress, and use role reversal, doubling, and whatever other techniques feel appropriate. This part of the role play can go back and forth. Role reversal interview can also be used by asking questions of the protagonist in role reversal:
    - "Do you think they deserve forgiveness?"
    - "Tell us a little about the part of yourself that seems unforgivable."
    - "Are you in any way afraid to forgive that part of yourself?"
    - "Why do you think that part of you wants forgiveness so much?"
4. When the scene seems to be coming to natural closure, ask the protagonist to end it. Say, "Say the last things you'd like to say for now to this part of yourself."
5. Have the role players return to their seats for deroling and sharing. Or you can do several role plays, one right after the other, and move into sharing after this.

Variations

- **Telehealth:** You can do this role play over telehealth, or you can use the same prompt for experiential letter writing.
- **One-to-One:** The client can use the empty chair technique.

CHAPTER 12

Learning Unhelplessness: Fostering Resilience

In working through the pain of a traumatic past, it is important for clients to identify not only what hurt them but also what sustained them. While it is indeed critical for a client to go back and rework significant issues that are blocking their ability to be present and productive in the here and now, focusing exclusively on the negative qualities in themselves and others can sometimes have the adverse effect of weakening the self and the client's relationships rather than strengthening them. Identifying and appreciating the qualities that they developed while meeting challenging circumstances, as well as the people who saw and helped them when they needed it, is an important practice.

Understanding what makes up resilience helps to counter what researchers refer to as the "damage" model: the idea that if someone had a troubled childhood, they are condemned to a troubled adulthood or are operating without strengths (Wolin & Wolin, 1993). In fact, adversity can help a person develop strengths if they learn to mobilize and make use of the supports that are at their disposal. Wong and Wong (2012) propose that certain qualities of behavioral resilience can only be developed from actual experience of having to overcome adversities.

Resilience seems to develop out of the challenge to maintain self-esteem. It is a dynamic and interactive process that builds on itself; it is not just a state of self, but a state of self-in-relationship. The ability to access and make positive use of family, friends, mentors, and community support is a significant part of what allows one child to do well where another might experience a tougher time. As Rutter (1993) argues, "Resilience may reside in the social context as much as within the individual" (p. 626). It is not that some children are "invulnerable" to adversity or trauma, as was proposed in the early days of resilience research; there is an interplay of individual differences and adaptive processes, as well as context factors (Wong & Wong, 2012).

Key to being a resilient person is realizing that many resilient characteristics are under one's own control, especially once the client reaches adulthood; they can consciously and proactively develop these qualities. And the more they do so, the more insulated they are against the effects of trauma. Resilient children tend to show these qualities as adults (Wolin & Wolin, 1995):

- They can identify the dysfunction in their family and are able to find ways to distance themselves from it; they don't let the family dysfunction destroy them.
- They work through their problems.
- They take active responsibility for creating their own successful lives.
- They tend to have constructive attitudes toward themselves and their lives.
- They tend not to fall into self-destructive lifestyles.

All of these qualities interweave to help lay a protective enough base so that a person can access, use, and continue to develop their strengths in meeting life's challenges.

For an adult, building resilience also includes processing what might be in the way of it—the old complexes that are still undermining their happiness (Crawford et al., 2006; Ungar et al., 2007). Actively taking responsibility for the effects that a painful past may have had on them, and taking the necessary steps to work through their conflicts and complexes, is part of creating resilience in adulthood. It is entirely possible for a person to go through painful life experiences and process as they go. By doing so, they actually build strength from facing and managing their own reactions to tough situations. They learn from their setbacks and mistakes and sharpen their skills for living successfully. Reviewing the growth they've had through encountering and facing challenges can help our clients to build resilience and consolidate their strengths.

How Optimism May Build Resilience

In his presidential address to the American Psychological Association in 1998, Dr. Martin Seligman, one of the world's leading scholars on learned helplessness and depression, urged psychology to "turn toward understanding and building the human strengths to complement our emphasis on healing damage." That speech rekindled an interest in the positive psychology movement, which had been founded in 1968 by Abraham Maslow, and sparked continued research into qualities that maintain resilience and positivity—how things go right rather than how they go wrong.

Optimists, as Seligman (1990/2006) explains, see life through a positive lens. They see bad events as temporary setbacks that can be overcome by their effort and abilities. Pessimists, on the other hand, tend to react to setbacks from a presumption of personal helplessness. They feel that bad events are their fault, will last a long time, and will undermine everything they do. Through his research, Seligman found that the state of helplessness was a learned phenomenon. He also realized that "unhelplessness"—and optimism—could be learned as well.

He offers a process through which someone can change their mindset from pessimism to optimism. First, they learn to notice (and even write down) the beliefs they have that block them from feeling good about themselves or their life—to pay attention to the negative "recordings" they are playing in their head. Then they write down the consequences of those beliefs—the toll those thoughts are taking on their emotions, energy, will to act, and so forth. Once the person becomes familiar with their pessimistic thought patterns, they can challenge them. They can recognize that a specific negative belief is not useful and generate alternative ideas and solutions that might be better.

In this way, they can choose to see problems as temporary, the way an optimist would, and that in itself provides psychological boundaries. This new type of thinking can interrupt the "loop" of negative tapes that were running through their head. Over time, this more optimistic thinking becomes engrained as their default position, and as they choose optimism over pessimism through repeated experiences, they are rewarded with new energy and vitality.

Mobilize and Build Resilience Through Sociometrics

It's my experience that most people who make it as far as embracing recovery have already developed many qualities of resilience. Even so, it is important to help them identify these strengths and develop more. Facing and healing trauma is no easy task; they can benefit from all the resources they can muster.

With sociometrics, skills-building and resilience-building are baked into the very process. Sociometric exercises:

- Feel welcoming and safe so that clients don't shut down immediately but can build trust in feeling feelings that might ordinarily overwhelm them.
- Teach skills of experiencing and tolerating intense emotion, translating triggered feelings into words, and talking about them rather than acting them out through projecting pain and blame.
- Get clients on their feet, grounded in the room, and exercising their initiative through choosing which feelings or symptoms they identify with.
- Teach about the psychological dynamics involved in PTSD, grief, resilience, and posttraumatic growth in a way that allows clients to take ownership of their own learning and healing.
- Give the body a stage on which to move and allow the body—including hurting, tight, anxious, or sensual parts—to feel and speak.
- Provide an embodied relational process through which the nervous system can feel calm, engaged, and grounded.

The sociometric exercises in this chapter are infused with ways to build qualities of resilience. They will help your clients identify and appreciate their strengths and supports, challenge and change their negative thinking, and lead a purposeful, meaningful life.

Clinical Exercise

Optimism Locogram

This resilience-building locogram, which is based on Martin Seligman's research, helps clients learn what optimism looks and feel like. Clients may want to "be" more optimistic, but they may not realize that optimism is something they can actually *do*—it's not a gift that they either were given or lack, but a skill that they can learn, practice, and strengthen. This activity makes optimism easy to learn by breaking it down into specific beliefs. It also encourages the group members to share and to offer each other motivation and support.

Goals

- Train clients in "unhelplessness."
- Give clients a direct experience of their own strengths or strengths they'd like to develop.
- Challenge clients to consciously develop optimistic attitudes.

Steps

1. Designate four areas on the floor to represent various aspects of optimism, such as:
   - Seeing life through a positive lens
   - Seeing setbacks as temporary
   - Feeling that I can overcome challenges
   - Other
2. Ask a criterion question and invite the group members to move to the area that best represents their response. If they feel ambivalent or between responses, they may want to stand between those areas. Possible questions include:
   - "Which quality do you feel you don't have enough of?"
   - "Which quality do you feel good about having or being in the process of developing?"
   - "Which quality do you envy in others?"
   - "Which quality do you wish you had but feel you don't?"
   - "Which quality do you feel shame about not having?"
   - "Which quality are you determined to develop?"

3. Invite them to share a sentence or two about why they are standing where they are standing. Group members may spontaneously double for each other if this seems useful to the process.
4. If you feel that the group wants to make another choice, you might say something like, "Has anything changed for you since you shared just now? If so, change places and share from where you are right now."
5. Continue asking criterion questions until the group is saturated; generally, for a locogram, two or three at the most is sufficient. You may then ask them to return to their seats for sharing or move into other processes.

Variations

- **Telehealth:** Display the options to the group using a whiteboard tool, a shared document, or another method that works for you. As you ask the criterion questions, group members can call out their answer and say a sentence or two about why they chose it. You can also create the locogram using an interactive whiteboard tool: Draw a large square, divide it into four sections, label the sections, then invite the group members to add a dot or other mark on the diagram to represent their answer and then share about why they are located at that point.

Clinical Exercise

Resilience Floor Check

It's so important that clients not only get in touch with their pain and anger, but also identify their special gifts and let them be seen by others. This floor check offers a way to claim and consolidate some of those personal strengths. Let this be lively and fun—let the group members brag a bit and bond over their strengths as well as their problems. Encourage them to share about how they mobilized or discovered their inner and relational qualities of resilience in getting their lives to work.

Goals

- Educate clients on the qualities and characteristics of resilience.
- Provide a format through which clients can choose for themselves which qualities they feel they experience in their own lives and relationships.
- Create opportunities to lay claim to personal strengths and consolidate the gains of growth and recovery.
- Encourage connection, engagement, and bonding.

Steps

1. On separate sheets of paper, write these characteristics of a resilient self, which are based on the Connor-Davidson resilience scale (Connor & Davidson, 2003):
    - I am able to adapt to change.
    - I can have close and secure relationships.
    - I believe sometimes fate, God, or another higher power can help.
    - I can deal with whatever comes.
    - Past successes give me confidence for new challenges.
    - I see the humorous side of things.
    - Coping with stress strengthens me.
    - I tend to bounce back after illness or hardship.
    - I believe things happen for a reason.
    - I make my best effort no matter what.
    - I can achieve my goals.

- When things look hopeless, I don't give up.
- I know where to turn for help.
- Under pressure, I can focus and think clearly.
- I prefer to take the lead in problem-solving.
- I am not easily discouraged by failure.
- I think of myself as strong person.
- I can make unpopular or difficult decisions.
- I can handle unpleasant feelings.
- I can act on a hunch/intuition.
- I have a strong sense of purpose.
- I am in control of my life.
- I like challenges.
- I work to attain my goals.
- I have pride in my achievements.
- Other

2. Place the papers a couple of feet apart, scattered around the floor.
3. Ask the participants to stand on or near a characteristic that describes them—a way that their resilience manifests in their life.
4. Invite them to share a sentence or two about why they are standing where they are standing. You may have them share with the full group, with those standing on the same characteristic, or a combination of these.
5. Repeat this process with additional criterion questions—for example:
    - "Which quality do you have that you feel really proud of?"
    - "Which quality do you feel you gained in 'the school of hard knocks' or through struggling?"
    - "Which quality do you lean on the most when you feel down to get you through?"
    - "Which quality do you feel is most present in your family?"
    - "Which quality do you feel might get you far in your life?"
    - "Which quality do you feel you do not possess?"
    - "Which quality do you want to develop more of?"

6. Say, "Walk over to someone who shared something that you identified with or that moved you, stand next to them, and share with them what moved you," or "Walk over to someone from whom you feel you could learn something and ask them for help."
7. When the group is saturated, invite them to sit down and share about the experience as a whole. Or, if they are warmed up for further work, you can move into role plays.

Variations

- **Resilience Walk and Talk:** Invite a protagonist to walk among the qualities and do a soliloquy. For example: "I'm starting at 'I see the humorous side of things' because I really lean into humor when I get sad or scared, and that has gotten me through some tough situations. But when something really terrible happens, it feels overwhelming and I can't think of jokes anymore. Then I feel like I'm not fun to be around, so I stop reaching out to the people I care about. I'm going now to 'I know where to turn for help' because that's what I want to work on . . ."
- **Telehealth:** Display the options to the group using a whiteboard tool, a shared document, or another method that works for you. As you ask the criterion questions, group members can call out their answer and say a sentence or two about why they chose it. Or, if the group is large enough, you can use the initial questions as a warm-up and then move into breakout rooms for continued sharing. You can also use the *Qualities of Resilience* journaling page: You can call out one question at a time and invite the group members to share their responses. If they might benefit from further sharing, they can do so in breakout rooms or they can continue the process of working through one question at a time in breakout rooms.
- **One-to-One:** The client can use the *Qualities of Resilience* journaling page, then you can unpack together in session.

Journaling Page

Qualities of Resilience

Resilience describes the kinds of qualities that allow a person to meet challenges in life and bounce back from setbacks. Research shows that resilience is an interplay between facing life's challenges head-on; mobilizing environmental relationships and supports in positive, life-enhancing ways; and adopting the kinds of attitudes that optimists tend to possess.

A great way to start building resilience is to take some time to recognize the characteristics of resilience that you already embody or practice, as well as those you wish to build. You may find that you're more resilient than you thought! Read through the list of qualities from the Connor-Davidson resilience scale (Connor & Davidson, 2003), then answer the questions that follow.

Resilience Qualities

- I am able to adapt to change.
- I can have close and secure relationships.
- I believe sometimes fate, God, or another higher power can help.
- I can deal with whatever comes.
- Past successes give me confidence for new challenges.
- I see the humorous side of things.
- Coping with stress strengthens me.
- I tend to bounce back after illness or hardship.
- I believe things happen for a reason.
- I make my best effort no matter what.
- I can achieve my goals.
- When things look hopeless, I don't give up.
- I know where to turn for help.
- Under pressure, I can focus and think clearly.
- I prefer to take the lead in problem-solving.
- I am not easily discouraged by failure.
- I think of myself as strong person.
- I can make unpopular or difficult decisions.
- I can handle unpleasant feelings.
- I can act on a hunch/intuition.
- I have a strong sense of purpose.
- I am in control of my life.
- I like challenges.
- I work to attain my goals.
- I have pride in my achievements.
- Other: ______________________________

Questions

Which quality do you have that you feel really proud of? Describe how you use this quality.

Which quality do you feel you gained in "the school of hard knocks" or through struggling? Explain.

Which quality do you lean on the most when you feel down? How does this help you get through?

Which quality do you feel is most present in your family? Describe what you have experienced or learned as a result.

Which quality do you feel might get you far in your life? What might it help you accomplish?

Is there a quality that you feel you do not possess, but you'd like to develop more of? What could you do to start developing this quality?

Clinical Exercise

Buffering Supports Spectrogram

Through this process, clients get in touch with experiences in their childhood that acted as "buffers" that helped them feel cared about or seen so that they could better manage challenging experiences. Some clients may not have had many protective factors or buffering supports. As with all spectrograms, there is a "how much/how little" format; hopefully, each client will be able to identify at least some of these resilience-building experiences to get in touch with and claim as their own. The criterion statements in this spectrogram are based on the resilience questionnaire developed by Mark Rains and Kate McClinn (2006/2013).

Goals

- Help clients identify sources of support from their childhood and in the present.
- Provide an experiential format through which clients can choose for themselves which qualities they feel they experience in their own lives and relationships.
- Create opportunities to lay claim to personal strengths and consolidate the gains of growth and recovery.
- Encourage connection, engagement, and bonding.

Steps

1. Designate an area in the workspace and explain to the participants that each end of this area represents an extreme—for example, one end represents 0 percent and the opposite end represents 100 percent. Next, draw an imaginary line bisecting the area, representing the midpoint (50 percent).
2. Read any of Rains and McClinn's (2006/2013) statements that you wish you explore with the group, and invite the participants to move to whatever point along the continuum of "how much" to "how little" best describes their response to the question. Possible statements include:
    - I felt loved by my parents.
    - I felt loved by other people who helped take care of me, like grandparents or older siblings.
    - Other adults—like teachers, coaches, youth leaders, or ministers—were there to help me.
    - If I felt bad, I felt I had someone to go to who'd help me feel better.
    - My family was supported by extended family, friends, or community members.

- I felt liked by neighbors, friends, or community members.
- People noticed that I was capable and could get things done.
- I was independent and a go-getter.
- I believed that life is what you make it.

3. After each question, allow people to share, either with the full group or in dyads or clusters with the people nearest to them (those they are sociometrically aligned with). Invite them to share a sentence or two about why they're standing where they're standing.
4. You can also ask, "Did anyone say something that particularly resonated with you? Or is there someone you feel you could learn something from? If so, walk over to that person, place your hand on their shoulder, and share why you choose them."
5. After you have explored as many statements as you wished to or the group has reached its saturation point, you can invite them to return to their seats and continue to share. You can also move into a role play.

Variations

- **Buffering Supports Floor Check:** This exercise can also be done as a floor check. Write the buffering statements on separate pieces of paper and scatter them around the floor. Then ask criterion questions like "Which statement are you drawn to right now?" "Which statement does not apply to you?" "Which statement did you long to have more of?" or "Which statement developed strength and hopefulness in you that you still draw from today?" With each question, invite the group members to stand on or near the statement they choose, then invite them to share a sentence or two about why they are standing where they are standing.
- **Telehealth:** You can simply ask the criterion questions and invite the group members to rate their degree of intensity by holding up one to five fingers (with one being the least intense and five being top intensity) or by holding their arm sideways across the screen in a lower or higher position. You can also create the spectrogram using an interactive whiteboard tool: Draw a line and label the two endpoints and the midpoint, then invite the group members to add a dot or other mark along the line to represent their answer.

Clinical Exercise

Resilience Timeline

This exercise helps clients claim their strengths and consolidate gains through recovery or what they have learned through facing the challenges of life. As clients create and share their resilience timelines, they gain a sense of how much they have learned and grown through being willing to show up for life, make good choices, and stick with them. There is a sense of survivor's pride (Wolin & Wolin, 1995) that you can hear in their voices. They feel proud of themselves and have a sense of themselves not only as survivors but as thrivers—as people who have chosen to live their best life, one day at a time.

Goals

- Give clients a way to embody and consolidate their strengths and gifts.
- Help clients identify personal qualities that they were able to call on to get through challenging times.
- Help clients identify relationships that were key or helpful in allowing them to move forward in positive ways.

Steps

1. Provide clients with copies of the *Resilience Timeline* journaling page (or blank pieces of paper) and writing utensils.
2. Explain how to create the resilience timeline: "Mark those times in your life when you rose to a challenge, made a good choice that led to more good choices, reached out for or received help or support, felt great about something you did, or showed your good qualities. Consider times when you drew on the kinds of qualities inside you that not only helped you get through but built strength, decency, perseverance, and grit. Identify relationships or relational moments along the way when you felt loved, seen, and supported and you were helped to move forward in positive ways. Write down all these moments or periods of time on your timeline."
3. Invite the group members to share their timelines. Sharing can be done in dyads or clusters or as a full group. Sharing on this subject can be deep and emotional; encourage your clients to really feel and claim their personal strengths.
4. If the participants are warmed up for further work, you can move into focused role plays or experiential letter writing, inviting the protagonist to talk to the self at any age or moment in time.

Variations

- **Telehealth:** The group members can complete their timelines on their own paper or digitally. They can then share them in the full group or share in breakout rooms before returning to the full group for further processing.
- **One-to-One:** The client can complete their timeline, then you can unpack together in session. Or use the timeline as a warm-up to an empty chair role play.

Journaling Page

Resilience Timeline*

Next to the appropriate, approximate ages, jot down moments or periods in your life when you built resilience. These might be times when you rose to a challenge, made a good choice that led to more good choices, reached out for or received help or support, or felt great about something you did. Consider times when you drew on the kinds of qualities inside you that not only helped you get through but built strength, decency, perseverance, and grit. Also identify relationships or relational moments along the way when you felt loved, seen, and supported and you were helped to move forward in positive ways.

______	80	______
______	75	______
______	70	______
______	65	______
______	60	______
______	55	______
______	50	______
______	45	______
______	40	______
______	35	______
______	30	______
______	25	______
______	20	______
______	15	______
______	10	______
______	5	______
______	0	______

* Reprinted from *Relational Trauma Repair Therapist's Guide* (revised edition), © 2014 Tian Dayton.

Clinical Exercise

Experiential Resilience Timeline

It is a simple process to move the resilience timeline from page to stage and make it a powerful group experience. In this activity, participants become sociometrically aligned with each other by age. They can observe common threads as they share with each other the strengths that they used or developed through facing life challenges at particular ages.

Goals

- Provide opportunities for group members to connect over common ages and share around their strengths.
- Help clients consolidate gains of making good decisions and taking positive actions.
- Acknowledge and celebrate a sense of "survivor's pride."

Steps

1. Place large number cards on the floor in a timeline progression at five-year intervals, starting at 0 and ending at a high enough number to cover all ages in the group (such as 90).
2. Invite the group members to go to a place along the timeline that represents their answer to any of the following prompts:
    - "Walk over to an age in your life when you made a good choice."
    - "Walk over to an age when something wonderful occurred."
    - "Walk over to an age when you learned to reach out for support."
    - "Walk over to an age when you felt that you were developing qualities of resilience and strength."
    - "Walk over to an age when you felt loved, supported, or seen."
    - "Walk over to an age when someone helped you in a way that you are grateful for."
    - "Walk over to an age when you struggled and that helped you become who you are today."
    - "Walk over to an age when you faced a challenge in a way that you're proud of."

- "Walk over to an age that you can draw strength from or a time when you had strength that you now worry you have lost."
- "Walk over to an age when you had an insight or aha moment that started you in a new direction, or when a door flew open in your mind and you could see new possibilities and choices that could lead you to a better life."

3. Invite them to share with those nearest to them on the resilience timeline. This allows them to (1) begin to talk from that age and emotional and psychological space in time, (2) give that part of themselves a voice, (3) receive identification, recognition, and support, and (4) listen to, learn from, and support others.
4. You can repeat this process with other prompts from the list.
5. Afterward, if group members are warmed up to do so, you can move into role play or experiential letter writing. Invite them to speak to themselves at any age when they want to congratulate themselves, connect with themselves, or thank themselves, or to another person they want to thank for supporting them.

Clinical Exercise

Walking the Resilience Timeline

This can be an important and moving exercise. Clients stand up, walk through their development, and create a spontaneous resilience narrative. It's just as important to create a resilience narrative as a trauma narrative, and these narratives should be experiential, embodied, and bottom-up. In order to heal from C-PTSD, words are not enough; clients need to *feel*, and feeling is a mind-body experience. Becoming comfortable identifying and owning their strengths is a powerful part of healing and creates a good base for moving forward.

This often serves as a warm-up to psychodrama, focusing the jumping-off point of the work at the age that is being explored. In some cases, the timeline began before the client's own timeline; for example, a client might say, "I have drawn so much strength from what my parents and grandparents faced and overcame." Or it can extend into the future, if the client wishes to talk to the self they want to be at a given future time.

Goals

- Provide an embodied experience of the resilience timeline.
- Give clients a stage on which to share their qualities of strength and resilience and have them witnessed.
- Focus small role plays to talk to the self or someone who helped along the way.

Steps

1. Place large numbered cards on the floor in a timeline progression at five-year intervals, starting at 0 and ending at a high enough number to cover all ages in the group (such as 90).
2. Ask for volunteers, then invite the first protagonist to start at the beginning and narrate their walk through the various ages of their life. They can say things like "I am two and I feel totally special and loved" or "I am eight and my father has just left—it's really tough, but I'm developing a lot of strength and coming through for my family."
3. Role plays can organically grow out of this process. If the protagonist passes an age where it looks like further investigation might be helpful, simply ask them, "Would you like to speak with yourself at this age?" or "Would you like to talk to that person you just mentioned being grateful to and thank them for their help and kindness?" Then have the protagonist choose a role player

and bring them (or an empty chair) alongside the protagonist. After the role play has come to closure, let the protagonist continue to walk along the timeline.

4. Invite the group to share, either after each person's walk or after multiple people have walked the timeline. The group can share directly with the protagonist about ways in which they identify and what was brought up for them while watching and witnessing.

Clinical Exercise

Gratitude Letter

This is the only letter writing exercise where the letter can actually be sent, and it offers unique benefits. Expressing gratitude, either out loud or in writing, seems to make positive emotions "sticky," countering the phenomenon of sticky negative thinking that I see so often. In one study, participants were asked to write and personally deliver a letter of gratitude to someone. The participants immediately exhibited a significant increase in happiness scores. This impact was greater than that from any other intervention, with benefits lasting for a month (Seligman & Tierney, 2017).

In another study, which specifically recruited participants who were seeking mental health counseling, the findings suggested that "gratitude writing can be beneficial not just for healthy, well-adjusted individuals, but also for those who struggle with mental health concerns. In fact, it seems, practicing gratitude on top of receiving psychological counseling carries greater benefits than counseling alone, even when that gratitude practice is brief" (Brown & Wong, 2017).

Goals

- Open the client's heart and mind to expressing gratitude to someone who deserves thanking.
- Allow clients to embody gratitude and make it into a meaningful role play.

Steps

1. Warm up the group using another process (such as the *Resilience Timeline*) or by simply inviting them to share about people toward whom they feel grateful.
2. Provide the group members with paper and writing utensils.
3. Ask the group members to write letters expressing their gratitude toward someone—perhaps a person they have never properly thanked for helping them at some point in their life.
4. Place two chairs facing each other—one for the person reading the letter and one to represent the person to whom the letter is written.
5. Ask the first protagonist to imagine that the person to whom the letter is written is sitting in the empty chair, or they can choose another group member to represent this person. Invite the protagonist to read their letter.
6. You can extend the role play and use doubling, role reversal, role reversal interview, or other techniques as appropriate.
7. Move into sharing, either after each letter or, more efficiently, after several letters have been read.

Variations

- **Telehealth:** Participants can write their letters on their own, then share either in the large group or in breakout rooms.
- **One-to-One:** The client can write their letter, then read it as part of an empty chair role play in session.

Clinical Exercise

Resilience Social Atom

This exercise helps clients remember and recognize times in their life when something positive happened, when they accomplished a goal, or when they just felt good. Sometimes in therapy we can have an emphasis on talking about what went wrong; this exercise lets us talk about and celebrate what went right.

It may be helpful to show your clients a sample social atom; you can find one in the *Basic Social Atom* exercise (page 84).

Goals

- Help clients build resilience through practicing optimism and gratitude.
- Help clients identify relationships that were key or helpful in allowing them to move forward in positive ways.

Steps

1. Provide copies of the *Resilience Social Atom* journaling page (or blank pieces of paper) and writing utensils to the participants.
2. Say, "Draw a social atom of a moment or period in your life when something terrific happened or when you just felt good—maybe you felt strong, successful, empowered, helped by someone, or happy with yourself or with a relationship dynamic."
3. Go over the symbols and what they represent: circle for female, triangle for male, diamond for another gender, square for an institution or group, and a symbol with a dashed line for someone who is deceased.
4. Say, "First, locate yourself on the paper anywhere that feels right to you."
5. Say, "Now locate your important relationships during this time of your life. You can place them as close to or distant from yourself as you feel them to be, and in the size or proportion that feels right. You may include parents, siblings, pets, in-laws, grandparents, friends, institutions, and so on. Write their name in or next to their symbol."
6. Once the participants feel that their atoms are finished, invite them to share, either in the full group or in dyads or clusters.
7. Creating and sharing the atoms is a full process in itself. Additionally, you can sculpt the atoms as described in *Sculpting the Social Atom* (page 93). Or you can move into simple role plays,

inviting participants to speak to themselves or to someone from their social atom whom they wish to thank or explore further.

Variations

- **Telehealth:** Give the group members time to complete their atoms on their own paper or digitally. Then invite them to share, either in the full group or in breakout groups.
- **One-to-One:** The client can use the *Resilience Social Atom* journaling page, then you can unpack together in session.

Resilience Social Atom

Think of a moment or period in your life when something terrific happened or when you just felt good—maybe you felt strong, successful, empowered, helped by someone, or happy with yourself or with a relationship dynamic.

Draw a social atom of this golden moment, using the key below. First, draw a symbol to represent yourself, placing this symbol anywhere in your diagram that feels right to you. Then consider the important relationships in your life at that time. These might be other people, pets, groups, institutions, and so on. Add them to the diagram. You can place them as close to or distant from yourself as you feel them to be, and in the size or proportion that feels right.

Once your social atom feels complete, reflect on the questions that follow.

Key

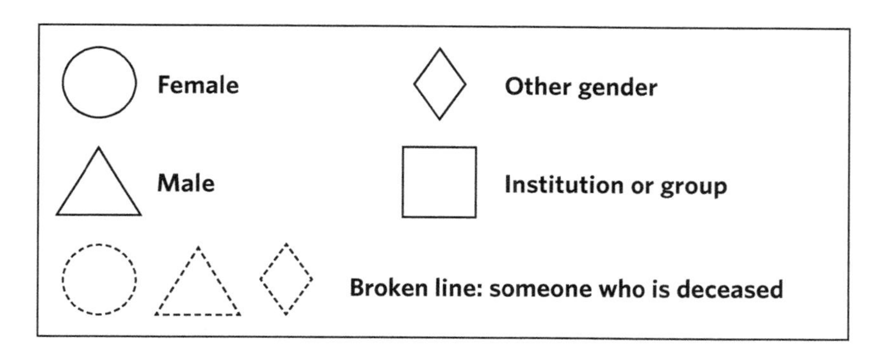

Diagram: Resilience Social Atom

Questions

How do you feel when you revisit this moment? Share about it.

Which personal strengths, relationships, or other features of this time in your life contributed to its being so positive or hopeful?

Is there someone in your atom whom you'd like to say something to? Say it now.

Is there someone else you would like to say something to? Say it now.

Clinical Exercise

Playing with Props

I like doing floor checks using props and costume pieces to introduce play into recovery. If you stay open and relaxed, group members come up with wonderful ways of using props, trying on identities, and bringing characters to life.

Goals

- Introduce creativity and play into the healing process.
- Allow group members to laugh and co-create fun moments.

Steps

1. On the floor, scatter any props and costume pieces you have collected. You might include hats, crowns, boas, capes, toy swords and shields, scraps of fabric, microphones—anything that you can imagine people creating characters around. Masks are especially helpful in representing characters or roles of all kinds, both feared and wished for. I recommend gathering a variety of Halloween masks, Venetian masks, blank-face masks, and so forth.
2. Ask criterion questions and invite the group members to stand near the prop that represents their answer. Possible questions include:
    - "Which prop draws you at this moment?"
    - "Which prop makes you feel brave?"
    - "Which prop represents a part of yourself that you hide?"
    - "Which prop represents a part of yourself you'd like to let out?"
    - "Which prop represents something or someone you wanted to be when you were a kid?"
    - "Which prop brings up anxiety in you?"
    - "Which prop emboldens you?"
3. After each question, invite the group members to share a few sentences describing why they chose the prop they chose. As they share, invite them to wear or hold the props to engage more senses. The atmosphere should be lively and fun—there are no goals here but to engage in an enjoyable process.

4. Once the group reaches a saturation point, have them return to their seats and share about the process. If group members get warmed up to doing role plays with some part of themselves they wish to talk to, that's fine, but just having fun and sharing about what that feels like is more than sufficient.

Variations

- **Telehealth:** Invite the group members to wander around their space and pick up something that represents their mood of the moment, a wished-for experience, a part of self, or any other criterion you may wish to explore. Each group member can share why they chose what they chose. You can also ask them to bring a mask to group that represents a part of self they might hide, fear becoming, or wish to become. This is an easy way to bring creativity, spontaneity, and warm-up into telehealth.

CHAPTER 13

Revisioning the Future: Looking Optimistically at What's Possible

In order to move into a better life, the client needs to be able to see that life in their mind's eye. One of the symptoms of PTSD is a sense of a foreshortened future, so part of healing from PTSD is somehow rekindling and restoring the sense that a positive future is possible.

Role play helps clients to not only think about but actually experience standing in and interacting with the future they would like to have. It lets them try on and explore new roles they might like to undertake. A client can, for example, step into the future momentarily and talk to and as their potential selves. They can also talk to the people they'd like to be with or meet. It is on-the-spot role training; clients experience and practice new ways of thinking, feeling, and behaving through role play.

Consolidating and Celebrating Posttraumatic Growth

Posttraumatic growth, a concept developed by Drs. Richard Tedeschi and Lawrence Calhoun in the mid-1990s, describes the positive self-transformation that people undergo through meeting challenges head-on. It refers to a profound, life-altering response to adversity that changes the person on the inside as they actively summon the kinds of qualities—like fortitude, forgiveness, gratitude, and strength—that enable them to not only survive tough circumstances but also thrive. While a quarter of people who experience some form of trauma will likely develop PTSD, two-thirds of this same group experience posttraumatic growth. They self-report personal growth in the areas of self-actualization, relationships, family, work, and community (Bloch-Jorgensen et al., 2018; Tedeschi & Calhoun, 2004).

Outcomes of posttraumatic growth can include:

- Having a greater appreciation for the value of one's own life
- Changing one's priorities about what is important in life

- Developing new interests
- Feeling more optimistic about the future
- Feeling more confident that one can accept and handle difficulties
- Developing stronger religious or spiritual beliefs
- Having greater appreciation and compassion for other people
- Feeling closer to others putting more effort into relationships
- Feeling both more self-reliant and better able to rely on others when needed
- Being more willing to express one's emotions

These qualities hearken back to Abraham Maslow's well-known hierarchy of human needs. According to Maslow and positive psychology, we human beings have a deep drive to grow into all that we can be. People often reported feelings such as "wonder, awe, reverence, humility, surrender, and even worship" in association with what Maslow called "peak experiences," which are moments of transcendent happiness and fulfillment (1964/1994, p. 65). It's why he placed self-actualization—"to become everything that one is capable of becoming"—at the top of the hierarchy (Maslow, 1943, p. 383).

Maslow's Hierarchy of Needs

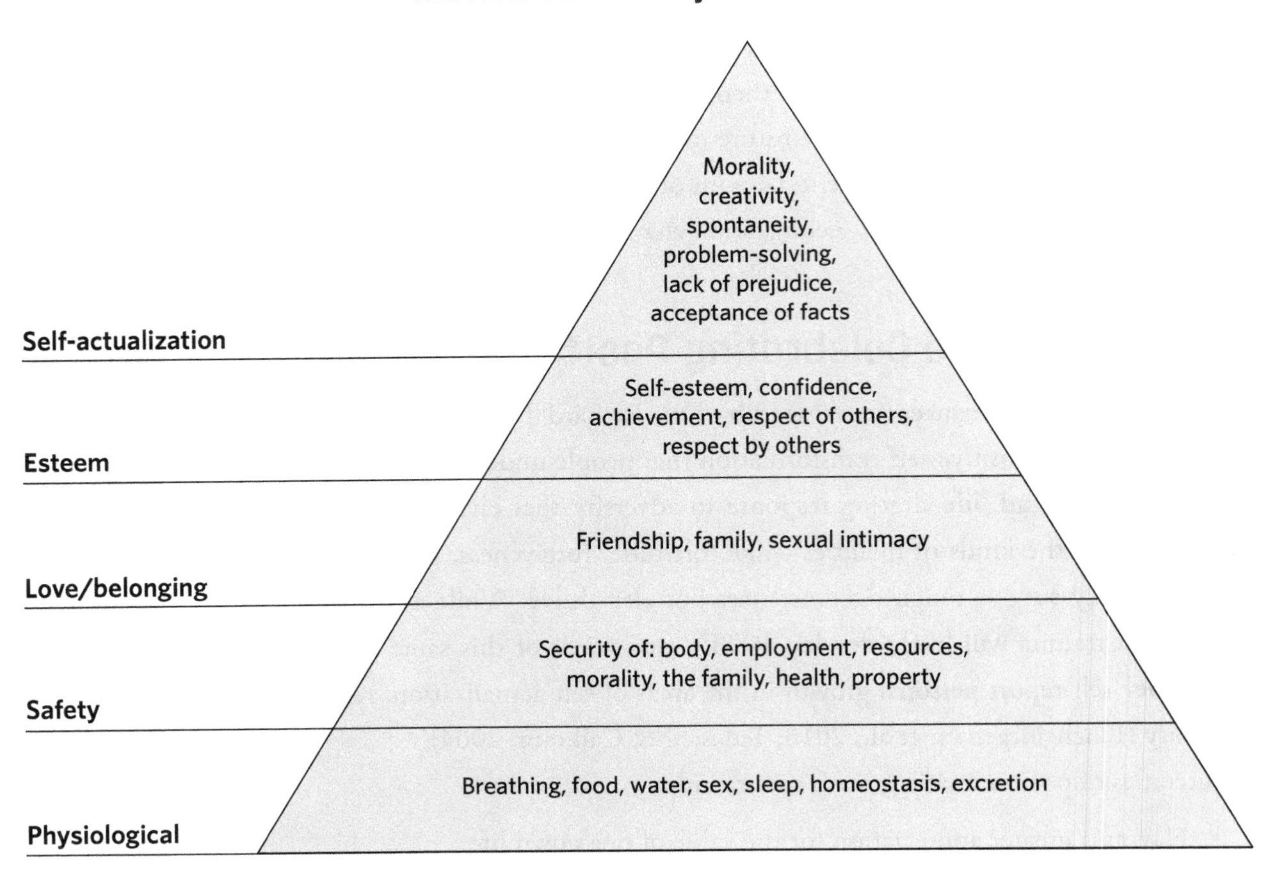

Maslow (1964/1994) observed that the self-actualizing individuals in his studies evidenced several personality traits. They tended to be reality centered (able to differentiate what is fraudulent from what is genuine), problem centered (treating life's difficulties as problems that demand solutions), comfortable being alone, and engaged in healthy personal relationships. They tended to have a small number of close friends and family members rather than a large number of shallow relationships. These individuals also had a deep acceptance of themselves, others, and the world. They were often private individuals who valued their personal time and developed inner resources. They were not too strictly bound to convention but able to strike their own path through life. They were spontaneous and creative.

One of the primary goals of psychodrama and sociometrics is to increase personal spontaneity and creativity, to get in touch with what Zerka Moreno (2012) called our "autonomous healing center." Psychodrama and sociometrics aren't only about resolving past wounds, they're about helping clients develop the kinds of skills that make their lives worth living—helping them become self-actualized individuals. The methods in this book, and in this chapter, offer a pathway toward self-actualization and posttraumatic growth, particularly when they are accompanied by the kind of spiritual awakening that many clients in recovery in general and twelve-step programs experience.

Clinical Exercise

Posttraumatic Growth Floor Check

The field of positive psychology looks at the kinds of personal strengths people can develop in meeting life's challenges. The posttraumatic growth inventory was developed by psychologists Richard Tedeschi and Lawrence Calhoun (1996) to bring awareness to and measure some of these gains. I have adapted their categories into an experiential group process so that group members can drop down into themselves and really feel, unpack, share, internalize, and consolidate some of these gains.

Goals

- Consolidate gains made through facing life challenges and trying to overcome them.
- Acknowledge and celebrate clients' personal growth.
- Help clients set goals for more growth.

Steps

1. On separate pieces of paper, write these outcomes of posttraumatic growth:
    - I changed my priorities about what is important in life.
    - I have a greater appreciation for the value of my own life.
    - I developed new interests.
    - I have a greater feeling of self-reliance.
    - I have a better understanding of spiritual matters.
    - I more clearly see that I can count on people in times of trouble.
    - I established a new path for my life.
    - I have a greater sense of closeness with others.
    - I am more willing to express my emotions.
    - I am more confident that I can handle difficulties.
    - I am able to do better things with my life.
    - I am better able to accept the way things work out.
    - I can better appreciate each day.
    - New opportunities are available to me that wouldn't have been otherwise.

- I have more compassion for others.
- I put more effort into my relationships.
- I am more likely to try to change things that need changing.
- I have a stronger religious faith.
- I discovered that I'm stronger than I thought I was.
- I learned a great deal about how wonderful people are.
- I better accept needing others.
- Other

2. Place the papers a couple of feet apart, scattered around the floor.
3. Say, "Walk over to a statement that draws you and share a sentence or two about why you choose it." You may have them share with the full group, with those standing on the same statement, or a combination of these.
4. Repeat this process with a few additional criterion questions, such as:
    - "Walk over to a statement you feel you have come a long way in mastering."
    - "Walk over to a statement that represents your growing edge."
    - "Walk over to a statement that you feel trauma took away from you and you are getting back."
    - "Walk over to a statement that you look forward to expanding in the future."
    - "Walk over to a statement that inspires you in your recovery."
    - "Walk over to a statement that makes you think of a parent, grandparent, mentor, or role model."
5. Say, "Walk over to someone who shared something that you identified with or that moved you, stand next to them, and share with them what moved you," or "Walk over to someone from whom you feel you could learn something and ask them for help."
6. When the group is saturated, invite them to sit down and share about the experience as a whole. Or, if they are warmed up for further work, you can move into role plays or experiential letter writing, inviting the participants to either thank someone else for their love and support or thank the self for making good choices and trying to get life to work.

Variations

- **Telehealth:** Display the options to the group using a whiteboard tool, a shared document, or another method that works for you. As you ask the criterion questions, group members can call out their answer and say a sentence or two about why they chose it. Or, if the group is large enough, you can use the initial questions as a warm-up and then move into breakout rooms for continued sharing. You can also use the *Posttraumatic Growth Inventory* journaling page: You can call out one question at a time and invite the group members to share their responses. If they might benefit from further sharing, they can do so in breakout rooms or they can continue the process of working through one question at a time in breakout rooms.

- **One-to-One:** The client can use the *Posttraumatic Growth Inventory* journaling page, then you can unpack together in session.

Journaling Page

Posttraumatic Growth Inventory

Posttraumatic growth is the positive self-transformation that people undergo through meeting challenges head-on. It is a profound, life-altering response to adversity that changes the person on the inside as they actively summon the kinds of qualities—like fortitude, forgiveness, gratitude, and strength—that enable them to not only survive tough circumstances but also thrive.

Many people who develop PTSD also experience posttraumatic growth. Identifying the ways in which you may have experienced this growth will help you to appreciate your own strengths and set goals for your future. Read through the list of posttraumatic growth outcomes, then answer the questions that follow.

Outcomes of Posttraumatic Growth

- I changed my priorities about what is important in life.
- I have a greater appreciation for the value of my own life.
- I developed new interests.
- I have a greater feeling of self-reliance.
- I have a better understanding of spiritual matters.
- I more clearly see that I can count on people in times of trouble.
- I established a new path for my life.
- I have a greater sense of closeness with others.
- I am more willing to express my emotions.
- I am more confident that I can handle difficulties.
- I am able to do better things with my life.
- I am better able to accept the way things work out.
- I can better appreciate each day.
- New opportunities are available to me that wouldn't have been otherwise.
- I have more compassion for others.
- I put more effort into my relationships.
- I am more likely to try to change things that need changing.
- I have a stronger religious faith.
- I discovered that I'm stronger than I thought I was.
- I learned a great deal about how wonderful people are.
- I better accept needing others.
- Other: ______________________________

Questions

Which statement do you feel most drawn to? Why?

Which quality do you feel you have come a long way in mastering or recovering? Share what this means to you.

Which statement represents your growing edge—a quality that you want to expand in the future? What steps are you planning to take to work on this?

Which statement makes you think of a parent, grandparent, mentor, or role model? What do you admire about this person?

Clinical Exercise

Future Projection Social Atom

We all carry future scenes around in our heads, whether wished for, feared, or dreamed of. This social atom invites clients to imagine a possible future and to concretize and interact with their desires, wishes, and plans. It encourages optimism for a future beyond the client's relational trauma, and it works well as part of a treatment or aftercare plan for clients in recovery.

It may be helpful to show your clients a sample social atom; you can find one in the *Basic Social Atom* exercise (page 84).

Goals

- Help clients concretize their goals for the future.
- Allow clients to experience future goals and interact with them in concrete form.
- Function as part of a treatment plan or aftercare plan.

Steps

1. Provide copies of the *Future Projection Social Atom* journaling page (or blank pieces of paper) and writing utensils to the participants.
2. Ask the group members to imagine their future as they wish it to be at some point; you could also specify a particular point (e.g., in six months, one year, three years, five years) for them to focus on. Invite them to make a social atom of their life as they would like it to be at that point in the future.
3. Go over the symbols and what they represent: circle for female, triangle for male, diamond for another gender, square for an institution or group, and a symbol with a dashed line for someone who is deceased.
4. Say, "First, locate yourself on the paper anywhere that feels right to you."
5. Say, "Now locate the important relationships that you want or expect to be in your life at a point in the future. You can place them as close to or distant from yourself as you feel them to be, and in the size or proportion that feels right. You may include parents, siblings, pets, in-laws, grandparents, friends, institutions, and so on. Write their name in or next to their symbol."

6. Once the participants feel that their atoms are finished, invite them to share, either in the full group or in dyads or clusters.
7. Creating and sharing the atoms is a full process in itself. Additionally, you can begin the *Talking to a Future Self* exercise (page 276) or move into simple role plays, inviting participants to speak to themselves in the future.

Variations

- **Sculpting the Future Projection Social Atom:** The future projection can also be moved into a sculpture as described in *Sculpting the Social Atom* (page 93). This allows the protagonist to gain a here-and-now experience of interacting with themselves and/or others that are part of a desired experience. In psychodrama this is referred to as "role training."
- **Aftercare Social Atom:** This type of atom can be done as part of a treatment or aftercare plan to reflect the sorts of life changes and relationships that a client may need or wish to create. Clients in recovery often need to make different decisions about whom they spend time with as part of staying sober; this might include friends, partners, and family members. Concretizing these changes and identifying people who might become part of a group of recovering friends can help them take the first step toward creating this group. Other activities that reflect positive life changes—such as twelve-step programs, exercise, and meditation—can be included in the atom as well.
- **Telehealth:** Give the group members time to complete their atoms on their own paper or digitally. Then invite them to share, either in the full group or in breakout groups.
- **One-to-One:** The client can use the *Future Projection Social Atom* journaling page, then you can unpack together in session.

Clinical Exercise

Support Network Floor Check

Building a support network is an important part of feeling sustained while working through relational trauma. Lots of feelings can come up over a fairly long period of time when a client is moving through C-PTSD. Knowing where their supports are, where they can reach out for help, and what activities feel nourishing to them is part of living differently. Let your clients know that there are twelve-step programs for all kinds of issues that they may be working through, such as codependency, eating issues, drug or alcohol issues, adult child issues (ACA), or spouse issues (Al-Anon). These programs provide a place to go to share feelings and feel cared for that has no dues or fees attached.

Goals

- Help clients revisit their support network and discuss which parts need strengthening and affirming.
- Work through any blocks around any aspect of the support network.
- Create an experiential process through which to engage with and explore the client's support network.

Steps

1. On separate pieces of paper, write various aspects of a support network, such as:
    - Twelve-step programs
    - Group therapy
    - One-to-one therapy
    - Personal time
    - Family time
    - Leisure and play activities
    - Passions and hobbies
    - Exercise
    - Good nutrition
    - Proper sleep
    - Self-soothing activities (e.g., massages, baths, yoga, walks, movies)
    - Time in nature
    - Soul nourishment
    - Other
2. Place the papers a couple of feet apart, scattered around the floor.

3. Say, "Walk over to a part of your support network that you feel is pretty strong but could still use some strengthening." Invite the group members to share a sentence or two about why they are standing where they are standing. You may have them share with the full group, with those standing on the same statement, or a combination of these.
4. Repeat this process with a few additional criterion questions, such as:
   - "Go to a part of your network that you are feeling a bit insecure about. Share what blocks or scares you in this area."
   - "Which part do you need to ask for help with or connect with others to get going?"
   - "Go to a part of your support network that you feel secure about and share what you've learned or gained."
5. When the group is saturated, invite them to sit down and share about the experience as a whole.

Variations

- **Telehealth:** Display the options to the group using a whiteboard tool, a shared document, or another method that works for you. As you ask the criterion questions, group members can call out their answer and say a sentence or two about why they chose it. Or, if the group is large enough, you can use the initial questions as a warm-up and then move into breakout rooms for continued sharing. You can also use the *Support Network* journaling page: You can call out one question at a time and invite the group members to share their responses. If they might benefit from further sharing, they can do so in breakout rooms or they can continue the process of working through one question at a time in breakout rooms.
- **One-to-One:** The client can use the *Support Network* journaling page, then you can unpack together in session.

Journaling Page

Support Network

While working through relational trauma, it's important to build a network of people, groups, resources, and activities that can support and nourish you. This activity invites you to recognize your current support network, as well as identify the types of support that you may need or want to add to your network. Read through the list of possible supports, then answer the questions that follow.

Types of Support

- Twelve-step programs (for addiction, codependency, eating issues, etc.)
- Group therapy
- One-to-one therapy
- Personal time
- Family time
- Leisure and play activities
- Passions and hobbies
- Exercise
- Good nutrition
- Proper sleep
- Self-soothing activities (e.g., massages, baths, yoga, walks, movies)
- Time in nature
- Soul nourishment
- Other: ______________________

Questions

Which parts of your support network are already pretty strong? Are there ways that you could strengthen these supports even further?

____

____

____

____

____

____

____

Which areas are you feeling a bit insecure about, or like you could use some help with to get going? What's blocking you from adding these elements to your support network?

____

____

____

____

____

____

____

What are your wishes or hopes for your support network? Which types of support would you love to have more of in your life? What would these types of support do for you?

____

____

____

____

____

____

____

What are some small, concrete steps that you can take right now to move closer to these supports?

____

____

____

____

____

____

____

Clinical Exercise

Embodying a Feared, Stuck, or Wished-for Role

All clients have roles they feel stuck or less alive in, as well as roles they long to play—these might be real roles they'd like to work toward or "impossible" dream roles they fantasize about. In this exercise, clients can play with these roles, explore them, and see what embodying them feels like.

This role play works well in conjunction with the next exercise, *Role Diagrams*. You might have clients use the *Diagramming Your Primary Roles* journaling page to generate ideas for roles they'd like to embody in this exercise, then use the *Revisioning Your Roles* journaling page afterward to further explore the changes they'd like to make in their life roles.

Goals

- Allow clients to concretize and embody a particular role for further exploration.
- Help clients work through the thoughts, feelings, and behaviors attached to a particular role.

Steps

1. Ask the protagonist to think of a role that they wish to explore, expand, or diminish. This might be a role that they currently feel stuck in or one that they wish or plan to experience in the future. Invite them to choose another group member or use an empty chair to represent this role.
2. Ask the protagonist to reverse roles and embody the role they have selected. You might say, "Show us what you look like in that role—how you're sitting or standing, and so forth. Now say something back to yourself from this role. Now reverse roles and answer this role from the role of self."
3. Continue with role reversals and doubling—the protagonist may double for themselves in either role, and you or other group members can double for the protagonist in either role as well.
4. Encourage the protagonist to speak fully and enjoy the experience of trying on a desired role or exploring a role they'd like to diminish.
5. While the protagonist is in their future self role, invite the group members to double for the protagonist or the protagonist in role reversal, in order to deepen their spontaneous experience of what the role feels like to be in. You can also do role reversal interviewing when the protagonist is in their future self role.
6. Ask the protagonist to end the scene in any way they choose.
7. Move into deroling and sharing as a group.
8. This exercise can be done repeatedly for a variety of roles.

Variations

- **Somatic Experiencing of a Future Self:** If you're familiar with Peter Levine's somatic experiencing work, you can add some somatic experiencing theory/therapy to this role play. Ask the protagonist, "What is going on in your body as you embody this role? Can you describe it? Can you place your hands there? If that part of you had a voice, what would it say? Does it have a color or a shape? Can you allow that color or shape to get bigger, then smaller—to pendulate along with your inward and outward breath so that it becomes more modulated?" Slowing this process down and allowing more of the body feeling to come forward into awareness can be very helpful to the protagonist.
- **Telehealth:** The somatic experiencing variation described above works well over telehealth because it can be made interior—it doesn't have to involve a lot of reversing roles, and the protagonist can use the role casting and embodiment as a warm-up to exploring what feelings come up while embodying a particular role. This can also help the protagonist understand that certain feelings are actually stimulated while in certain role relationships (e.g., talking to their mother may stimulate different emotions from talking to their friend). Alternatively, you can have the group members write letters to their chosen roles and share them, rather than doing a role play.
- **One-to-One:** This works well in one-to-one therapy. For example, if the client is talking about a circumstance they fear or wish for, you can say, "If you were talking to the part of yourself that is afraid, what would you say?" or "If you could talk to yourself in the future actually being who you wish to become, what would you like to say?" Then proceed as normal with an empty chair role play. Additionally, this can follow up the *Role Diagrams* exercise (page 257) if it was done previously.

Clinical Exercise

Role Diagrams*

Your clients play many different roles in their lives. Some of these roles may feel rewarding and satisfying, while others may feel draining or overwhelming. Through role diagrams, clients can take inventory of their life roles; explore feelings, thoughts, and behaviors related to them; and identify the steps they can take in order to balance these life roles so they become better aligned with their goals and values. Well-adjusted people tend to play a variety of roles, and those roles can adapt throughout stages of life. By creating a visual representation of their life roles, the client can come to understand how their roles are shaping their experience, and then they can revision them and play them with more awareness.

This intervention is broken into two parts: *Diagramming Your Primary Roles* and *Revisioning Your Roles*. In the first part, *Diagramming Your Primary Roles*, each client designates a primary role that they play in their life and breaks it into its subroles. In the second part, *Revisioning Your Roles*, clients can reshape their subroles and revision how they wish to play them.

Goals

- Create a visual representation of how clients experience the context and quality of the roles they play in their daily lives.
- Allow clients to explore their feelings, thoughts, and behaviors around the various roles they play in their lives.
- Empower clients to envision and work toward a more fulfilling and balanced set of life roles.

Steps

1. Provide the participants with writing utensils and copies of either the *Diagramming Your Primary Roles* journaling page or the *Revisioning Your Roles* journaling page, depending on where you are in the process.
2. After giving them time to journal, invite them to share, either in the full group or in clusters.
3. After sharing, clients can have the option of moving into role plays by talking to any aspect of their role. They can either choose someone to play the role or subrole or use an empty chair, first

* This exercise is adapted from Robert Siroka, PhD, TEP (personal communication, 1990).

talking to the role and then reversing roles and talking as the role. Doubling can be incorporated. Follow the process for the *Basic Role Play* (page 35).

4. Have the role players return to their seats for deroling and sharing.

Variations

- **Role Sculpture:** The client can use their diagram as a jumping-off point to create a sculpture of their roles. They can choose a role player to represent each role in their sculpture, placing them accordingly based on how the role feels for them. If a role feels big and overbearing, for example, or small and distant, that can be embodied both by the distance or closeness on stage and the position the role player assumes. Follow the steps in *Sculpting the Social Atom* (page 93). After you have done the process to whatever extent you wish to, invite the client to "redo" the sculpture by reshaping the roles as the client would like to experience them. The client can also choose reformed auxiliary egos to represent and interact with a more ideal form of the role.
- **Roles Before and After a Life-Altering Event:** Significant life events—such as a traumatic event; marriage, divorce, or remarriage; the birth of a child; the loss of a loved one; changing jobs/professions; returning from active duty; sobriety; or significant weight loss/gain—can change the roles we play and the way we play them vis-à-vis others in our lives. In this variation, invite each client to create two primary role charts: one for before the event and one for after. Start with *Diagramming Your Primary Roles* and follow up with *Revisioning Your Roles*. Clients can use the questions as they appear in these sections and/or add their own.
- **Life Stages Role Diagram:** Any stage of life can be examined using a role diagram. For example, a midlife crisis can be examined to explore which roles have been underfulfilled and which roles need to be added to or expanded upon in order to find balance and satisfaction.
- **Couples' Role Diagrams:** In couples work, give each person *Diagramming Your Primary Roles* followed by *Revisioning Your Roles*, in two different sessions or in the same session. Their primary roles in this case could be spouse/partner, and the wedges within those roles might include friend, co-parent, cook, driver, sexual partner, planner, playmate, social partner, breadwinner, spiritual partner, sharer of household tasks, nurturer, or in-law, for example. The completed diagrams can be examined together to discover which roles are compatible within their partnership and which are conflictual. You can also use a percentage rating system by asking each person to assign a percentage in terms of their sense of compatibility for each wedge of their respective roles (e.g., sexual partner 85%, social partner 43%).

  It is helpful to build on the couple's strengths by examining which roles are going well and which roles need attention. One important takeaway for couples is that while some role compatibility in a relationship may need work, it does not mean the entire relationship is unhealthy or unproductive. Role diagrams may also help the couple understand that a successful long-term relationship requires adaptability as the couple moves through their life stages together and roles shift: Some get larger and some smaller; some are added and some reduced. Understanding this will empower the couple to learn how to allow for role changes without losing the relationship.

- **Telehealth:** Share the journaling page electronically for the participants to print out, fill in digitally, or simply reference as they write on their own paper. Then invite them to share, either in the full group or in breakout groups.
- **One-to-One:** The client can use the journaling page, then you can unpack together in session. Empty chair role plays can be incorporated if desired—this gives a fuller, 360-degree, embodied experience of how developmental roles got set up, and clients can "do, undo, and redo" (Moreno, 1946/2019).

Journaling Page

Diagramming Your Primary Roles

You likely play many different roles in your life. Maybe you're a parent, a partner, an employee, a therapy client, a runner, an avid reader, and a budding chef. Some of these roles may feel rewarding and satisfying, while others may feel draining or overwhelming. There may also be roles that you'd like to play but that aren't currently a part of your life. In this activity, you'll take inventory of your life roles, explore your feelings around them, and identify the steps you may wish to take in order to balance these life roles according to your goals and values.

Think of the main roles you currently play in your life—such as parent, partner, child, professional, student, and so on—whatever you see as your primary roles in life right now. List those roles here:

____

____

____

____

____

____

____

____

____

____

Most primary roles break down into multiple aspects, titles, or responsibilities that make up that role, called *subroles*. For example, the primary role of parent could be broken into the subroles of teacher, playmate, cook, nurturer, organizer, event planner, chauffeur, nurse, and so on.

In the diagram that follows, choose one of your primary roles to explore further. First, label the pie chart with the primary role you're exploring. Then divide the circle into wedges to represent each subrole, making the size of the wedge relative to the time you currently spend in that subrole. For example, within the primary role of parent, you might draw a large wedge for teacher because you help your children with their homework every day, and a smaller wedge for nurse because your children are generally healthy.

Once you've completed your wedges, rate your current internal level of satisfaction, aliveness, burnout, and chaos with each of your subroles using a scale from 1 to 10 (where 10 is the highest).

- **Satisfaction (S):** This subrole is generally good. You are okay with your current status.
- **Aliveness (A):** You find this subrole joyful, meaningful, and purposeful. It feels natural and brings a smile to your face.
- **Burnout (B):** You feel fatigued, listless, and tired of this subrole.
- **Chaos (C):** This subrole is unclear, messy, and a source of stress. You wish it were different.

An example of a completed diagram is included next, followed by a blank template for you to fill in. Once you have completed your own diagram, reflect on the questions that follow.

Example

Primary role: Mother

Meal Provider
S = 5
A = 5
B = 6
C = 4

Nurturer
S = 9
A = 10
B = 2
C = 0

Playmate
S = 10
A = 10
B = 0
C = 0

Taxi
S = 6
A = 4
B = 2
C = 2

Secretary
S = 4
A = 3
B = 8
C = 7

Teacher
S = 8
A = 7
B = 0
C = 1

Diagram: Roles and Subroles
Primary role: ___________________________

Questions

Which subroles in your life do you enjoy, and why? What pleasure are they giving you?

Which subroles are you not enjoying, and why? Do they feel unsatisfying or even oppressive?

Which subroles do you wish took up less time and space in your life? How would you like them to change? What is in the way of making that change?

Which subroles do you wish you could give more time to? How much more time would you like to have for them? What is in the way?

Are there subroles not represented here that you'd like to add to your life? What are they and how might you add them? What is in the way of adding them?

Consider the ratings in your pie chart. Would you like to say more about why you rated certain subroles as you did? How does that make you feel?

Which subroles take up the most space/time in your life?

Which subroles do you feel most alive in?

Which subroles are waning, becoming smaller in your life? How do you feel about that?

Which subroles are growing, becoming larger in your life? How do you feel about that?

Which subroles do you feel most shut down in?

What kinds of thoughts do you have while in each subrole?

What kinds of emotions do you experience while in each subrole?

How do you act when you are in each subrole?

Journaling Page

Revisioning Your Roles

Now that you've explored your current experience of your subroles, use the following diagram to create another pie chart—this time adjusting the size of each wedge, or subrole, to reflect the relative amount of time or space you *would like* this subrole to take in your life. Feel free to expand or reduce roles according to your preferences. Once you've completed your revised wedges, rate the internal level of satisfaction, aliveness, burnout, and chaos you *would like* to feel with each of your subroles. As before, use a scale from 1 to 10 (where 10 is the highest).

- **Satisfaction (S):** This subrole is generally good. You are okay with your current status.
- **Aliveness (A):** You find this subrole joyful, meaningful, and purposeful. It feels natural and brings a smile to your face.
- **Burnout (B):** You feel fatigued, listless, and tired of this subrole.
- **Chaos (C):** This subrole is unclear, messy, and a source of stress. You wish it were different.

Once you have completed your new diagram, reflect on the questions that follow.

Revisioned Diagram: Roles and Subroles

Questions

How does it feel to look at your reshaped role diagram?

Do you think you could make some of these changes in your life? What challenges do you expect to face?

Identify some supports that might help you cope with these challenges. What strategies or steps could help you start making these changes in your life?

What kinds of thoughts do you imagine you will have while playing these roles?

What kinds of emotions do you imagine you will experience while playing these roles?

How do you imagine you will act when you're in these roles?

How do you feel about making conscious changes in your roles and how you play them?

Do you have any anxieties or fears about making these changes? If so, what are they?

Do you have hopes or excitement about making these changes? Say a little about that.

Clinical Exercise

Play It Through to the End

Being able to imagine the consequences of a behavior, and then use that insight to make choices that will lead to other good choices, is an invaluable life skill. Trauma can make it difficult for clients to envision the future and make the kinds of choices that will lead to personal satisfaction. Losing connection with parts of themselves that they've shut down can interfere with how well they know themselves and what will make them feel productive, relevant, and happy. This exercise will help clients rebuild those connections and understand the probable outcomes of their decisions, empowering them to move forward in a positive direction.

This exercise was created by Bill Coleman MSW, TEP, and it is used in the addictions field to explore the consequences of addiction by designating one side as "continued use" and the other as "recovery." By renaming the sides "continued dysfunction" and "the future I want to create," you can broaden the scope of this exercise and allow clients to explore virtually anything—from changing careers, to leaving a relationship, to working on any unhelpful behaviors or thought patterns they have. Keep this flexible and nonprescriptive. This is not the time for clients to make big life decisions, simply to explore the potential outcomes of each option.

Goals

- Allow clients to "play it through to the end" experientially.
- Help clients understand that their actions have long-term consequences.
- Give clients an opportunity to experience different futures and test hypotheses.
- Compare and contrast time spent in recovery with continued use or dysfunction.

Steps

1. Place six chairs in two rows of three, in a long "V" shape.
2. Call one row "recovery" or "the future I want to create" and the other row "continued use" or "continued dysfunction." Explain to the group members that they will be embodying each path into the future, and that they can experience how different decisions impact their lives as they do.
3. Invite the first protagonist to designate a period of time for each chair in the row. Any length of time can be represented—weeks, months, years, and so on.
4. Invite the protagonist to sit in the first chair on the "continued use" or "continued dysfunction" side and share about how their imagined life looks at this point, then do the same for the next

two chairs on that side. For example: "I am one year out and my relationship with my dad hasn't changed . . . Now I'm two years out and still giving him money whenever he asks . . . Here I'm three years out and I'm still worried about making ends meet . . ."

5. Next, invite the protagonist to choose the "recovery" or "the future I want to create" side and narrate their progress through each chair. For example: "I am one year out and I've told my dad that I won't give him money if he won't get help for his drinking and gambling . . . Now I'm two years out and maintaining that boundary . . . Here I'm three years out and I've saved enough to go back to school like I wanted . . ."
6. At each interval, the protagonist can use role reversal and stand up and talk back to the part of themselves sitting in the chair. They can also double for themselves or accept doubling from other group members.
7. Once the protagonist has moved through both trajectories, invite them to sit down and move into sharing. Alternatively, you can have several protagonists go through the trajectories before sharing.

Variations

- **Telehealth:** Share the *Play It Through to the End* journaling page with the clients so that they can print it out, fill it in digitally, or simply reference it while writing on their own paper. Then invite them to share.
- **One-to-One:** The client can use the *Play It Through to the End* journaling page, then you can unpack together in session.

Journaling Page

Play It Through to the End

Being able to imagine your future—and predict the likely outcomes of the decisions you're making in the present—is a valuable life skill that will help you make the kinds of choices that will lead to contentment, happiness, and fulfillment. In this activity, you will practice this skill by mentally walking through two hypothetical scenarios. This isn't meant to rush or pressure you into making any decisions; it's simply a tool that you can use to explore your options and build the skill of looking to the future.

Use the following diagram to envision two possible futures for yourself. First, choose a span of time that you'd like to explore—this might be a matter of weeks, months, or years—and label the circles accordingly (e.g., today, year 1, year 2, year 3). You can think of these as the time markers along each path.

Next, focus on the path labeled "Continued Use/Dysfunction." Imagine that in the future you continue to repeat the patterns you're in today, whether that involves substance use, compulsive behaviors, painful relationship dynamics, or any other aspect of the status quo that you're finding difficult or unsatisfying. At each point along the path, write down what you expect your life will be like at that time—again, assuming that you *don't* make any changes.

Now turn to the second path. This represents the future you'd like to have, which might involve recovery, healing from relational trauma, or other changes that you believe would make your life better. At each point along this path, write down what you imagine your life will be like at that time if you *do* make the changes you're considering.

Once you've completed both paths, reflect on the questions that appear after the diagram.

Diagram: Play It Through to the End

Continued Use/Dysfunction

Recovery/Life Changes

Where I Am Now

Questions

How do you feel when you think about the path of continued use/dysfunction?

How do you feel when you consider the future you'd like to have?

What blocks are in your way of choosing the more desirable path? Can you envision overcoming them or working around them?

Did completing this exercise motivate you to work on some of the changes you've been considering? If so, identify three specific steps you can take right now that will help you start on the path toward your better future.

Clinical Exercise

Talking to a Future Self

Trauma can interfere with the client's ability to visualize a future. This is something that they can explore through psychodrama. The client can not only talk to a future self but embody and actually inhabit a future self through role reversal. Actually experiencing sitting in that chair, or standing in that space, can open up the energy to walk into it.

Goals

- Provide a direct experience of embodying a wished-for or desired future role.
- Counter the trauma sense of having a foreshortened future.

Steps

1. Use this as a follow-up to *Play It Through to the End* or ask the group members to close their eyes and relax. Invite them to connect with a self that they'd like to be or a role they'd like to play at some point in their future.
2. Invite the protagonist to choose another group member to embody this self, or they can use an empty chair.
3. Ask the protagonist to reverse roles and show how this self sits and looks.
4. Ask the protagonist (still in role reversal) to say something back to their current self, then reverse roles and answer as their current self.
5. Continue the drama, using both role reversal and doubling (by you, the protagonist, or other group members). Encourage the protagonist to speak fully and enjoy the experience of trying on a new role.
6. When the protagonist is in their future self role, you can do role reversal interview or invite the group members to ask questions of the protagonist in order to deepen their spontaneous experience of what the role feels like to be in.
7. Ask the protagonist to end the scene in any way they choose.
8. Move into deroling and sharing, either after each role play or after several role plays.

Variations

- **Telehealth:** This can be done as an experiential letter writing exercise wherein clients write letters to their future selves and take turns reading them, either in the full group or in breakout rooms.
- **One-to-One:** If the client has done the *Play It Through to the End* journaling page at home or if the subject of wanting to become something or someone in the future comes up spontaneously, simply invite the client to talk to themselves at some point in their future, using an empty chair. Do the role play as you normally would, incorporating doubling and role reversal. Once it has come to closure, you can unpack the experience with your client, letting them share fully about how it felt to be in their future role, what might be in the way for them, and how they might be able to see themselves differently and take steps toward becoming who they would like to be. This is also a good follow-up to the next exercise, *Visualizing the Life You Want*.

Clinical Exercise

Visualizing the Life You Want

Those who have experienced relational trauma can unconsciously imagine more bad things happening as they get lost in negative forecasting. By learning to imagine life working out, they can counter this tendency. This exercise helps them consciously imagine a positive future. It also shows them that a very important part of future happiness or contentment is to learn to feel that way in the present. The client may not always have control over the circumstances of their life, but they do have control over what they carry on the inside.

One possible script is included in the steps below. For additional free guided imageries you can use with your clients, visit tiandayton.com.

Goals

- Train the mind to see future circumstances in a positive and possible light.
- Help clients embrace possibilities and actually see the life they would like to live.
- Counter the tendency for negative forecasting by replacing it with positive forecasting/visioning.

Steps

1. Invite the group members to find a position in which they feel relaxed. Ask them to uncross their legs and arms. They can sit in a chair or lie on the floor on their back.
2. Ask them to focus on their breath and take deep, even breaths. Say, "Breathe in and out easily and completely, and as you do, allow yourself to relax and let go of any tension your body may be carrying."
3. Invite them to think about any situation in their life that they would like to experience change in or create. Ask them to see it as they would like it to be.
4. Continue to remind them to breathe in and out easily and completely and to simply allow that vision to flow naturally and easily in and out of their consciousness.
5. Invite them to see this scene or vision as if it were already true, already happening, already fulfilled. Say, "Feel it, sense it, enjoy it, taste it, touch it, and let it go over and over again."
6. Next, invite them to release the vision and leave it entirely to the universe to manifest it. Let them know that their only job is to feel what is possible, not to make anything happen but to open to allowing for new possibilities to come into being.
7. You can invite them to share about the experience, or this can be used as a warm-up for the *Talking to a Future Self* exercise (page 276).

References

For your convenience, purchasers can download and print the handouts and journaling pages from **www.pesi.com/ACORT**

Anda, R. F., & Brown, D. W. (2010, July 2). *Adverse childhood experiences & population health in Washington: The face of a chronic public health disaster.* Washington State Family Policy Council.

Anda, R. F., Felitti, V. J., Bremner, J. D., Walker, J. D., Whitfield, C., Perry, B. D., Dube, S. R., & Giles, W. H. (2005). The enduring effects of abuse and related adverse experiences in childhood. *European Archives of Psychiatry and Clinical Neuroscience, 256*(3), 174–186. https://doi.org/10.1007%2Fs00406-005-0624-4

Babyak, M., Blumenthal, J. A., Herman, S., Khatri, P., Doraiswamy, M., Moore, K., Craighead, W. E., Baldewicz, T. T., & Krishnan, K. R. (2000). Exercise treatment for major depression: Maintenance of therapeutic benefit at 10 months. *Psychosomatic Medicine, 62*(5), 633–638. https://doi.org/10.1097/00006842-200009000-00006

Bloch-Jorgensen, Z. T., Cilione, P. J., Yeung, W. W. H., & Gatt, J. M. (2018). Centeredness theory: Understanding and measuring well-being across core life domains. *Frontiers in Psychology, 9,* Article 610. https://doi.org/10.3389/fpsyg.2018.00610

Bowlby, J. (1982). *Attachment and loss: Vol. 1: Attachment* (2nd ed.). Basic Books.

Brown, J., & Wong, J. (2017, June 6). How gratitude changes you and your brain. *Greater Good Magazine.* https://greatergood.berkeley.edu/article/item/how_gratitude_changes_you_and_your_brain

Carnes, P. (1991). *Don't call it love: Recovery from sexual addiction.* Health Communications.

Connor, K. M., & Davidson, J. R. T. (2003). Development of a new resilience scale: The Connor-Davidson resilience scale (CD-RISC). *Depression and Anxiety, 18,* 76–82. https://doi.org/10.1002/da.10113

Crawford, E., O'Dougherty Wright, M., & Masten, A. S. (2006). Resilience and spirituality in youth. In E. C. Roehlkepartain, P. E. King, L. Wagener, & P. L. Benson (Eds.), *The handbook of spiritual development in childhood and adolescence* (pp. 355–370). Sage.

Dana, D. (2018). *The polyvagal theory in therapy: Engaging the rhythm of regulation.* W. W. Norton & Company.

Dayton, T. (2005). *The living stage: A step-by-step guide to psychodrama, sociometry and experiential group therapy.* Health Communications, Inc.

Dayton, T. (2011, November 17). *Adult children of alcoholics (ACoAs): Qualities and traits.* HuffPost Contributor. https://www.huffpost.com/entry/adult-children-of-alcohol_b_300572

Dayton, T. (2022). *Sociometrics: Embodied, experiential processes for healing trauma and addiction.* Central Recovery Press.

Fava, M., & Rosenbaum, J. F. (1999). Anger attacks in patients with depression. *Journal of Clinical Psychiatry, 60*(Suppl. 15), 21–24.

Giacomucci, S. (2021). *Social work, sociometry, and psychodrama: Experiential approaches for group therapists, community leaders, and social workers.* Springer. https://doi.org/10.1007/978-981-33-6342-7_5

Gilbert, P. (1998). What is shame? Some core issues and controversies. In P. Gilbert & B. Andrews (Eds.), *Shame* (pp. 3–38). Oxford University Press.

Greenspan, S., & Breslau Lewis, N. (2009). *Building healthy minds: The six experiences that create intelligence and emotional growth in babies and young children.* Da Capo Lifelong Books.

Greenspan, S. I., Wieder, S., & Simons, R. (1998). *The child with special needs: Encouraging intellectual and emotional growth.* Perseus Books.

Hart, K. E. (1999). A spiritual interpretation of the 12-steps of Alcoholics Anonymous: From resentment to forgiveness to love. *Journal of Ministry in Addiction & Recovery, 6*(2), 25–39. https://doi.org/10.1300/J048v06n02_03

Harvard Health Publishing. (2022, January 10). *How genes and life events affect mood and depression.* Harvard Medical School. https://www.health.harvard.edu/depression/how-genes-and-life-events-affect-mood-and-depression

Herman, J. (1997). *Trauma and recovery: The aftermath of violence—from domestic abuse to political terror.* Basic Books.

Herrenkohl, T. I., Jung, H., Lee, J. O., & Kim, M-H. (2016, January 1). *Effects of child maltreatment, cumulative victimization experiences, and proximal life stress on adult crime and antisocial behavior* (NIJ 250506). National Institute of Justice. https://www.ojp.gov/pdffiles1/nij/grants/250506.pdf

Johnson, S. (2016, February 4). *Love sense: From infant to adult (Sue Johnson and Ed Tronick)* [Video]. YouTube. https://www.youtube.com/watch?v=OyCHT9AbD_Y

Kübler-Ross, E. (2014). *On death and dying: What the dying have to teach doctors, nurses, clergy & their own families.* Scribner. (Original work published 1969)

Levine, P. A., & Frederick, A. (1997). *Waking the tiger—healing trauma: The innate capacity to transform overwhelming experiences.* North Atlantic Books.

Levine, P. A., & Phillips, M. (2012). *Freedom from pain: discover your body's power to overcome physical pain.* Sounds True.

Maslow, A. H. (1943). A theory of human motivation. *Psychological Review, 50*(4), 370–396. https://doi.org/10.1037/h0054346

Maslow, A. H. (1994). *Religions, values, and peak-experiences.* Arkana. (Original work published 1964)

Maté, G. (2010). Foreword. In P. A. Levine, *In an unspoken voice: How the body releases trauma and restores goodness* (pp. xi–xiv). North Atlantic Books.

Montessori, M. (1995). *The absorbent mind.* Holt Paperbacks.

Moreno, J. L. (2019). *Psychodrama* (4th ed., Vol. 1). Psychodrama Press. (Original work published 1946)

Moreno, Z. (2012). *To dream again: A memoir.* Mental Health Resources.

National Institutes of Health. (2002, November 6). *Mimicking brain's "all clear" quells fear in rats* [Press release]. https://md.rcm.upr.edu/wp-content/uploads/sites/52/2016/07/NIMH-2002.pdf

Osbon, D. K. (Ed.). (1991). *Reflections on the art of living: A Joseph Campbell companion.* HarperCollins Publishers.

Payne, P., Levine, P. A., & Crane-Godreau, M. A. (2015). Somatic experiencing: Using interoception and proprioception as core elements of trauma therapy. *Frontiers in Psychology, 6,* Article 93. https://doi.org/10.3389%2Ffpsyg.2015.00093

Porges, S. W. (2003). Social engagement and attachment: A phylogenetic perspective. *Annals of the New York Academy of Sciences 1008*(1), 31–47. https://doi.org/10.1196/annals.1301.004

Porges, S. W. (2004). Neuroception: A subconscious system for detecting threats and safety. *Zero to Three, 24*(5), 19–24.

Porges, S. W. (2011). *The polyvagal theory: Neurophysiological foundations of emotions, attachment, communication, and self-regulation.* W.W. Norton & Company.

Rains, M., & McClinn, K. (2013). *Resilience questionnaire.* https://www.sos.wa.gov/_assets/library/libraries/projects/earlylearning/resilience_questionnaire_in_english.pdf (Original work published 2006)

Reivich, K., & Shatté, A. (2002). *The Resilience Factor: 7 keys to finding your inner strength and overcoming life's hurdles.* Broadway Books.

Remen, R. N. (2006). *Kitchen table wisdom: Stories that heal* (10th anniversary ed.). Berkley. (Original work published 1996)

Rosenthal, N. E. (2002). *The emotional revolution: How the new science of feelings can transform your life.* Citadel.

Rutter, M. (1993). Resilience: Some conceptual considerations. *Journal of Adolescent Health, 14*(8), 626–631. https://doi.org/10.1016/1054-139X(93)90196-V

Schore, A. N. (1994). *Affect regulation and the origin of the self: The neurobiology of emotional development.* Lawrence Erlbaum Associates.

Schwartz, R. C. (2021). *No bad parts: Healing trauma & restoring wholeness with the internal family systems model.* Sounds True.

Seligman, M. E. P. (1998). President's address to the 1998 American Psychological Association's annual meeting. *The APA 1998 Annual Report, American Psychologist 54*(8), 559–562.

Seligman, M. E. P. (2006). *Learned optimism: How to change your mind and your life.* Vintage Books. (Original work published 1990)

Seligman, M. E. P., & Maier, S. F. (1967). Failure to escape traumatic shock. *Journal of Experimental Psychology, 74*(1), 1–9. https://doi.org/10.1037/h0024514

Seligman, M. E. P., & Tierney, J. (2017, May 19). We aren't built to live in the moment. *The New York Times.* https://www.nytimes.com/2017/05/19/opinion/sunday/why-the-future-is-always-on-your-mind.html

Shakespeare, W. (2019). *Hamlet* (2nd Norton critical ed.; R. S. Miola, Ed.). W. W. Norton & Company. (Original work published ca. 1601)

Siegel, D. J. (1999). *The developing mind: Toward a neurobiology of interpersonal experience.* Guilford Press.

Tedeschi, R. G., & Calhoun, L. G. (1996). The posttraumatic growth inventory: Measuring the positive legacy of trauma. *Journal of Traumatic Stress, 9*(3), 455–471. https://doi.org/10.1002/jts.2490090305

Tedeschi, R. G., & Calhoun, L. G. (2004). Posttraumatic growth: Conceptual foundations and empirical evidence. *Psychological Inquiry 15*(1), 1–18. https://doi.org/10.1207/s15327965pli1501_01

Tippett, K. (Host). (2013, July 11). Bessel van der Kolk: Trauma, the body, and 2021. *On Being* [Audio podcast]. The On Being Project. https://onbeing.org/programs/bessel-van-der-kolk-trauma-the-body-and-2021/

Ungar, M., Brown, M., Liebenberg, L., Othman, R., Kwong, W. M., Armstrong, M., & Gilgun, J. (2007). Unique pathways to resilience across cultures. *Adolescence, 42*(166), 287–310.

van der Kolk, B. A. (1985). Adolescent vulnerability to posttraumatic stress disorder. *Psychiatry, 48,* 365–370. https://doi.org/10.1080/00332747.1985.11024297

van der Kolk, B. A. (1987). *Psychological trauma.* American Psychiatric Publishing.

van der Kolk, B. A. (2014). *The body keeps the score: Brain, mind, and body in the healing of trauma.* Penguin.

van der Kolk, B. A., Perry, J. C., & Herman, J. L. (1991). Childhood origins of self-destructive behavior. *American Journal of Psychiatry, 148*(12), 1665–1671. http://eqi.org/p1/abuse/vanderkolk_childhood_origins_of_self_destructive_behavior_1991.pdf

van der Kolk, B. A., van der Hart, O., & Burbridge, J. (1995). The treatment of post traumatic stress disorder. In S. E. Hobfoll & M. W. de Vries (Eds.), *Extreme stress and communities: Impact and intervention* (pp. 421–444). Kluwer Academic Publishers.

Williams, Z. (2021, September 20). Trauma, trust and triumph: Psychiatrist Bessel van der Kolk on how to recover from our deepest pain. *The Guardian*. https://www.theguardian.com/society/2021/sep/20/trauma-trust-and-triumph-psychiatrist-bessel-van-der-kolk-on-how-to-recover-from-our-deepest-pain

Winnicott, D. W. (1965). *The maturational processes and the facilitating environment: Studies in the theory of emotional development.* International Universities Press.

Wolin, S., & Wolin, S. J. (1995). Morality in COAs: Revisiting the syndrome of over-responsibility. In S. Abbott (Ed.), *Children of Alcoholics: Selected Readings* (pp. 223–233). National Association for Children of Alcoholics.

Wolin, S. J., & Wolin, S. (1993). *The resilient self: How survivors of troubled families rise above adversity.* Villard Books.

Wong, P. T. P., & Wong, L. C. J. (2012). A meaning-centered approach to building youth resilience. In P. T. P. Wong (Ed.), *The human quest for meaning: Theories, research, and applications* (2nd ed., pp. 585–617). Routledge.

Yablonsky, L. (1976). *Psychodrama: Resolving emotional problems through role-playing.* Basic Books.